A Book of Many Uses

In the prisons: "A great theologian once said that the most important task of the Christian is to be able to communicate the Gospel to children. What he meant was that it should be simple, direct, truthful, and easily understood. That is a wonderful description of this clear, teachable, and easily read book on the tenets of Christian life that my good friend, Carol Vance, has written. We will enthusiastically use it in the prisons."

> **Charles W. Colson**
> Author and Founder of Prison Fellowship

In the church: "Your discipleship book is excellent. I was stunned at the quality yet the simplicity of what you have done."

> **Ed Young**
> Author and Pastor, Second Baptist Church of Houston

With professional and business people: "Carol Vance has penned a powerful book. Each chapter will enable the reader to become a 21st-century reproducing disciple."

> **John Tolson**
> Founder of The Gathering, U.S.A. (an organization dedicated to bringing Christ to business and professional men)

On mission fields: "We are excited about reproducing this vital work in various languages to use in training new converts in churches and discipleship groups in Africa, India, and other foreign fields. It is a simple, powerful, usable tool."

> **Shad Williams**
> Shad Williams Evangelistic Association and Global Field Evangelism

For evangelism and growth: "With a rare combination of no-nonsense biblical standards and sensitive mercy, Carol Vance has given us one of the best books on the basic Christian life to be found anywhere."

> **C. Peter Wagner**
> Author, International Leader of Evangelism and Prayer, and Professor of Church Growth at Fuller Theological Seminary

AFTER THE LEAP

Growing in Christ: The Basics of Discipleship

CAROL VANCE

Cook Communications

Victor is an imprint of
Cook Communications Ministries, Colorado Springs, Colorado 80918
Cook Communications, Paris, Ontario
Kingsway Communications, Eastbourne, England

Cover and Interior Design: Smith/Lane Associates
Cover and Interior Illustrations: Nishan Akgulian
Editor: Afton Rorvik

Printed in the United States of America.

1 2 3 4 5 6 7 8 9 10 Printing / Year 04 03 02 01 00

CIP data applied for
ISBN 0-78143-392-4

CONTENTS

*To Carolyn Vance, my wonderful wife who
has put up with me for 45 years
and has been my in-house expert on the Bible.*

Acknowledgments

I would like to acknowledge my wonderful family—my daughter Lynn Goodson and son-in-law Mark and Carrie, Camille, and Carly; son Carroll III and Janet and Carroll IV and Thomas Berry Vance; daughter Karen Geoca and son-in-law Ted and their boys, Nicholas, Peter, and Christian; son Harold; and daughter Cheryl Tucker and son-in-law Brian and Andrew, Sarah, Carolyn, and Benjamin Tucker; my mother Fanelle Burgess, who taught me about sacrificial love; my stepfather R. Lee Chance, who taught me about telling the truth and the importance of an education; my wonderful in-laws, Mae Kongabel and father-in-law Harold Kongabel, who is still here and going on 95; my grandfather Joseph Philp, who walked the walk and had such a strong influence in my life; my grandmother Allie Philp, who started off each day with about three hours of prayer and Bible study; my other grandfather Winston Vance, who was a lifelong Methodist preacher of the old school; my father, who was a Methodist minister and died when I was two from pulling a person out of a hotel fire; my uncle Marvin Vance, who was my first pastor at First Methodist Church in Austin, Texas; all of the Philp family, who taught me what a Christian family should be like and particularly, my aunt Corrine, who tried to teach me true theology at a time when I was offtrack and thought everyone would go to heaven; friends from childhood, including Orman Taylor, Gus Schill, Jimmy Brill, Bryan Strode, and Bill Wilde, who tried to keep me humble; my many dear friends in the Harris County District Attorney's Office where I served for 21 years and where we started one of my first Bible studies; my dear friends at Bracewell & Patterson, L.L.P., the law firm where I practiced law the last 20 years and where we also had a Bible study; my pastors through the years who were very dear friends—Dr. Charles King, who is now with the Lord, Jack Lancaster of First Presbyterian, David Dorst and Bob Petterson of Christ Evangelical Presbyterian, Dick Druary and Rufus Smith of the City of Refuge, an Evangelical Presbyterian Church.

Because this is a book on discipleship, special mention should go to: John Tolson, a Presbyterian minister who founded The Gathering of Men and who personally discipled me for several years; Shad Williams, who dragged me off to Malawi and Kenya and tried to make an evangelist out of me as we preached the Gospel from loudspeakers on the top of a car in the boondocks; Chuck Colson, who took me to see the first all-Christian prisons in the world in Brazil and Ecuador and who courageously walked into crowded maximum security prisons without guards to share the Gospel and with whose able staff I worked to help bring the first prison with all-Christian programming to the United States; the Texas Board of Criminal Justice and the wonderful people in that department who have helped open the Texas prisons to roughly 40,000 volunteers, who annually come in to share Christ with the inmates (this includes the Chaplain Corps of 130 Christians who love to share the Gospel); my friend, Skip McBride and his pastor Ed Young, who encouraged me in trying to have this book published; so many wonderful Christian seminars and books that have influenced my walk, including those by Peter Wagner, a delightful friend and wonderful teacher; all the fellow elders I served with in three churches over the last 30-plus years; guys like Jim Carroll, Ron Auvenshine, Dan Tidwell, and others that I have gone out to the prison with to hold church; and all the guys in prison who have found Jesus, particularly those at Jester III and the Carol S. Vance Unit outside Houston. Last but not least, my secretary of many years, Adell Milam, who was a big help with this book.

As I reflect on my walk, God worked through many other people to disciple me. That is the way it works. Jesus commanded us to make disciples of all believers. I need to be discipled and then go disciple others. That is what the Christian life is all about and why I want to give credit to those who discipled me. But of course, all the glory belongs to Jesus.

Introduction:
What This Book Is About

First of all, this book is based on the Bible and the Bible alone for everything that is being taught. It covers 26 essential topics that Christians should know about and apply to their lives.

Each chapter has two inspirational verses, one at the beginning and one at the end, for readers to memorize. Each chapter concludes with several personal and challenging discussion questions for readers to answer.

This book can be presented to a class as a six-month formal study, using the lecture method, or it can be undertaken by a small study group. The course can be presented one-on-one by a mentor to the student, or it can be self-taught. Appendix A in the back of the book contains practical suggestions for teaching the book. This book can be used to help disciple new Christians but will also challenge mature Christians to grow in their faith.

The book is easy to follow and easy to teach. The order of presentation is a natural flow as the chart in Appendix B indicates. The reader who takes these biblical principles to heart will be on the road to a lifetime of Christian discipleship. Jesus said, "If you abide in My word, you are My disciples indeed. And you shall know the truth, and the truth shall make you free" (John 8:31-32). Abide in His Word. Abide in Jesus. Be free to be His disciple.

I

THE BIG PICTURE
AND KNOWING YOU ARE SAVED

"For God so loved the world that He gave his only begotten Son, that whoever believes in Him should not perish but have everlasting life"
(John 3:16).

FIRST OF ALL, LET'S LOOK AT THE BIG PICTURE OF THE
CHRISTIAN LIFE.

Are you saved? Do you know if you are going to heaven? However one asks it, this is the most important question you'll ever have to answer. The good news is that you can know for certain.

Jesus said, "Most assuredly I say to you, unless one is born again, he cannot see the kingdom of God" (John 3:3). What does this mean? Jesus also said, "I am the way, the truth, and the life. No one comes to the Father except through me" (John 14:6). How exactly does salvation work? How can you know you are saved? Is Jesus the only way to an eternal lifetime in heaven?

Before we get into the basics of the Christian faith, we need to see the big picture of what the Christian life is all about. If we can stand on top of the mountain and look down and see how the Christian life works, then we will be able to see where we are going and how we will get there. Let's paint a picture of what happens to us when we become believers in Jesus Christ.

God loves us so much that He sent His Son to die for our sins. God meets us where we are, that is in our sinful state. Then He draws us to Himself for an eternal relationship that includes everlasting life. We come into this world with a sinful nature, and only God can save us from our sin and reconcile us to Himself. So becoming a Christian is a totally new beginning. At the moment of conversion, we give up our citizenship in this world and become citizens of the kingdom of God. Then we start a new and growing relationship with Jesus as we begin our journey in the Christian faith.

Let's start at the beginning. The moment we are saved, we have a new birth. When we become Christians, we are spiritually born again into the kingdom of God (John 3:1-10). When this happens, we are like a little child—first we learn how to crawl and then how to walk before we learn to run. Through obedience and our love of Jesus, we will begin to grow and mature as a Christian. This takes time. Some new believers remain infants in the faith all their lives. Others are faithful, available, and teachable and mature into Christians that are useful in the kingdom of God.

Imagine a large flowerpot that sits on the back porch and has not been attended to. The soil in the pot is parched, and the only life in it is a few weeds. We are like that pot. We are meant to bloom into a beautiful flower, but without Christ, we are just parched soil and weeds. When we are saved and born again, Jesus comes to live inside us for the first time. It is like planting a flower seed in the pot. The clay pot takes on meaningful life. This little seed, if properly tended, will grow into full bloom, bear flowers, and be a blessing to all who see it. In order to flourish and grow, the seed and then the tender roots must be watered and fed. The weeds and the rocks must be removed from the pot.

This new seed is the most important thing that ever happened in our lives. This new seed is the Spirit of God that comes to live in us and gives us new life. As 2 Corinthians 5:17 says, "Therefore, if anyone is in Christ, he is a new creation; old things have passed away; behold, all things have become new." Thus, when we believe in Jesus, Jesus comes to live in us, and He gives us real life for the first time.

Even though we have this new life in Christ, we still must deal with our old old ways. The weeds need to be removed once and for all so they do not return. Jesus came not only to save us, but also to free us from weeds that would strangle us. Also, the tender roots of the plant need a fertile soil. Only God and His Son can send the life-giving food and the living water so the plant will grow. Only the Father and the Son, Jesus, can protect the plant from the bugs or birds that would eat the leaves and destroy it altogether. Stop and read Matthew 13:1-23.

As we go through this life-changing process, God will reach down and change our hearts and our minds. Jesus will take us over more and more. As this occurs, the plant will grow and become strong and healthy. We must also

After the Leap

remember that Jesus must become the root from which the plant grows. Jesus described Himself as the vine of life to which we cling. He said, " I am the vine, you are the branches. He who abides in Me, and I in him, bears much fruit; for without Me you can do nothing" (John 15:5). The vine, meaning Jesus, is strong and perfect. The vine is what the branches are attached to and where the branches receive their life. Thus, when we turn over our lives to Jesus, our branches will be alive and bear fruit as God intended. This is how dependent we must be on Jesus. Jesus must be that vine on which all of our life depends.

Our purpose in life is to be saved and then to go out into the world to produce fruit for the glory of the Father. That is what the Christian life is all about. To do this we have to learn about the vine—Jesus. We have to learn how to tend the soil. We have to learn how to get food and water to the plant, and we have to learn how to get rid of the weeds. All of this requires the power of the Holy Spirit and a close personal relationship with our Savior, Jesus Christ. We must be open, vulnerable, and receptive to the changes that God wants to make in our lives. This is what is meant by fertile soil.

Learning to walk with Jesus is not easy, but Jesus will bring us great peace, joy, and happiness. We were born to be children of God. We have a destiny to fulfill. God has a plan for each of our lives. To be the person we were created to be, we must know the Father, the Son, and the Holy Spirit and what They want to do with us. Now is the time to begin.

Like the flowerpot with the flower that doesn't bloom overnight, we must live our Christian walk day by day to bloom in the faith. The extent to which we get rid of the junk in our lives determines how we will grow in Christ and become more like Him. As Christians, we will face plenty of challenges, but in all things we can be conquerors of this life on earth through Jesus Christ.

JESUS ALONE IS NECESSARY FOR OUR SALVATION.

The last half of this chapter will focus on salvation and why Jesus is necessary. Why does God require us to believe in Jesus for salvation? Why can't we do good works and earn our way to heaven? To answer these questions we must look at what the Bible says about the basic nature of man and a fundamental problem called sin.

In the beginning, God created the world. Read the first three chapters of Genesis to see how God created the heavens, the earth, the seas, the mountains, and the animals. Before God finished His creation, He created man and then a woman after His own image, named Adam and Eve, and put them in charge of the animals and the things on earth. For a while, Adam and Eve lived in perfect harmony with God. At that time everything on earth was peaceful, including the animals, and the earth was a perfect place to live.

Then one day Adam and Eve disobeyed God. On that day the devil, who is also called Satan, disguised himself as a serpent. He lied to Eve and convinced her that she and Adam should eat from the one tree in the garden that God had said they should not eat. The devil told Eve that she and Adam would be like God if they ate from this particular tree. Adam and Eve were rebellious and disobedient, and they ate the forbidden fruit. They acted out of a selfish pride, wanting to be like God and be independent. This was the first sin. When Adam and Eve defied God, the beautiful relationship and wonderful life God had provided for them ended. Sin, that is their rebellion against God, separated Adam and Eve from God. From that time forward, life on earth has not been easy, as man has been in a constant struggle with sin and its terrible consequences.

Also, from that time forward, all mankind, that is all of Adam and Eve's descendants, have sinned. We all have a sinful nature. In fact, we sin every time we have a bad thought, think more of our own needs than of others, fail to pray, envy others, say something mean, get angry, look lustfully, fail to use time wisely, or refuse to love others as God commanded. This list goes on and on. Jesus was the only One on earth who never sinned, and He was born of woman and God. All of us are sinners (Romans 1:18-32; 3: 9-23). Romans 3:23 tells us that all of us have sinned and fallen short of the glory of God, and Romans 3:10 says that there are none who are righteous.

GOD SAYS THE PUNISHMENT FOR SIN IS DEATH, BUT JESUS SHOWS US A WAY OUT.

Now God is a perfect God. He does not want sin in His heaven or on the earth or anywhere. In fact, God hates sin so much the Bible says, "The wages of sin is death" (Romans 6:23). Death is the punishment for sin, according to what the Bible teaches. But God is also love (1 John 4:16). From His great love for us and His grace and mercy, God provided a solution to man's problem of sin and its punishment of death. To put it another way, sin always requires a punishment— someone must pay the price for sin. This is a basic truth that God teaches. And without Jesus, the individual who sinned pays that price.

The good news is that God sent His Son Jesus to pay the price for our sins when Jesus died on the cross (John 3:16, 1 Peter 3:18, 1 John 2:2). In other words,

After the Leap

Jesus died on that cross in our place. We who deserve to die for our many sins are spared that punishment because Jesus, who was sinless, died for each of us. Jesus tells us that if we will repent of our sins and put our faith and trust in Him for our salvation, then we will be saved (Ephesians 2:8). Faith in Christ is the only way we can be saved, and it is not by any good works we do.

Jesus led a sinless life even though He was fully human and fully God. Jesus willingly gave up His life to become the only perfect and acceptable sacrifice for the sins of all believers for all times. Today, all believers receive the free gift of eternal life and full benefit of that sacrifice. Nonbelievers do not. On that cross at Calvary some 2,000 years ago, Jesus was crucified and put to death to pay the full price for your sins and mine (Romans 4:25). The response God requires from us in return is that we put our faith and trust in Jesus alone for our salvation. We must come to God in true humility, recognizing we cannot save ourselves or make it to heaven on our own (Romans 10:9). God loved us so much that He sent His Son to die for you and me. In John 3:16, Jesus said, "For God so loved the world that He gave His only begotten Son, that whoever believes in Him should not perish but have everlasting life."

The truth is we cannot save ourselves. We cannot earn our way to heaven. Jesus is the only way to heaven. As Jesus said in John 14:6, "I am the way, the truth, and the life. No one comes to the Father except through Me." That is really specific, isn't it? Jesus tells us that the gate is narrow (Luke 13: 23-28). We only enter through that gate into heaven by believing in Jesus for our salvation. There is no other way to gain eternal life.

So what must we do to have eternal life? We must recognize who God is, who Jesus is, and what Jesus did for us. Then we must put all our faith and trust in Jesus for salvation. Putting our faith in Jesus is not a simple ritual or a mental exercise we engage in. This faith that we are to put in Jesus is more than an intellectual recognition that Jesus is the Son of God. Even Satan and the demons know Jesus is the Son of God (Luke 4:41). They know all about Jesus and they are not saved. Likewise, we can know in our minds exactly who Jesus is and still not be saved.

There is a big difference between *knowing* Jesus and knowing *about* Jesus. When we put our faith in Jesus, we turn our lives over to Jesus. We start to live for Jesus and not for ourselves. We must repent, confess we are sinners, and have a change of heart. We are human and will continue to sin, but we are changed. We are now forgiven, and through the sacrifice of Jesus, we are now acceptable to a holy and perfect God. Thanks to Jesus, we start our life anew. That is why Jesus wants us to ask Him to come in and live in us.

What do we mean by "putting our faith in Jesus" and "being born again?"

Webster's Dictionary defines faith as "belief and trust in God." Faith also means believing in and acting on that which we cannot see. We step out in faith when we live our lives in obedience to Christ even though we cannot see Him.

Since faith is believing in what we cannot see, the Bible says we are to walk by faith and not by sight (2 Corinthians 5:7). In other words, we must have faith in Jesus in accordance with what the Bible says and not just our own understanding. Proverbs 3:5 says, "Trust in the Lord with all of your heart, and lean not on your own understanding." When we believe in Jesus and follow Jesus even though we cannot see or touch Him, that is the living faith which the Bible says we are to have.

When we put our faith in Jesus, we are born again. (Read the story of Nicodemus in the third chapter of John.) Jesus says we must be born again. Like newborn babies, we still have to learn and mature in the faith to become who God wants us to be. We become new creatures in Christ because Jesus, through the Holy Spirit, has come to live in us (2 Corinthians 5:17).

Our individual salvation experiences differ. One person may undergo a very dramatic conversion with great emotion at the time of accepting Jesus as his Savior. Another may simply feel a sense of peace in the realization she has passed from death to life. Read about Paul's dramatic conversion when he was struck down on the road to Damascus (Acts 9:3). Next, look at how Timothy came quietly to be a believer because of his grandmother (2 Timothy 1:5). How you come to put your faith in Jesus is not important. What matters to God is that you put our faith in Jesus and then follow Him the rest of your life.

Those who are saved have their names written in the Book of Life (Philippians 4:3). When you meet Jesus face-to-face and should He ask you why you should be permitted into heaven, you can tell Him that you should be allowed to enter heaven because you put your faith and trust in Him alone. No other answer will be needed (Ephesians 2:8).

We will spend our eternity in either heaven or hell. Which one will you choose?

Jesus promises us in John 14:1-2 that there is a heaven: "Let not your heart be troubled; you believe in God, believe also in Me. In My Father's house are many mansions; if it were not so, I would have told you. I go to prepare a place for you."

Jesus tells us about heaven on numerous occasions. Jesus also tells us there is a hell (Matthew 25:31-46). The reality is that both places do exist. Every human will go to one place or the other when he or she dies. Jesus does not lie. Jesus tells us the way it really is. God's Word is the truth and the final authority on all matters because God wrote the Bible through His Holy Spirit. And the Bible tells us time and time again that each of us will spend eternity in either heaven or hell.

Jesus makes it clear that when we die, there will be a day of judgment. We will go to heaven or to hell. There will be no second chance. The Bible says our judgment will be final. Another reality that we must face is that we cannot simply choose to die and go to sleep forever. That is not an option. If we die, our lives do not end. Our souls go on forever into eternity, and there is nothing we can do to change that fact. That is why we must put our faith and trust in Jesus and only Jesus for our salvation. Only Jesus' paying for our sins by His death on the cross enables us to escape the judgment of death for our sin.

The Bible says that someday "every knee should bow . . . and every tongue should confess that Jesus Christ is Lord" (Philippians 2:10-11). Those who are saved and go to heaven will bow before King Jesus and confess He is Lord. Likewise, those who go to hell will confess Jesus Christ is Lord. The difference is that when we as humans on this earth confess that Jesus Christ is Lord on earth, then we have eternal life in heaven. If a person dies and does not know Jesus, he will confess Jesus is Lord from the depths of hell. It is only a matter of time before everyone will acknowledge Jesus is Lord. That is why it is urgent for any unbeliever to make a decision for Jesus while he is still alive. Otherwise, the Bible teaches it will be too late. Doesn't it make more sense to confess Jesus is Lord right now and be saved, instead of having to confess Jesus is Lord from the depths of hell?

Hell is such a bad place that many people, if not most of those in the world, try to convince themselves that hell does not exist. Some who claim to be Christians today now say hell no longer exists. If this is true, we do not need Jesus. If there is no hell, there is no need for a savior. The truth is our oldest and biggest enemy, the devil, does his best to deceive us by saying hell does not exist. Do not let the devil spread his favorite lie, which is that neither he nor hell exists. The Bible says hell is a place of constant torment. In hell we can cry out to God, but there will only be silence. We will be separated from God for an eternity. Can you imagine being in misery and pain in the pit of hell and not being able to call out to God? (Luke 16:19-31)

John, the apostle, was taken up to heaven, and based on his experience he wrote the Book of Revelation. Revelation gives us a partial look at heaven. What a beautiful image it is. You need to read the descriptions of heaven in the Book of Revelation. The Apostle Paul tells us in 1 Corinthians 2:9: "Eye has not seen, nor ear heard, nor have entered into the heart of man the things which God has prepared for those who love Him." Heaven is an indescribably wonderful place where we will live in the presence of Jesus for eternity.

When Jesus was dying on the cross, He told a criminal on another cross beside Him, that the criminal would join Jesus in heaven that very day. Instantly, that man was saved in the final moments of his life. He went on to live in heaven forever where he has enjoyed life to the fullest during these last 2,000 years. There was a second thief on a cross on the other side of Jesus. In his pride and stubbornness, he rejected Jesus. For his last 2,000 years and for all eternity, he will suffer in hell. One made a good choice and one made a bad choice. We have to make a choice too. The good choice, of course, is to believe in Jesus.

There is a heaven and a hell, and each one of us will spend eternity in one place or the other. Eternity is a long time. The song "Amazing Grace" says it so well: "When we've been there [in heaven] 10,000 years . . . we've no less days to sing God's praise than when we first begun."

Jesus said: "I am the resurrection and the life. He who believes in Me, though he may die, he shall live"
(John 11:25).

DISCUSSION QUESTIONS

1. Share how you came to know Jesus as your Lord and Savior.

2. How has that experience changed your life?

3. What do you think is your main purpose for being alive and here on this earth?

4. If you should die today and Jesus were to ask you why you should be admitted to heaven, what would you say?

2

REPENTANCE AND FORGIVENESS

*"If we confess our sins, He is faithful and just to forgive us our sins
and cleanse us from all unrighteousness"
(1 John 1:9).*

To understand why we need repentance and forgiveness,
we must first understand sin.

Repentance and forgiveness are both essential to receiving Jesus into our hearts. In fact, repentance and forgiveness are foundational to the salvation process. One follows the other. First we are to repent, and then we are to ask for forgiveness when we confess our sins to God. In this chapter we will discuss repentance, confession, and forgiveness from God, and last we will discuss our need to forgive others. First, let's have a look at sin so we can understand why we need repentance and forgiveness.

If it were not for sin, there would be no problems in the world. People would live in peace and happiness and live forever because sin would not have destroyed their relationship with God. Sin is a serious thing. Sin is something God hates. Sin brings down nations, cities, homes, families, marriages, and individuals. Sin always has its victims. Among the victims, we always find the sinner, who suffers the consequences of the sin.

Sin in its most basic form consists of disobedience to God. To sin is to rebel against God. To sin is always to choose man's way over God's way. Ever since Adam and Eve sinned in the Garden of Eden, we have had a basic desire in our hearts to do our own thing and to follow our own desires instead of God's perfect law. Doing it our way leads to death, destruction, depression, and disappointment. At its very root, sin separates us from God. Nothing could be worse for anyone than to be separated from God. With this separation comes hopelessness and a life of futility that ends in death unless and until we are reconciled with God.

Therefore, when sin occurs, it must be dealt with—the quicker the better. Our past sins are dealt with for all time when we repent, confess, and put our faith in Jesus as our Lord and Savior. Then we must deal with each new sin as it comes up if we are to stay close to God and receive the blessings He has in store for us. A quick and full confession of new sins is necessary to restore that right relationship with God. When things are made right again, God will restore our joy and our peace. The way we deal with sin is a process. It is a simple process but very profound. Within this process, we are called to humble ourselves, seek God's face and God's will for our life, repent, confess, and then receive the forgiveness that makes the world right side up once again.

Remember that sin is a serious business with God. That is why we must understand how to deal with our sin through repentance, confession, and forgiveness.

JESUS TAUGHT THAT REPENTANCE IS NECESSARY FOR FORGIVE-NESS AND FORGIVENESS FOR SALVATION.

Repentance is necessary in order to receive forgiveness. Repentance precedes forgiveness. And we must be forgiven by God to escape God's penalty for sin, which is death. In Luke 13:3 Jesus said, "Unless you repent you will all likewise perish." Jesus came to call sinners to repentance (Luke 5:32). Jesus at the start of His ministry said, "The Kingdom of God is at hand. Repent, and believe in the gospel" (Mark 1:15). Jesus thought repentance was so important that at the end of His days on earth, He instructed that "repentance and remission of sins should be preached in His name to all nations" as part of His great commission (Luke 24:47). In other words, not only is confessing that we are sinners important to our salvation, but repentance is also a must. Repentance involves a change of heart—that is, a determination to leave our old and sinful ways and become obedient to God. Because it is so essential, we need to know what repentance means and what we must do to repent.

What is repentance, and why did Jesus say it was so important? Repentance is turning from one's old sinful ways to follow God's ways and God's commands. The Bible has described repentance as a "godly sorrow" for our sin (2 Corinthians 7:10). The concept of repentance is simple to understand. God hates sin. God wants us to pursue righteousness. To repent is to recognize just how bad the sin in our lives is and to desire change. Repentance involves a radical change in our outlook on sin. Repentance also involves a realization of the perfect holiness and righteousness of God and just how far we have fallen short due to our sin.

Repentance is more than just sorrow for our sin. Most anyone who commits a serious sin will feel bad about such an act. Repentance is feeling godly sorrow so deeply that we desire to tell God how sorry we are for that sin. Repentance includes that state of mind in which we commit ourselves not to repeat that sin again. True repentance also brings about a desire to make things right with any person we have harmed. Repentance is a matter of the heart where down deep we want to follow Jesus and not our own fleshly desires.

Repentance and forgiveness always lead to a fundamental improvement in our relationship with God. The reason is that we become separated from God when we sin. God wants us to be reconciled to Himself so that our relationship with Him will be restored. When that relationship is restored, God provides us with a clean slate and a fresh start. And repentance involves a commitment to start over and do things right, that is do them God's way.

After we are saved, we continue a process of coming to God to seek His forgiveness. Each time we do this, we need to repent and resolve to submit to God's will. When our hearts are right, and we come to God in humility and truth, God forgives us, and our relationship with Him is restored once again. Although we receive our salvation when we first put our trust in Jesus, repenting and confessing our sins is a lifetime process. To repent is to be broken. Through repentance and a sorrow for our sins, we are broken of our pride and our self-dependence. Our fleshly ways are nailed to that same cross on which Jesus died. Then when we are broken and have turned from our sinful ways, Jesus will come to live within us in greater power through the Holy Spirit.

After we repent, John the Baptist tells us in Luke 3:8:"Therefore bear fruits worthy of repentance." Peter said that when we repent and are baptized in the name of Jesus, we will receive the gift of the Holy Spirit (Acts 2:38). The Bible also tells us in Acts 26:20 that our works will be related to our repentance. One who truly repents will no longer be involved in habitual sin. Acts 3:19 says that when we repent and turn to God, our sins will be wiped out and our repentance will be followed by times of refreshing from the Lord. The Bible makes it clear that blessings flow when we repent. When we repent, we will feel cleansed. Because repentance helps remove our guilt and shame, the very act of repentance brings forth a deep personal peace as our relationship with our Father is restored.

Repentance not only applies to each one of us as individuals, but repentance can also apply to a sinful nation. Second Chronicles 7:14 says that healing will come to a nation if the people will confess their sin, pray, seek God's face, and turn from their wicked ways. Then God will forgive their sin and heal their land. Repentance is a powerful and life-changing act. The Bible often uses the terms *forgiveness* and *repentance* interchangeably because we must repent to receive forgiveness. To seek forgiveness and not to repent is to play a deceptive mind game with God. If we ask for forgiveness, but have every intention of committing the same old sins, that in itself is a sin. That is not repentance. God forgives those who come with a clean heart, are truly sorrowful for their sins, and honestly want to change.

GOD WILL FORGIVE US OF ANY SIN, NO MATTER HOW BAD, IF OUR HEARTS ARE RIGHT.

Mary Magdalene's story is a remarkable example of how God's forgiveness and repentance works. We do not know a lot about Mary's early life except that she was deep into sin and those sins had been with her for a long time. In fact, Luke 8:2 tells us that she was oppressed by demons. She was such a sinner that Jesus had to deliver her of seven separate demons. Jesus loved her so much He not only saved her, but He also freed Mary from her slavery to sin. Once Jesus set Mary free, Mary went on to serve Jesus.

Even though Mary had many sins, Jesus forgave her of each and every sin. Mary went on to serve Jesus in mighty ways. She had the great honor of ministering to Jesus (Mark 15:40-41), of being present at the cross (John 19:25), and of being the very first person to whom Jesus appeared after the Resurrection (Mark 16:9). Not only did Jesus totally cleanse her of sin, but He also totally changed her life.

The important principle here is that Mary was not some highly religious person who led a moral and godly life. She was a longtime sinner with many problems in her past. After Mary's encounter with Jesus, she had a new heart. Jesus did a mighty work in her life, and He now stands ready to do the same for you and me. Jesus wants to forgive us just as He forgave Mary. Jesus takes us where He finds us. When we repent, Jesus cleans us up and makes us whole again. When Jesus forgives us, our sins are forgotten. This is what happened to Mary. Jesus no longer saw the old Mary because she had been forgiven. She was pure once again in God's eyes.

God says that when we are forgiven, He does not remember our sins any longer. He dumps those sins in the sea of forgetfulness. The Bible also tells us those sins are removed forever. They are no more. They are gone. The Bible tells us those sins are removed as far as the east is from the west (Psalm 103:12). That is how complete God's forgiveness is.

When we seek forgiveness, we should name each one of our sins and bring them up before the Lord one at a time. We need to be reconciled with God by this forgiveness process so it is important to be specific and confess each sin. Naming each sin drives home the seriousness of that sin and helps us recognize how much we need God's mercy. This is a healthy process that God commands us to undergo. After we have confessed, with a deep sense of humility and gratitude, we should ask for His forgiveness. God is faithful and just and will forgive us of our sins (1 John 1:9). He will forgive the worst of our sins as He did for Mary Magdalene.

The forgiveness of sins is such a miracle that even the Jews took Jesus to task for telling someone that his sins had been forgiven. The Jews accepted the fact that Jesus was capable of performing miracles of healing; however, when Jesus said that He had forgiven someone of his sin, the Jews were shocked and wanted to kill Him for blasphemy (Luke 5:21). The point is that forgiveness was considered a greater miracle than making the blind to see or the crippled walk. Today, many people believe that they have lived such a terrible life that God could never forgive them. Nothing could be farther from the truth.

Please understand that we cannot keep anything a secret from God. God knows our every sin. Thinking we can hide a sin from God is a sin. Proverbs 28:13 tells us that if we try to cover up our sin, we will not prosper. On the other hand, this same passage tells us the good news. If we confess and forsake our sins (forsaking means to repent) God will extend His mercy.

WHEN GOD FORGIVES US, WE ARE FORGIVEN. WE MUST MAKE CERTAIN THAT WE FORGIVE OURSELVES.

If God has forgiven us, then we are forgiven; therefore, we must forgive ourselves. Judgment of sin is up to God, not us. People who will not forgive themselves are guilty of blasphemy and pride. This practice is blasphemous because forgiveness of sin is totally within the hands of God. We have no divine power to overrule the sovereignty of God. Also, we have the sin of pride if we do not forgive ourselves. Not to forgive ourselves is to think our standards are higher than God's. We should not think we are so good that we cannot forgive ourselves. Do not let Satan deceive you by leading you to believe you are so bad that you cannot forgive yourself. If God has forgiven you, accept it, and go on to follow Jesus.

We must have faith and confidence in God's ability to forgive. God tells us in the Bible that the wages of sin is death (Romans 6:23). We escape death only because of the fact that Jesus' death on the cross paid for our sins. The last thing Jesus said on the cross was, "It is finished!" (John 19:30) This meant Jesus' work was complete and fulfilled. The debt for the sins of mankind had been paid in full for all who believe. Since Jesus paid the debt in full, we can now stand in God's eyes as totally forgiven people. Never let selfish pride separate you from God's mercy.

EVEN THOUGH GOD FORGETS OUR SINS WHEN HE FORGIVES US, CONSEQUENCES CAN REMAIN.

When we are forgiven, will the consequences of our sin be blotted out? No, not usually. If we have sinned against another, such as having injured another person, the consequences of that sin may remain for years to come. That is why sin is such serious business. The Bible says the iniquities, that is the sins, of the father are passed on even to the third and fourth generation (Exodus 20:5). That is a reality we have to face. If we face that reality without God's forgiveness, it is unbearable. When we accept God's forgiveness deep in our hearts, then we can go on in life. Not only will we be able to make peace with God and with our-selves, but like Mary Magdalene, we can even be useful in the work of God's kingdom here on earth.

After we are forgiven, God does not want us to go around looking like whipped dogs. We should be humble, but being depressed over our past sins is not an act of humility. Every human who ever lived has been a sinner; but when God restores our relationship with Him, we can go on living with joy and thanksgiving.

WHEN WE SIN AGAINST ANOTHER, WE SHOULD CONFESS IT, THEN TRY TO RESTORE THE OTHER PERSON TO WHOLENESS AND WORK TO RECONCILE OUR RELATIONSHIP WITH THAT PERSON.

When we sin against another, the Bible tells us we should go confess that sin to the other person and tell him or her we are sorry and seek forgiveness (James 5:16). The Bible tells us it is our responsibility to put that person in the place he or she would have been had we not sinned. Sometimes this is impossible as no amount of money could pay for a life wrongfully taken. To the extent we can, we have a biblical obligation to make restitution. This is a simple instruction and

After the Leap

needs no further explanation except to seek guidance from the Lord as to how to go about it. Part of this restorative process is to repent and ask the person you have wronged to forgive you. That act of forgiving you is important to that person and necessary to restore the right relationship between you and the other person. God wants all human relationships to be restored. You need to give that person the opportunity to forgive you.

The forgiving of sins is part of a healing process, bringing us to reconciliation and wholeness. James 5:16 says that we are to confess our sins to one another and pray for one another that we may be healed. So often, the asking for forgiveness and forgiving of another brings forth the healing and reconciliation that God so deeply desires. Forgiveness leads to wholeness. Unforgiveness is like a sickness or cancer growing within us. If we believe the Bible and believe that God's principles for our lives are true, we will be quick to forgive and forget. God wants us to do that for our own good as well as for the good of the other person. This is because He loves us.

WHEN ANOTHER SINS AGAINST US, WE MUST FORGIVE THAT PERSON OR GOD WILL NOT FORGIVE US.

Forgiving a person who has hurt us deeply is usually the most difficult issue with which to deal. When another sins against us, we will naturally feel that person should be punished. Knowing that we have been wronged, our fleshly tendency is to hold a grudge. Our fleshly tendency may be to hate the person who has wounded us deeply. Our fleshly reaction is to want to get even. This is the world's way of reacting to the situation. Our man-made laws are based on this concept to a large extent. God's law in the Old Testament speaks of an eye for an eye and a tooth for a tooth. Jesus, however, made it clear under His new covenant that judgment is up to the Lord. Judgment, revenge, and getting even are something Jesus tells us not to do (Matthew 7:1-20). The government and courts are called to make earthly judgments, but only God makes the eternal judgments. We are not called to be the judge or the executioner.

God has a different way for us to react to our enemies. God wants us to forgive those who have wronged us. In fact, God demands that we forgive anyone who has sinned against us. God makes this principle clear throughout the Bible. Three passages in the Bible explain this clearly. First, in Matthew 6:15, Jesus tells us that the Father will not forgive us unless we forgive those who have wronged us. Jesus tells us God is going to treat us just as we treat someone who has sinned against us. If we forgive our trespassers, God will forgive us. The second passage,

Mark 11:25-26, says, "If you have anything against anyone, forgive him, that your Father may also forgive your trespasses. But, if you do not forgive, neither will your Father in heaven forgive your trespasses."

The third biblical passage illustrating this point is found in the parable in Matthew 18:21-35. In this parable, Jesus said that we should forgive someone not once, twice, or three times, but seventy times seven. Jesus doesn't mean we are to keep score, forgiving someone 490 times, and then stop. He uses this high number to illustrate that we must always keep on forgiving. This same passage tells about the master who forgave his servant of a huge debt, which amounted to thousands of dollars. Right after this particular servant had been forgiven of his large debt, he began to choke another servant who owed him some small pocket change. Jesus used this illustration to explain the absurdity of our failing to forgive someone for a few sins when God has shown us great mercy by sparing us from death for our many sins. God demands we extend the same mercy to others. Remember, the trespass another person commits against us will never be as serious as the sins we have committed against God.

The point is that when God forgives sin, it is a huge blessing because God hates sin so much. God is willing to forgive us many times for serious sins. God's forgiveness demonstrates His great love for us. God wants us to love the other person just as God loves us even when that person has wronged us. When we will not forgive that other person, we are simply not following Jesus. When we refuse to forgive, we act out of our selfish nature and not in the image of Jesus. If this occurs, we need to take a close look at ourselves and seek God's forgiveness for our stubbornness. Then we must forgive that other person.

To harbor unforgiveness is to bring on bitterness and discontent.

God gives us another great benefit when we forgive the other person. That benefit is the peace of mind that flows from our act of forgiveness. This benefit alone is reason enough to forgive and forget. If we keep on harboring a grudge and hatred in our hearts, we will become defiled (Matthew 15:18-20). Unforgiveness breeds bitterness, resentment, and grief. Chances are this bitterness will grow worse every day if it is not dealt with. The quicker you deal with the sin of unforgiveness, the better off you will be. The Bible says, "Do not let the sun go down on your wrath" (Ephesians 4:26). The same is true with unforgiveness. Each day you hold on to unforgiveness, you keep on sinning in defiance of God's instruction to you. Is it any wonder that unforgiveness brings such turmoil and torment to our minds. Our mental hospitals are full of people who cling to unforgiveness and hatred and who will not forgive and forget and turn this burden over to Jesus.

When you run into people who feel as if the world is against them, look for the root of unforgiveness. It begins as a seed and then grows and flourishes until it produces all kinds of personal grief. The results can be so serious that only prayer and the powerful work of the Holy Spirit can restore these people to wholeness. Unforgiveness can grow like a cancer and spread to other areas of people's lives. The enemy has a field day as hate replaces love, and bitterness keeps people from pursuing a normal life. Those suffering from the inability to forgive need prayer and help from fellow Christians within the church body.

If you have unforgiveness in your life, confess it as a sin, then forgive that person, and turn the matter over to Jesus. Go to that other person in love and tell her that she is forgiven. Have your heart and mind and soul grafted to the vine of Christ and not to the root of unforgiveness. When you forgive, forgive totally as God has forgiven you. Do not bring the matter up again. Put the whole thing behind you just as God did with your sins.

Unforgiveness is a hard burden to carry. It is like a garbage sack that gets a little heavier every day. Let it go. Give it to Jesus. He can withstand all of our burdens. Forgiveness makes things right. Always choose forgiveness. And God always stands ready to forgive us of any sin when we repent and confess. Jesus gave us an example of that total forgiveness and beautiful reconciliation of father and son even after the son had squandered his life. Read this story in Luke 15:11-32.

"For if you forgive men their trespasses, your heavenly Father will also forgive you. But if you do not forgive men their trespasses, neither will your Father forgive your trespasses" (Matthew 6:14-15).

Discussion Questions

1. Are you currently holding any grudge, bitterness, resentment, or anger against any other person? Make a list. Write out each person's name and what it is you are having trouble forgiving that person for.

2. What are you going to do about your unforgiveness? What do you think the result will be if you hold on to unforgiveness?

3. What continuing sin in your life do you need to repent of and confess right now? Are you willing to do this? If not, why not?

4. How will God see you after you have repented, confessed, and asked for His forgiveness?

3
GOD, OUR CREATOR AND FATHER

"God is love" (1 John 4:8).

To understand God we need to know about the Trinity. The Trinity refers to God, Jesus, and the Holy Spirit.

How big is your God? What is your idea about who God is? Your relationship with God will depend in no small part on your understanding of His nature and character. You must know the truth about God and you must know God.

God is all-powerful and all-knowing. He is the Creator of all things. Also, God is love. To understand God, we must understand what the Trinity is. The Trinity refers to the only three Divine Beings that exist. The three are God, Jesus, and the Holy Spirit. There are other supernatural beings such as angels and demons, but there are only three Persons who have the nature of God. As Christians, we believe in God, we believe in Jesus, and we believe in the Holy Spirit. There is a mystery here because humans have trouble understanding how God, Jesus, and the Holy Spirit are separate, and yet at the same time the Three are One. The Three are One because Jesus and the Holy Spirit always reflect God perfectly in their character. The Three are so identical in thought and deed that to know One is to know the Others. Jesus and the Holy Spirit are so close to God that They know Him perfectly and know what His will is in every situation. They have both been with God from the beginning. And, of course, Jesus is God's only Son.

All Three are essential to our salvation as explained fully in Romans (chapters 1 through 8). All Three are totally unified in mind and will. They act together in complete agreement on all things. Jesus and God are One (John 10:30), and God and the Holy Spirit are One (John 16:13).

In this chapter, we will look at what the Bible says about God, the Father. Then, in the next two chapters we will focus on His Son Jesus and the Holy Spirit.

GOD IS ALL-POWERFUL AND ALL-KNOWING AND CAPABLE OF BEING EVERYWHERE AT THE SAME TIME.

God is known by many names in the Bible. Each name describes an important character trait of God. In fact, there are so many names, it would be difficult to make a list. Some of the names are Creator, Healer, Provider, King, Judge, Giver of Life, Love, Truth, All-Knowing, All-Powerful.

The Bible says that God has such infinite wisdom that no man is capable of understanding the mind of God (Job 36:26). Although no one can fully understand God, God has revealed to us all that we need to know about Him. God, the Father, wants us to know Him intimately. He wants us to be able to hear His voice and to obey Him (Deuteronomy 30:20). The Bible tells us many things about God. We will focus on some of those things that we need to understand about God. When you read the Bible in its entirety, you will have a clearer picture of who God is.

First, God created all things (Genesis 1). Every creature and every thing is His and under His control. That means He knows what you are thinking right now (Hebrews 4:13). He knows every hair on your head, and not a sparrow falls that He does not know about. God knew us before we were in our mother's womb. He knows every time we sit down or stand up. God knows all things about us.

God is God. He described Himself to Moses simply as "I AM" (Exodus 3:14). That is the only name He needs. "I AM." God can do anything He wants. He is totally sovereign. He is totally in control of the universe, of history, and of everything that exists or will ever exist.

GOD IS LOVE. HE IS ALSO FAITHFUL AND JUST.

God is not only totally in control of the universe, but He is also faithful and just (1 John 1:9). He is totally dependable. God is the King and Lord. He is the judge of every person. He hates sin. As a God of justice, He will punish sin. The Bible tells us "the wages of sin is death" (Romans 6:23). Only through Jesus Christ, who paid the price for our sins on the cross, can believers avoid that certain pun-

After the Leap

ishment of death for sin. God is to be feared. According to the Old Testament Scripture, the only thing we should fear is God (Deuteronomy 6:13). He is indeed an awesome God.

God is love as the Bible tells us (1 John 4:8). That is probably the most important characteristic for each of us to understand. Our most basic need is to love and be loved because God made us that way. The fact that God loves sinners like us so much is beyond our worldly comprehension. God's love is powerful. His love, through His Son Jesus, gives peace and purpose to our lives on this earth and also gives us eternal life. God loves us the same whether we are saved or not saved. Remember, Jesus came to die in order to save sinners, and we are all sinners. God, by sending His only Son to die for you and me, shows how very much He does love each one of us (John 3:16).

God is merciful. By forgiving our sins each time we confess them and ask for forgiveness, God demonstrates His endless mercy as He cleanses us (1 John 1:9). He forgets our sin and remembers it no more, so we are able to enter His presence spotless and pure.

God wants the best for each of us. He always has our best interests at heart. He wants to see us grow and mature in our Christian walk. He wants to enlist us as part of His army to carry out His agenda and His plan for His kingdom. God has a plan for each of our lives. God is always at work and calls us to be a part of His team in doing His work. We need to listen to Him to know what He has called us to do and then do it.

OUR GOD IS A JEALOUS GOD WHO DESIRES THAT WE PRAISE AND WORSHIP HIM.

God demands our worship and praise of Him alone. He is a jealous God. He does not want us to worship false gods of any kind. God commanded each one of us to love Him with all of our heart, strength, soul, and mind. This is called "The Great Commandment." Jesus said this was the most important commandment (Matthew 22:37-38).

Our God is a generous God whose storehouse of blessings and gifts is unlimited. He may not shower us with material gifts, but He wants us to have whatever we need in order to serve Him. He will give us spiritual gifts and blessings in accordance with our needs. He wants us to come to Him in prayer and be dependent on Him instead of ourselves. When we obediently follow Him, God will equip and empower us to carry out the mission to which He has called us.

GOD IS ALSO OUR FATHER, OUR DADDY.

Above all else, God wants our hearts. He wants each of us to have a warm, close, and intimate relationship with Him. God describes himself as our Father. When Jesus gave His disciples the Lord's Prayer, Jesus told the disciples to refer to God as "Abba" (Matthew 6:9). Abba was the Greek word for *Daddy*. The Jews had not used such a familiar term to refer to God before. Jesus wants us to call our all-powerful and holy God "Daddy." The use of this term shows just how caring, how tender, and how loving our God is.

God is all-knowing, all-powerful, and is outside of time and space as we know it because God created time and space. God is the Great Healer. He is our Deliverer from the enemy, the devil. He is our Savior, and that is why He sent His Son. He is perfect. God is our Rock and our Refuge and a Mighty Fortress. God knows everything about us, including all our sins, yet God still chooses to love us in the midst of all our shortcomings.

We do not have the mental capacity to understand the mind of God. God is so much greater and so much smarter than we are that we cannot hold a candle to His ways or His thoughts. "My thoughts are not your thoughts, nor are your ways are my ways," says the LORD (Isaiah 55:8). God looks at things differently than we do. God looks at things perfectly. We do not. We can learn so much about God through the Bible and the life of Jesus, but we will never fully understand His ways. The important thing is to know Him the best that we can. That is more important than memorizing factual knowledge about Him. We get to know Him by loving Him, obeying Him, and spending time with Him through the Bible, through prayer, and through serving others in Jesus' name. That is what is important. God is smarter than all people, all angels, all books, and all computers put together. In fact, He is billions and billions of times smarter than that. There is absolutely nothing too complicated for God to understand. Is it any wonder that man's chief end in life is to glorify God and enjoy Him forever?

GOD IS SO MERCIFUL THAT HE SENDS US A WAY TO BE SAVED IF WE WILL JUST LISTEN.

Some people say that God is not fair or just because some people are saved and go to heaven and some will spend an eternity in hell. This is simply not a true statement. We all deserve death because of our sins. Yet God through His endless love and mercy sent Jesus to show us a way out of death for our sins. All we have to do is repent and put our faith and trust in Jesus. As sinners, we are all on a boat that is sinking into the deep waters of hell. God tells us through His Word that all of us are doomed to go down with the ship unless we do what God tells us. We must follow God's instructions and get on the lifeboat that He has sent to save us.

When we reject Jesus and turn our backs on God's provision for salvation, then we choose our own fate and seal our own death. If you were on a ship and the ship started sinking, what would you do? You would want to climb on a lifeboat and get off that sinking ship. God has sent us a lifeboat in the person of Jesus Christ. He can save us from hell. When we hear that Jesus is the only way to avoid death and hell, we need to get on board. We do this by believing in Jesus alone for our salvation. If the ship is sinking and we refuse to get in the lifeboat, how can we complain? God wants to draw everyone to Himself (2 Peter 3:9). When God offers us a way to escape the punishment of our sins, we simply must do what God says. If we refuse to obey, that is our own fault. We cannot blame God for our own stubbornness, our own pride, and our own hardness of heart. How can we complain when we refuse to do what God asks of us? We deserve whatever we get either due to our hardheaded pride or to our deliberate rebellion from our Father in heaven.

WE SHOULD NOT FEAR ANYTHING OR ANYBODY EXCEPT GOD.

Because of God's greatness and His power, we are called to fear Him. He is the only Person we should fear. To fear God means to hold Him in awesome respect for His holiness and who He is. To fear God is to realize how much He hates sin and the penalty of death that He has prescribed for sin. Proverbs 9:10 tells us the fear of the Lord is the beginning of wisdom and understanding. That is how basic this command to fear God is. Fear of God leads to long life, humility, wisdom, and all kinds of blessings. The fear of God gives us an appreciation of the seriousness of sin.

Ecclesiastes 8:13 says that the ungodly do not fear the Lord and without such a fear life will not go well for these fools. A big difference between the godly person and the ungodly person is that the godly person fears the Lord. This fear of God means to have a deep sense of reverence and awe for God. The person who takes the Lord's name in vain is a fool because he obviously has no fear of the Lord. At the same time we are to fear nothing but God. Nothing else in this world, including any person, should cause us fear. We should fear only God.

Jesus put it this way: "Do not fear those who kill the body but cannot kill the soul. But rather fear Him [God] who is able to destroy both soul and body in hell" (Matthew 10:28). We are told to fear God because of His perfect justice and His perfect holiness, which are essential to His character. Even when we come into His presence in prayer or worship, we should do so with awe and with a deep realization of His greatness and His holiness.

OUR GOD IS A HOLY GOD WHO WANTS US TO KNOW AND UNDERSTAND HIS CHARACTER.

God is holy. God is righteous, and God is just. Until we can understand just how much God hates sin and that God's punishment for sin is death, we cannot appreciate the magnitude of God's love, mercy, and grace. God gave us His law, which we will study later in the chapters on the Ten Commandments. God's law is perfect. God's standards are perfect. There is no compromising of His law. All of this is part of God's character and essential to our knowing Him. Without God's perfect standards and perfect law, there would be no need for His grace or His mercy and no need for a Savior, that is Jesus, to save us from our sins. We must never fall for the lies of this world or the enemy that a little sin is all right. Sin is never all right with God, and that is why we always need to confess any sin and receive God's forgiveness. God's holiness is awesome and an essential part of His character.

Although we are not capable of fully understanding either the holiness of God or His unsearchable depths, God did describe Himself in many ways in the Bible. The more we understand about who God said He was, the greater will be our love for Him, the greater will be our total dependence on Him, and the greater will be our appreciation of who He really is.

The most common name God used in the Bible is the name **Jehovah,** which means "the One who is always present." God is present with us when we get up in the morning and when we go to bed at night. This name was used several thousand times. The next most common name is **Elohim**, which describes God's power and might. His power and might are unlimited. **El Shaddai**, literally meaning "God of mountains," also carries with it the message that God is all-powerful.

The name **El Olam** signifies that God is everlasting. We find our security in the fact that God will always be there for those of us who are His children. **Jehovah-shalom** is the name of God that means He is the Lord of peace, and that the only way we will ever find true personal peace will be by putting our trust in His Son, Jesus Christ.

Jehovah-tsidkenu speaks of God's perfect righteousness. It is because of

After the Leap

God's perfect righteousness that God is a Holy God. God is holiness personified. Until we understand something about God's holiness and righteousness, we cannot appreciate the severity of sin, particularly our own sin. Also, God imparts His righteousness to us through His Son's death on the cross. We have no righteousness on our own, but we become righteous through the power of the death and resurrection of Jesus and through the total forgiveness God gives to us in His grace.

We also know God as our **Adonai**, that is our Master. His authority is total and absolute over all things. We are to serve Him as a servant serves His master. At the same time God is also our loving **Abba Father**. This is how we address God in prayer as Jesus taught us in the Lord's Prayer. Our mental image of God should always include one of the Loving Father.

El Elyon means Most High. This name also signifies that God is the Creator of heaven and earth. **Jehovah-nissi**, which means "the Lord is my banner," signifies that God is always victorious and that it is by God's might and not our own that victory comes. And with God on our side, we are always assured of victory although at times we must wait on the Lord.

These are just a few of God's many names that characterize His majesty, His greatness, and the vastness of His Being. What a miracle it is that in light of His infinite greatness and our smallness, this Loving Father reaches down to love us and provides for us and calls us His children. As Psalm 8:4 says, "What is man that You [the God of the Universe] are mindful of him?"

Perhaps Isaiah 40:28 sums it up at least in part with this beautiful passage: "Have you not known? Have you not heard? The everlasting God, the Lord is the Creator of the ends of the earth, neither faints nor is weary. There is no searching of His understanding."

GOD WANTS AN ONGOING AND CLOSE PERSONAL RELATIONSHIP WITH EACH OF US THROUGH HIS SON.

Take a moment to think about why we are here. We are here because God made us. His main purpose in creating us is so we would have an intimate and loving relationship with Him. Yet, since the time that Adam sinned, all of us have let God down and pursued a lie instead of His truth. That is our nature. Even so, in our rebellion and disobedience, God calls us today to be reconciled to Him through His Son, Jesus, who died for our sins. Through that great miracle and process, we are now welcomed into His kingdom where we will be seated in heaven with Jesus as we receive those wonderful blessings that He has for each of us. What an awesome God we serve.

"Blessed is the man who fears the Lord, who delights greatly in His commandments" (Psalm 112:1).

Discussion Questions

1. Name as many of the characteristics of God as you can. Be specific.

2. What are the three things about God that mean the most to you personally?

3. Why is knowing God intimately more important than knowing factual information about God?

4. What is it about God that causes us to love Him and yet also to fear Him?

4
JESUS, OUR LORD, SAVIOR, AND FRIEND

"In the beginning was the Word, and the Word was with God, and the Word was God" (John 1:1).

"And the Word became flesh and dwelt among us" (John 1:14).

JESUS IS GOD'S ONLY SON, AND JESUS HAS BEEN WITH GOD FROM THE VERY BEGINNING.

Jesus is the only Son of God. The Gospel of John begins by telling us that Jesus has been with God from the very beginning. *Word* as used in the above memory verse refers to Jesus. John 1:3 tells us that it was through Jesus that everything in the world was made. The first chapter of the Gospel of John tells us about the character and identity of Jesus. Please read it. About 2,000 years ago, Jesus took on the form of flesh and dwelt among us on earth (John 1:14). Jesus is also described as King and Lord (Revelation 19:16). Jesus will also be the Judge of each of us when we die on this earth. The Bible tells us that Jesus is our Prophet, Priest, and King. He is also our closest personal Friend (John 15:15). He is our Savior. Jesus is our all in all. He is the most important thing in our life.

Long before Jesus came down to this earth and was born in that manger in Bethlehem, the Bible had prophesied the coming of Jesus. The Bible has many prophecies about Jesus. The Bible told us hundreds of years in advance what Jesus would be like, where He would be born, how He would live, how He would die, and how He would save us from our sin. The prophecies about Jesus all came true. One of the major purposes of the Old Testament is to point to Jesus and lift Him up as the Savior.

JESUS ALONE PROVIDES SALVATION, ETERNAL LIFE, AND TOTAL FORGIVENESS OF OUR SINS.

If we put our faith and trust in Jesus, we will live joyously and victoriously in heaven. We will be with Jesus forever. The Bible tells us that someday "every knee should bow . . . and every tongue should confess that Jesus Christ is Lord" (Philippians 2:10-11). This is because Jesus is Lord. Whether we are in heaven or hell, each one of us someday will acknowledge the truth about Jesus.

Jesus came to die for our sins, and if we believe in Him for our salvation, we will have eternal life. Jesus willingly came to die for you and me. Jesus told His disciples long before His death that "No one takes it [My life] from Me, but I lay it down of Myself. I have power to lay it down, and I have power to take it again. This command I have received from My Father" (John 10:18).

Jesus' perfect sacrifice paid for the sins of all believers for all time, including all the years in the past and all the years to come in the history of mankind. This is because Jesus led a perfect life. Jesus was the only person who ever walked on the face of the earth without sin. Everyone else has sinned. Thus, Jesus became the perfect sacrifice, like the perfect lamb that was the object of sacrifice in the Old Testament. Jesus is that perfect Lamb. That is why the Bible refers to Jesus as the Lamb in the Bible. He is also referred to as the Lion of Judah. Through His perfect strength and power, He reigns over everything in the universe more than the lion reigns over the animals of the jungle. Because Jesus was perfect and because His suffering on the cross was so great, Jesus made the only sacrifice sufficient to pay for all the sins of the world. In fact, the sacrifice of Jesus was greater than all the sins of the world.

JESUS' LIFE ON THIS EARTH IS AN AMAZING STORY.

Jesus was born in Bethlehem (in Judea) not very far from the holy city of Jerusalem. His mother was Mary, a virgin. Jesus' Father was God because Mary was made pregnant by the Holy Spirit. Mary's husband, Joseph, was not Jesus' natural father, but Joseph served as Jesus' earthly father.

To understand how Jesus lived and what He did and what He said, you must read the four gospels, which are the books of Matthew, Mark, Luke, and John. Jesus' first goal was to call sinners to salvation. Jesus did this through His preaching, teaching, and performing of many miracles. He had the same human emotions that all of us are born with. He wept, cried, and rejoiced. He had compassion every time He saw someone who was hurting or who was not saved. In short, He loved others like no one has ever loved before. In the short span of only three years of ministry, Jesus accomplished all that He set out to do, all that God the Father desired.

As one author put it, Jesus never wrote a book, never traveled far from His place of birth, never was a king, never held any public office, never was rich, and never had a place He could call home. He chose to work through a small band of men, whom we call the twelve disciples. They were not famous either. They were ordinary men. Yet through His ministry and the small group of men and women who surrounded Him, Jesus changed the world. All honest historians and scholars recognize this. Unfortunately, many who recognize His greatness do not recognize Him as Lord and Savior and God's only Son. Jesus spent only 33 years on earth, and the gospels vividly describe His ministry during the last three years of His life.

At the end of His time on earth, Jesus gave up His life on the cross to die for our sins. Even though He was condemned to death and put to death by the authorities, it was Jesus who voluntarily gave up His life for our sins and fulfilled the promises of the Old Testament. Three days later Jesus was raised from the dead exactly as He had foretold His disciples. By doing this He claimed victory over death for all who believe in Him (Mark 10:33-34). Jesus, after His death on the cross, was put into a tomb that was sealed with a huge stone and guarded by well-armed soldiers. Nevertheless, Jesus rose from that tomb. His body was never found.

The resurrection of Jesus is a historical fact. First Corinthians 15:1-8 gives a good account of the many witnesses who saw Jesus after He rose from the dead. These witnesses included His disciples, several of the women who were very close to Him, and many others, including a crowd of 500 people. As John said in 1 John 1:1, "The One who existed from the beginning is the One we have now heard and seen. We saw Him with our own eyes and touched Him with our own hands. He is Jesus Christ, the Word of life" (*The Book*). All these eyewitnesses could attest that Jesus returned from the dead in full physical form including being able to eat food. They also saw that He had nail scars on His hands. Jesus remained on earth during this 40-day resurrection period and then was taken to heaven (Acts 1:9).

No one has ever been able to prove that Jesus did not arise from the dead. The body of Jesus was never found because it was not anywhere to be found.

Before Jesus died on the cross, most of His disciples were so frightened that they went into hiding; however, after the Resurrection, the disciples were so convinced that Jesus was the Son of God that all but one disciple suffered a cruel death as a result of witnessing to the world about Jesus. The evidence points to the fact that Jesus was exactly who He said He was—the Son of God and the long-awaited Messiah. The name "Jesus" means He will save us from our sins. He is our Savior and our Lord.

JESUS IS ONE IN THOUGHT AND SPIRIT WITH THE FATHER AS JESUS DID ONLY WHAT THE FATHER TOLD HIM.

When Jesus was on earth, He relied totally on the Father. Jesus only spoke on the authority of the Father (John 12:49). Jesus did only what the Father told Him to do. Jesus did nothing without the Father's direction (John 5:19). Jesus looked to the Father every day and every hour for specific direction as to what He was to do (John 5:20). Jesus in His human form on earth was totally dependent upon the Father for everything (John 8:28-29). Jesus constantly prayed to the Father. Jesus would take periods of time to get away and pray, fast, and seek the Father's will.

Therefore, when we look at the life of Jesus and understand how Jesus lived and how He thought, we know God. Jesus revealed the Father as never before. Every time Jesus made a statement or performed an action, it was just like the Father was doing it.

From Jesus' example we also learn that we must always look to the Father and hear His voice to know how we should live. Jesus set the perfect example for us in how He lived on this earth. We are called to follow that example. Jesus commanded us to take up our cross and follow Him (Matthew 16:24). That is not an easy saying because it means we are to crucify our flesh and live in the Spirit. This means we have to put down the things of this world and follow Jesus.

Jesus wants to live inside us and make His home in us (John 14:23). Jesus loved us so much that He came as a humble servant, even though He is our King and Lord. Now He wants to be the center of our lives. Through the work of the Holy Spirit, He wants to be a part of everything we do. He wants to take up residence in our lives and bodies. That is why our bodies are referred to as holy temples (2 Corinthians 6:16). When Jesus does live in us, others will see Him in us. And if they really see Jesus, they may also want to know Him.

JESUS CAME TO FREE US FROM OUR SLAVERY TO THE SIN OF OUR FLESHLY NATURE.

God had planned in advance for Jesus to come to earth to provide for our salvation. The prophets in the Old Testament told the Jewish people years in advance about the coming of Jesus, who was also called the Messiah. The Jews were expecting a mighty king to overthrow the Roman conquerors of Israel, but Jesus came as a humble servant who brought not worldly power but eternal salvation to believers (Isaiah 61:1-3). Jesus did not accomplish His mission by military power. Jesus showed us the way to God through the power of His love. And by that same power, Jesus came to free us from our sinful ways.

As humans we are all drawn to sin. Sin can enslave us as it has with so many who are obsessed with alcohol, drugs, sex, pride, money, and power. The Prophet Isaiah told us in chapter 61 that God would send a Messiah who would heal the sick and brokenhearted, make the blind see, and set the prisoners free. In Luke 4:18, we read about Jesus at the beginning of His ministry. He read those same words from Isaiah 61:1-2 and declared that He, Jesus, was the One who had come to set the prisoners free. Then through His death on the cross, Jesus did just that. Jesus set us free of the sin and idols of this world so we can follow Him (John 8:32).

The truth about Jesus is that He came to do far more than save us. He came to heal us and deliver us so that we might be good and faithful servants. He wants to heal us of the deep emotional wounds of the past. He wants to deliver us from the enemy. He wants to free us of our addictions. He wants to free us from worshiping the things of this world that will rust and decay. He wants to free us of our pride, which comes from our fleshly nature. He wants to be our Savior and the Lord of our lives. Jesus has the power and the desire to set us free from anything and everything that keeps us from being the people God wants us to be. Jesus wants to free us so we can be effective disciples for Him. Jesus also came to destroy the works of the devil, Satan. It was the work of the devil that brought Adam and Eve and mankind into sin, and Jesus came to defeat this age-old enemy (1 John 3:8).

The most important question anyone will ever ask is, "Just who is this Man, Jesus"? Jesus asked that question of Peter, and Peter got the answer right (Matthew 16:15-16). If you have not put your faith in Jesus, Jesus is asking you this question right now. You cannot avoid Him. You must either accept Him as your Lord and Savior or deny Him. To be undecided about Jesus is to deny Him. The most important decision you will ever make is to decide who Jesus is. Is He an impostor, a liar, or exactly who He said He was? The answer is clear. He is the Christ, the Messiah, and the Savior who will rescue you from hell and give you eternal life from the moment you first believe. He now says to each of us, "Take up [your] cross daily and follow Me" (Luke 9:23). Will you?

After we are saved, we are called to develop a personal relationship with Jesus, whom we are to serve and obey, and who desires to be our closest friend.

Jesus wants each of us to have a close, intimate, and personal relationship with Him. The extent to which we come to know Jesus will determine our Christian growth. Above all, Jesus wants our hearts. How do we give Him our hearts? We start by developing a personal relationship with Jesus by spending time with Him. Since Jesus wants to be our closest friend, we must understand what it is that forms an intimate friendship.

To have a close friendship with someone, we must really know the other person. We must know how the other person thinks and what his priorities in life are. We must know what that person likes to do. We must spend time, in fact, a lot of time, with that person to build a close relationship. All communication between two friends should be honest, open, and loving. We must be willing to reach out to that friend, and we must care about our friend in order to build a friendship. It is the same with Jesus.

Jesus told His disciples that He came to serve. Jesus made it clear to His disciples and to all believers that we are all called to serve: "Just as the Son of Man [Jesus] did not come to be served, but to serve and to give His life as a ransom for many" (Matthew 20:28). When we minister to others in His name, we serve Jesus. When we visit the sick or the prisoners or feed the poor, we serve Jesus. One basic way we love Jesus is to do for others as Jesus has done for us. Jesus commands us to love Him, love others, and serve Him. He also tells us if we love Him, we will obey His commands (John 14:21; 15:10.)

Jesus should be our best friend. He saved us. He always wants to do what is best for us, and He takes great interest in how we live our lives and if we obey Him. He is always there to forgive us for our sins if we will truly repent and ask for that forgiveness (1 John 1:9). He is always available when we take our problems to Him. He is faithful in His friendship. He is consistent. He never gives up on us. We are the recipients of His perfect love and His grace and His endless mercy. All Jesus asks is that we love Him as He first loved us (1 John 4:19).

We are His sheep. He is the loving and caring Shepherd (John 10:14). If we

After the Leap

stray, He will go out of His way to retrieve us. He cares about every single thing we do and every single thought we have. We must be available to Him to serve Him. We must be open to Him so that He can change our lives. We must be teachable so that He can mold us into His followers. Jesus wants us to know Him so well that we recognize His voice over all others (John 10:27-28).

The more we know Jesus, the more we appreciate His greatness, His holiness, His perfection, and, of course, His love, grace, and mercy. The closer we draw to Jesus, the more humble we become and the more important He becomes in our lives. How can you draw closer to Jesus and love Him more? The Bible mentions several ways:

- We can draw closer to God through frequent, regular prayer.

- We can draw closer to God through the daily reading of His Word, the Bible.

- We can draw closer to God through constant praise and worship of Jesus and the Father.

- We can draw closer to God through ministering to others in love in the name of Jesus.

- We can draw closer to God through fellowship with close friends who hold each other accountable.

- We can draw closer to God through participation in the church, which is the body of Christ.

The more we know God, the more His presence increases in our lives. The more He increases, the greater our joy becomes. What kind of friend is Jesus to you? What are you doing to draw closer to the Savior? Is He just another acquaintance, or is He the center of your life? Is He the Lord of your life? Do you know His voice? Can others look at you and know you are close to Jesus? Can they look at you and see Jesus? How would you describe your personal relationship with Jesus?

As this chapter closes, focus on who Jesus described Himself to be. Jesus said He is **the truth**, which means we can believe everything that He tells us. Jesus described Himself as **the way**, which means that Jesus is the only way to the

Father and to heaven. Jesus said He is **the life**, which means He is the provider of eternal life (John 14:6). Jesus also declared that He is **the bread of life**, and said that "he who comes to Me will never hunger" (John 6:35). Jesus said He is **the gate,** because Jesus is our gateway into heaven and eternal life. In John 8:12 Jesus said He is **the light of the world,** and that no one who follows Him will ever walk in darkness. Jesus also said He is **the vine** and that we are the branches (John 15:1-8). Of course, branches have no life apart from being attached to the vine. Finally, Jesus declared Himself to be **the good shepherd** (John 10:11) and tells us that the good shepherd lays down His life for His sheep, which, of course, is all of us who believe. These declarations and promises of our Lord and Savior, Jesus Christ, sum it all up. Truly, Jesus is our all in all and invites us to believe in Him and to know Him as we have never known anyone else.

To capture the depth of what Jesus did for us and who Jesus is, turn to Colossians 1:13-18 and read this passage right now. Truly, Jesus has reconciled us to the living God for an eternity of love and peace.

"I am the vine, you are the branches. He who abides in Me, and I in Him, bears much fruit; for without Me you can do nothing"
(John 15:5).

Discussion Questions

1. Describe your personal relationship with Jesus right now and then discuss how you can get to know Him better.

2. What do you see that Jesus has done for you according to Colossians 1:13-18? List each thing that you discover.

3. What are you doing for others right now to show your love for Jesus?

5
THE HOLY SPIRIT, OUR COUNSELOR AND HELPER

"And I will pray [to] the Father, and He will give you another Helper, that He may abide with you forever, even the Spirit of truth, whom the world cannot receive because it neither sees Him nor knows Him. But you know Him, for He lives with you and will be in you" (John 14:16-17).

JUST WHO IS THE HOLY SPIRIT?

Did you know you cannot live for Christ without the Holy Spirit in you? Did you know that it is the Holy Spirit who will empower you for life, counsel you, comfort you, and convict you of sin? To be a Christian, you must understand who the Holy Spirit is.

The Holy Spirit is the third person of the Trinity. Usually, it is this person of the Trinity that Christians know the least about. This is natural because the Bible puts the focus more on God and Jesus, whom we are called to worship. What we need to remember is that the Holy Spirit is our friend, who also serves as our Comforter and Counselor. Also, we need to remember that it is only through the power of the Holy Spirit that we receive true spiritual life. The Bible teaches that life only comes to us through the Holy Spirit (John 6:63).

The way that Jesus comes to live in us is by the Holy Spirit. It is only by the power of the Holy Spirit that is Jesus Christ in us, that we are able to walk and live in Christ. All of the Christlike character traits we possess, such as love, faithfulness, and goodness, come to us through the work of the Holy Spirit. When we have Jesus living in us, we have the Holy Spirit and vice versa. The Holy Spirit always reflects and points to Jesus.

The Holy Spirit and God and Jesus are so completely identical that they are one. When we talk of God or Jesus or the Holy Spirit, we see the same character-istics. This is because the Bible teaches God, Jesus, and the Holy Spirit are one. The Holy Spirit is sent out by the Father to do the work of the Father and of Jesus. Jesus, of course, only does the will of the Father. The three are alike in thought, and the three work together in total harmony to carry out God's purposes.

The Holy Spirit is a spirit and capable of being everywhere at once. At the same time, the Holy Spirit is a person. Let us look at what the Bible says about the Holy Spirit. The Holy Spirit is a person just as Jesus was a person and was also sent to do the will of God. The Holy Spirit has great power and participat-ed in the earth's creation. God created the earth when He breathed His Spirit on the waters (Genesis 1:1-2). This third person of the Trinity is the power that draws us to Jesus. Without the Holy Spirit, we would remain blind and unable to see or understand that Jesus is truly our Savior. Only through the Holy Spirit are we given eyes to see and ears to hear the truth about Jesus to be drawn to Him for our salvation. The Holy Spirit testifies about Jesus.

This person of the Trinity was sent to be with each of us in a very personal way. The Holy Spirit is always there for us. He immediately takes residence within us when we invite Jesus to be our Savior. It is through the power and presence of the Holy Spirit that Jesus lives in our hearts. The Holy Spirit relates to us individually, intimately, and personally. He has all the power and authority of the Father and is also extremely sensitive, gentle, and caring.

The Holy Spirit is the main way God communicates with us. The Holy Spirit teaches us in various ways, but usually through that quiet voice within us (John 14:26). As we walk more in the Spirit, we come to the point where we hear more clearly what God is telling us. When the Holy Spirit communicates with us, this is God and Jesus talking to us (John 16:12-15).

You will have a deeper appreciation of what the Holy Spirit can do in your life if you look up and study the following passages about the Holy Spirit.

THE BIBLE GIVES US WONDERFUL DESCRIPTIONS OF WHAT THE
HOLY SPIRIT DOES FOR US.

• The Abiding Guest (John 14:16)
The Holy Spirit abides permanently in the hearts of all believers. He lives within us. In fact, Jesus lives inside us through the Holy Spirit.

• The Teacher (John 14:26)
The Holy Spirit is our teacher. When we read the Bible, the Holy Spirit will

make clear to us important biblical truths. The Holy Spirit teaches us in many ways. He uses the Bible, sermons, Christian friends, Bible studies, prayer, and praise. The Holy Spirit can speak to us anyway He chooses.

- **Convicter of Sin (John 16:8)**

When we sin, the Holy Spirit lets us know we have done wrong. If we are walking with Jesus, our conscience will hurt when we sin because of the work of the Holy Spirit. The Holy Spirit convicts us of our sin.

- **The Testifier (John 15:26)**

The Holy Spirit always glorifies and honors both the Father and the Son. The Holy Spirit prepares the hearts of those who are lost and draws them to Jesus. Without the work of the Holy Spirit, people in their natural state would not be able to see Jesus for who He is. The Gospel is just foolishness to the lost without the work of the Holy Spirit (1 Corinthians 1:18).

- **The Spirit of Truth (John 16:13)**

God is truth. Jesus is truth. Whatever the Holy Spirit does is truth. The Holy Spirit is to be trusted to communicate the truth to us.

- **The Empowerer, Anointer, and Giver of Gifts for Service to Others (1 Corinthians 12:1–11)**

We can do nothing for Jesus in our own power, without the Holy Spirit working in us. The New Testament, particularly the Book of Acts, describes how Christians were empowered and anointed to preach, to teach, to heal, to minister to others, and to do the things that Jesus commanded all of His disciples to do. Our gifts for ministry and our power to minister come through the Holy Spirit. These gifts are available to us today as God chooses to impart them and are to be used for the glory of God and Jesus.

- **Our Helper (Romans 8:26)**

The Bible tells us that even when we do not know how to pray, the Holy Spirit will pray for us. Jesus describes the Holy Spirit as our helper when in John 14:16 He tells us: "He [the Father] will give you another Helper, that He may abide with you forever." The Holy Spirit helps us in ways that we don't even notice.

- **Our Counselor (John 16:13)**

Scripture tells us that the Holy Spirit is there to "to guide us into all truth."

When we go to the Father in prayer, the Holy Spirit will be our counselor. He is the best counselor we will ever have, so we should let Him lead and direct us in the decisions of life.

- ### Giver of Life (John 6:63)
In our flesh we are dead. The Holy Spirit is the power of God and imparts the only real life we have.

God wants to fill us with the Holy Spirit (Ephesians 5:18). In the Bible we see that it is only through the power of the Holy Spirit that we can live the Christian life. In fact, apart from the Holy Spirit, we cannot be used by God. All we can do without the Holy Spirit is stay in our old fleshly ways and live for ourselves (1 Corinthians 2:12-16).

Turn to 1 Corinthians 2:9-16 and read this wonderful description of the powerful and complete work of the Holy Spirit. The Holy Spirit searches out the deepest secrets of God Almighty. In fact, no one can know God's thoughts except through the Spirit of God. The Holy Spirit also gives us the gifts or the knowledge or whatever we need to carry out God's purposes for our lives. The Bible says we should not cause the Holy Spirit any sorrow by the way we live because He is the one who marks us to be with God on that day when salvation from all sin will be complete (Ephesians 4:30).

When Jesus was getting ready to leave this earth, He said He was going so the Holy Spirit would come (John 16:7-9). At that time Jesus referred to the Holy Spirit as the Helper. Now, all believers have a Helper in the Holy Spirit. And the closer we stay to God and the more we love Him, the greater the role the Holy Spirit will play in our lives.

WE WHO BELIEVE KNOW THE HOLY SPIRIT EVEN THOUGH THE WORLD DOES NOT.

Jesus said that the world cannot receive the Holy Spirit "because it neither sees Him nor knows Him" (John 14:16); but when we know Jesus, we know the Holy Spirit. As Jesus said, "He dwells with you and will be in you" (John 14:16). Jesus promised us the Holy Spirit. Jesus said He would ask the Father, and the Father would give us a Counselor (the Holy Spirit) to be with us forever. That means that from the time we wake up in the morning until we go to bed at night, we have a Counselor who can advise us and direct us. With the Holy Spirit in us, we are present with God. That is why a believer's body is described as a holy temple because the Holy Spirit inhabits that body. Jesus lives in us through the Holy Spirit. When we speak of Jesus in us and the Holy Spirit in us, we are talking about the same thing.

THE HOLY SPIRIT IMPARTS LIFE TO OUR DEAD FLESH AND EMPOWERS US FOR SERVING GOD.

The Holy Spirit always stands ready to do a new thing and a new good work in our lives. The Holy Spirit is the giver of life. Apart from the Holy Spirit we are dead in our flesh. Paul tells us in the Bible that we are to crucify the flesh (Romans 6:6). Basically, we crucify the flesh when we step out in faith and follow Jesus. When we are obedient to God and love Him from our hearts, we begin to kill off more of our flesh, and we become able to walk more in the Spirit. The more we know and love Jesus, the more the Spirit will be within us.

We are like a camel that must go to the well for water in order to survive. We are also like a car that needs to be gassed up in order to keep running. We must go to the well of the living water that Jesus spoke of in the Gospel of John (John 4:10-14). God will fill us and refill us with His Spirit, which empowers us for life. The only way we can preach or teach the Word with power is to be empowered by the Holy Spirit (1 Corinthians 2:4).

To understand the Holy Spirit, imagine an electric power plant that provides light for an entire city. God created the plant and also made the electricity and the power. Then God put His Son, Jesus, in charge of operating the plant and deciding who would get the electricity. The Holy Spirit is like the electricity that is sent out to light up each and every home in the city. This is not a perfect analogy because the Holy Spirit is a loving Person who does so much for us; nevertheless this analogy illustrates how the Holy Spirit comes from God, glorifies Jesus, and provides power and light to all believers simultaneously. The Holy Spirit is our connection to God's unlimited power supply so we can be light in the world for Jesus. Jesus said that we need to shine and not hide our light because God wants to use us as His light to bring others out of darkness (Matthew 5:14-16).

The Holy Spirit comes into our lives to help develop our Christian character and those Christlike traits necessary to live the Christian life. Galatians 5:22 tells us the fruit of the Holy Spirit is love, joy, peace, longsuffering, kindness, goodness, faithfulness, gentleness, and self-control. It is only through the Holy Spirit that we take on these characteristics. Galatians 5:25 exhorts us to walk in the Spirit since we live by the Spirit. Even Jesus did not begin preaching or doing anything until He heard from the Holy Spirit. The Spirit directed Him. For our ministry and service to Jesus to become effective, we too must be directed as well as empowered by the Holy Spirit.

"It is the Spirit who gives life; the flesh profits nothing. The words I speak to you are spirit, and they are life" (John 6:63).

DISCUSSION QUESTIONS

1. Discuss any experience you have had with the Holy Spirit.

2. Discuss how the Holy Spirit has been at work in your life.

3. How do you know when you are hearing from the Holy Spirit?

4. Look at the list on pages 46-48 of what the Holy Spirit does and consider what you need most right now from the Holy Spirit.

6

THE WORD OF GOD—THE BIBLE

*"For the word of God is living and powerful and sharper than any
two-edged sword, piercing even to the division of soul and spirit,
and of joints and marrow, and it is a discerner of the thoughts and
intents of the heart" (Hebrews 4:12).*

WHAT IS THE BIBLE, AND WHAT IS ITS PURPOSE?

The Bible is the Word of God. We refer to the Bible as the Word because it came from God. It is His Word. Out of all of the books ever written, we can rely only on the Bible as being totally true and totally inspired by God. God, Jesus, and the Holy Spirit are the only originators of truth. God, through the Holy Spirit, imparted through the Bible all the basic truths we need for living. That is why the Bible is so special. As Jesus said, "If you abide in My word, you are My disciples indeed" (John 8:31).

The Bible is the story of the redemption of sinful man by a just and perfect God. It is our instruction book, our training manual, and our guidebook as to how we should live. The Bible begins with God's creation and the fall of man and continues on through time to the coming of Jesus and the life of the early church. The major theme of the Bible is the reconciliation of God and His people through the work of Jesus Christ who saved us from our sin and makes us acceptable to the Father.

Every page and every verse of the Bible were written by God through the power of the Holy Spirit. The Holy Spirit put the words and thoughts on the hearts of the writers, who in turn wrote this great book. The Bible is God's love letter to each of us about how to be saved and how to live our lives. The Bible is also a book of history, describing important spiritual events as they unfolded. The Bible is an amazing and exciting book that brings us into the presence of

God where we can receive His truth in our hearts. This Book always points to Jesus and glorifies the Father, Son, and Holy Spirit. The Bible is also a book that provides great comfort at all times, particularly in times of need and distress.

GOD WROTE THE BIBLE THROUGH HIS HOLY SPIRIT.

The most important thing we can realize as we pick up a Bible is that God wrote the Book. As 2 Timothy 3:16 tells us, all Scripture is inspired by God. Revelation 19:13 refers to Jesus as "The Word." This is how we know the Bible is true. Another strong confirmation comes from the mouth of Jesus. We know the Bible is true because Jesus constantly referred to the Old Testament, and He quoted from it as the Word of God. Jesus knew Scripture, using it constantly as a source of authority from God, His Father. He treated it with reverence and confirmed it is God's Word. Although Jesus constantly exposed things that were not true, He never once criticized the Bible. The Bible was a big part of Jesus' life. In fact, Jesus never referred to another book. So if we believe Jesus is who He said He is, then we must accept the Scripture as the Word of God.

As to the New Testament, Jesus told His disciples that the Holy Spirit would remind them of all things that needed to be remembered (John 14:26). When the Holy Spirit did this, He inspired the disciples to write about the life of Jesus; this new writing became known as the New Testament. Jesus didn't write down anything during His lifetime, but Jesus knew God would send the Holy Spirit to remind His disciples of exactly what to write. Now we can pick up the New Testament and know the truth about Jesus and His life.

THE BIBLE IS AN AMAZING BOOK AND THE MOST ACCURATE BOOK OF ANCIENT HISTORY.

The Bible is simply amazing. It is incredible that this one Book was written over a period of 1,500 years by authors from many different places and varied walks of life. No book has ever had so many authors of such diverse backgrounds. Most of the writers did not have previous writing experience. They included a tax collector, others who were unemployed, uneducated fishermen, kings, priests, prophets, and judges. Just think how unlikely it would be for such a diverse group of nonprofessional writers to compose such a book that transformed the world. The only plausible explanation is that the writers were inspired and directed by the Spirit of God.

There is no other book of ancient history in which events are recorded in such detail and passed down from generation to generation. The writers of the Old Testament and New Testament went to great effort to record every event perfectly. No subsequent event in history ever brought any discredit to the Bible. Even though most of the authors did not know each other, the entire book came together as a single unfolding story of God and His purposes. The Bible is a miracle—a miracle God wrote. It is also a miracle that it has been so well preserved. Many ancient manuscripts have been recovered in the last several decades, and these manuscripts show the Bible is the same today as it was centuries ago. Finally, the Bible is a perfect work. Second Samuel 22:31 says, "The word of the Lord is proven."

THE BIBLE IS AN ORGANIZED INSTRUCTION MANUAL ON HOW WE SHOULD LIVE.

The Bible tells us all that we need to know about God, Jesus, and the Holy Spirit. The Bible tells us about the sinful nature of man and the mistakes that man has made in the past. The Bible tells us how to live our lives and instructs us on what we should do and what we should not do (Psalm 119:11). The Bible is a comfort in time of trouble. The Bible tells us about the future and how God will cast Satan into the pit and triumph over evil. The Bible also tells us how to overcome the problems of this world (Deuteronomy 8:3). The Bible is the only book that God wrote, and it is without error. The Bible is the one standard of truth against which all things must be measured.

As you read your Bible, understand the way the Bible is organized. The Old Testament consists of those books recorded before the time of Jesus. In the Old Testament, the first five books are known as the Books of Law. The creation story and the early history of God and man are found in these five books. The next books, starting with Joshua and going up to the Psalms, are books of history. These books cover the various reigns of the kings of Israel and Judah.

The next grouping of books, including the Psalms and ending with the Song of Solomon, are poetic books in nature and provide readers great comfort. Then, the remainder of the Old Testament from Isaiah through Malachi consists of the prophets, who told the truth about the times in which they lived and the truth about what was to come. Through the prophets and throughout the Old Testament, Jesus' coming was frequently predicted. The prophets foretold such details as where Jesus would be born and numerous details about His life and His death. Jesus fulfilled these prophecies and hundreds of other ones that had been written centuries earlier and recorded in the Old Testament. Then, just as the

Bible had predicted, Jesus came and lived among us.

The New Testament is the story of the life of Jesus and the early history of the church. The New Testament starts with the four gospels, which are Matthew, Mark, Luke, and John. In the gospels, four separate authors give detailed accounts of the life of Jesus. Of the four gospels, Matthew gives us the most complete picture of the events in Jesus' life. John tells us the most about the character of Jesus and exactly who He is. Some consider Luke to be the most colorful writer as he retells so many of Jesus' beautiful parables. The Book of Acts, which follows the gospels, is the dynamic history of the early church. Then, the next group of books is the letters of Paul, written for instruction and encouragement to the early church as well as to the church today. After Paul's letters comes the Book of Hebrews, and then the writings of James, Peter, John, and Jude. The Bible ends with Revelation which gives us a glimpse of heaven, prophecy of the end times, and the final judgment of Jesus Christ.

One thing we learn from the characters of the Bible is that none was perfect except Jesus. They all had their struggles and their failures. Some developed into men and women of God while others died in their sins. Many of the biblical characters fell away from God and ended tragically. Of the men and women of faith who followed God, some committed terrible sins. Through the history of all of the men and women of the Bible, we see the reality of life, the reality of sin, and the reality of God's love and mercy. Throughout the Bible we see the basic weakness of man and the faithfulness of God. We also learn that those who stepped out in faith were dependent on God, and humbly received great blessings. The Bible is a story of how the faithful turned failure into triumph through the power of God. It is also a story of tragedy, darkness, and death, which accompany the godless life.

The Bible needs no one to defend it. It has and will stand the test of time.

The Bible is the truth and needs no one to defend its authenticity. This Book has stood the test of time and is still unchallenged in the face of criticism by those alienated from God. The Bible stands alone among all books and all writings as the one unique account of the character and nature of God. There may be millions of volumes of law books in thousands of law libraries, but all of them put together do not hold a candle to the Bible, which is the ultimate and final word on the law. The Bible is our source of knowledge for salvation as well. The Bible tells us how we must repent, confess we are sinners, and then place our entire faith and trust in Jesus Christ as our Lord and Savior to obtain salvation. The Bible gives us assurance that if we believe in Jesus, we will be saved and have eternal life. What we must do is open our Bibles and start reading every day.

Make sure that you have your own Bible if at all possible. Consider each chapter of the Bible as a personal letter to you from God. God will talk to you on each page. As you deepen your relationship with God, you will find that nothing can hold you back from reading the Word. The Word will cut you to the quick like a two-edged sword because of its power that comes from God (Hebrews 4:12).

GOD COMMANDS US TO READ HIS WORD AND TO FOLLOW IT. HERE ARE SOME GOOD SUGGESTIONS.

Before you read the Bible, pray that the Holy Spirit will speak to you through the words and assist you in your understanding.

Expect that God will speak to you about your own life and reveal special truths about Himself every time you read His Word.

Set aside a special time and develop a method for daily Bible study. Write out your plan of study and be disciplined as you follow that plan.

In addition to your regular study, spend some of your quiet time with God by reading a psalm or another passage. Then reflect slowly and carefully on the passage so that God may speak to you.

Pick one of the gospels to read and reread in order to really understand who Jesus is and how He spent His time reaching out to the lost and hurting and drawing new believers to Himself.

Memorize verses that will become a part of you. Then you will always have these passages in your heart as situations arise.

Underline verses in your Bible and take notes. Keep a journal of the important things that God speaks to you about in your prayers and Bible time.

Think of ways you can share what you have learned with others. Look forward to the day when you can teach the Bible to others.

Get into a Bible study with others so that you can discuss the Bible and its application to your life, but do not let this substitute for your own private time of reading the Bible.

Understand the basic fundamentals of the faith so you can explain them to others. See the big picture of the Bible and understand how it is put together.

Always know that God will speak to you through His Word (John 17:17). God is no further from you than that Bible on your desk or by your bedside. Keep your Bible handy. Always take your Bible to church. Keep it close to share with others. Know where you can find passages that can comfort others in times of trouble (Psalm 119:105). Make your Bible a spiritual food that you digest every day of your life. Peter tells us in 1 Peter 2:2: "As newborn babes, desire the pure milk of the word, that you may grow thereby." Hunger and thirst after God's Word as the newborn babe does for milk.

AS YOU READ THE BIBLE, HERE ARE SOME HELPFUL INSTRUC
TIONS FOR A CLEARER UNDERSTANDING.

1. Understand the historical setting. In other words, what is going on in this part of the Bible, in this chapter, and in the preceding verses? Who is struggling with what problem and what is happening in general?

2. God is always at work doing something for somebody. What is God trying to do specifically in the life of the particular individual or individuals about whom you are reading?

3. When a passage seems unclear, look for those surrounding points and messages that *are* clear to you. If you know the major truths and major points, things that may at first seem confusing may fall into place. If you do not understand some point that seems to be important, ask for help.

THERE ARE HELPFUL BOOKS ABOUT THE BIBLE, BUT ALWAYS
READ THE BIBLE. NO BOOK IS A SUBSTITUTE.

There are many helpful books written about the Bible. There are commentaries that can give you insights into the history and customs of the times. There are Bible dictionaries, concordances, and Hebrew and Greek dictionaries that can

After the Leap

give you the meaning of words as written in the original language. As you grow in the faith, you may find help from such sources, but outside references are not essential to your Bible reading. Keep in mind that reading the Bible is not like reading any other book. The Bible is more than a learning experience. It is the Word of God that provides power for your life (Jeremiah 23:29). God actually touches your heart and soul through experiencing His Word. Reading the Bible with a passion for God will be an experience that touches you at a deep level. Never underestimate what God will do for you when you study His Word.

Handle carefully the truths of the Bible because they are a precious gift from God (2 Timothy 2:15). Be a doer and not merely a listener to the Word (James 1:22). Remember grass withers and flowers fade, but the Word of God lasts forever (Isaiah 40:8). Finally, know that when God's Word goes out, it is God speaking; therefore, God's Word never returns empty, but accomplishes what God desires (Isaiah 55:11).

You cannot open your heart and read the Word of God without it being a life-changing experience. In fact, reading from the Bible is an experience with God. God wrote this Book for you. Enjoy it, relish it, learn from it, and look forward to every minute spent with it.

"All Scripture is given by inspiration of God, and is profitable for doctrine, for reproof, for correction, for instruction in righteousness"
(2 Timothy 3:16).

DISCUSSION QUESTIONS

1. How do you know the Bible is truly the Word of God?

2. How would you describe your knowledge or familiarity with the Bible?

3. Write out a detailed plan for your study of the Bible on a daily and weekly basis. Share your ideas with the group.

4. Read Psalm 119. Now make a list of each different thing that this psalm says about God's Word, God's law, or God's statutes.

7

SEEKING A DYNAMIC PRAYER LIFE

"Rejoice always, pray without ceasing, in everything give thanks; for this is the will of God in Christ Jesus for you"
(1 Thessalonians 5:16-18).

U<small>NDERSTAND THE FOLLOWING THREE BASIC PRINCIPLES FOR AN</small>
EFFECTIVE PRAYER LIFE.

First of all, be fully aware of a very special position that you have with both God and Jesus as you come to them in prayer. Because you are a believer, you will be praying to a loving Father, one Jesus said in the Lord's prayer we should address as Abba ("Daddy"). When you address Jesus in your prayers, you are talking not only to your Lord and Savior but also to your brother and best friend. Just knowing what a special relationship you have with God and Jesus and how much they want the very best for you should give you great joy and confidence as you pray.

The **second** foundational principle you should hold onto is that the Father and Jesus are concerned with your heart. They want to hear from your heart. They want you to come to them not in some staged voice or with some needless repetition or babble, but they want you to speak to them in truth and sincerely from your heart. Your worship and your prayers should be in spirit and in truth, from your heart to God's heart.

The **third** foundational principle for prayer is to realize it is God's will that is important and not your own will. God always knows what is best for you, and if you want to seek the best for your life, you need to do it His way and not your way. You need to be tuned into Him. Have an attitude in prayer of looking to God for the answers instead of relying on your own limited and fleshly desires. Come before His throne as a needy child, facing a loving Father who understands all of your faults and still chooses to love you anyway. These three states of mind and heart will serve you well.

With these foundational realizations, come before His throne in prayer with boldness. Lay before God the deep things of your heart. And out of His love for you, He will respond. This is what prayer is about. So when you pray, be aware of where you stand with God and His great desire to provide you with what you need to draw closer to Him. Keep in mind it is God who should receive the glory, and pray in Jesus' name, lifting Him up.

GOD USES PRAYER TO CHANGE OUR LIVES. GOD CALLS US TO PRAY UNCEASINGLY.

If there is one thing that is important about prayer, it is that God uses our prayers more than anything else to work supernaturally in the life of His people. Prayer does more to change the world and to change human hearts than anything else. If you don't pray, don't expect much change in your life.

If there is one thing that helps us to know Jesus better, it is prayer. God is always there waiting for His children to come to Him through prayer (1 Corinthians 7:5). God will hear our every word. God will answer all prayers offered in faith in His own way and in His own timing and according to His will (Matthew 21:22). Nothing much happens in the life of the Christian without prayer. God uses the power of prayer to change our lives, change our nations, bless our families, heal our wounds, and forgive our sins (2 Chronicles 7:14). In short, prayer unleashes the power of God through His Holy Spirit to do miracles or grant simple requests. Prayer keeps us close to God and is the way we have intimacy with the Father. We should pray constantly and always give thanks for what the Father has done for us.

If our prayer goes unanswered, then we should wait on the Lord, but not give up (Psalm 27:14). God encourages us to just keep on praying and coming back to Him for our needs. In Luke 18:1-8 Jesus tells a story about a widow who never gave up. In this story the widow kept going back to the same judge time and time again to get justice. Finally, the judge, who was not a godly man, gave her what she wanted because she was so persistent. God wants us to be like this widow; He wants us to keep coming back to Him in prayer.

The reason Jesus told the story was to make the point that we should take everything to the Lord in prayer, and we should keep on praying until our prayers are answered. Of course, God is sovereign and is not going to answer a prayer for something that is not right. Even so, God wants us to come to Him for everything. Nothing is too large or too small to ask for in prayer. He wants us to be totally dependent on Him to supply our every need. We are to ask, seek, and knock (Matthew 7:7-8). He wants us to come to Him with the faith of knowing He is fully capable of answering our prayers (James 5:15). God's timing in answering may be different from ours, but He always hears us and answers our prayers in accordance with His will (Matthew 7:9-11).

Jesus not only prayed constantly, but He also always listened to His Father.

Jesus demonstrated the importance of prayer. He prayed constantly. Jesus did not make a move without going to the Father. Through prayer, Jesus heard from the Father who guided Him every step of the way. Often Jesus would be on His way to one place, but God would give Him another mission or change the plans for the day. Sometimes God would direct Jesus to suddenly leave a particular place for Jesus' own safety. Often the disciples did not understand why Jesus would stop in His journey to spend time with someone like the woman at the well (John 4:6-38). The reason was that Jesus always listened to the Father and did what the Father said to do. Jesus always kept His prayers in total accord with the Father's will, even when He faced the agony of the cross and did not want to "drink of that cup" (Matthew 26:42).

Jesus realized that prayer was like a conversation in which we not only talk to God, but we also listen to what God has to say. God wants us to bring all our needs to Him, but we don't use prayer just to ask God for the things we want. Through prayer, we should listen to God. He usually speaks to us in the quietness of our soul.

The Bible says to pray unceasingly. This means to have a constant awareness of God and to go to Him throughout the day with those things He puts on our hearts. Also, God wants us to set aside time for prayer on a daily basis. Prayer is the ideal way to get started in the morning and the best way to close out the day at night.

Prayer brings us into the presence of Almighty God. Through prayer, we are there with Him.

Through prayer we have instant access to the throne room of God (Hebrews 4:16). That is hard to imagine. We can pick up a phone to call a loved one and hear what the loved one has to say. Prayer is just as easy as picking up the phone.

We can pray silently by saying the words in our minds, or we can pray out loud. If your mind seems to wander when you are praying silently, pull out your prayer list and whisper your prayers out loud in the privacy of your room or closet. We should talk to God as we would talk to someone in the same room.

Prayer can take many forms. When we have our main prayer time, which should be on a daily basis, it is helpful to have a plan for prayer. One outline for prayer is to remember the letters in the word "ACTS." The letters stand for the words, *adoration, confession, thanksgiving*, and *supplication*. Using this outline, we should begin by adoring and praising God—focusing on His greatness, love, and mercy. Next, we should confess each of our sins and ask for forgiveness. Third, we should always give thanks for everything. Finally, we should pray for the needs of others as well as our own needs.

THE LORD'S PRAYER IS THE PERFECT OUTLINE FOR OUR PRAYERS.

Jesus taught His disciples how to pray, teaching them the Lord's Prayer, a beautiful prayer with endless depth, found in Matthew 6. We often repeat the Lord's Prayer in church, but the primary purpose of the Lord's Prayer is not simply reciting memorized words. The primary purpose of the Lord's Prayer is to give us a perfect model of how to pray. Let's examine this prayer, which is found in Matthew 6:5-15. If you have never done so, memorize the Lord's Prayer. Each verse will remind you to cover certain basic subjects in your daily time of prayer.

Our Father
Jesus referred to the Father with the term "Daddy," the dearest and most familiar term that could be used at the time. As you pray, focus on how loving and caring God is. He is the creator of the universe and the judge of all mankind, yet you are told to call Him "Daddy." A daddy loves his children and wants the best for them. That is the God you serve. He is your daddy. When you focus on a daddy's tender love and mercy for his child, you will start your prayer off right.

in heaven,
Focus on the majesty of God, sitting on His throne in heaven. Picture all things being subject to Him. He is all-powerful, and His Son, Jesus, sits there at His right hand. Around the Father and Son are endless numbers of angels

singing praise. Imagine the majesty of heaven, where all believers will someday live forever with the Father and the Son who died to save them.

Hallowed be Your name.

God's very name is holy. *Hallowed* means to be revered and held in highest esteem. We bow down before Him and worship Him simply because He is who He is. His name is hallowed. His name is wonderful. Use this time to focus on the character of God.

Your kingdom come. Your will be done on earth as it is in heaven.

God wants to bring His kingdom right down here on earth. Thus, this is an ideal time to pray for your nation, your leaders, your city, your neighborhood, and individuals in need of God's will for their lives. Always pray that God's kingdom will come in your life, your workplace, your neighborhood, your city, and your nation.

Give us this day our daily bread.

This is the time to pray for your own needs and for the needs of others. God promises to supply all our needs. Keep your prayer list handy and talk to God about those needs you are asking Him to provide.

And forgive us of our debts as we forgive our debtors.

Confess every known sin to God and ask His forgiveness. He is faithful to forgive when we repent and come to Him with a clean heart. Then, of course, He demands that we forgive others for their sins against us. Search your heart, and if you have any unforgiveness or anger toward anyone, then get rid of it by forgiving that other person.

And do not lead us into temptation.

Think of the weakest areas in your life and ask for God's help to overcome temptation and to avoid situations where you may be tempted. Ask God to steer you from any place, person, or circumstance that might lead you into sin. Ask God to keep your mind off fleshly desires, and ask Him to keep you from evil influences and sinful opportunities.

But deliver us from evil. (*Or deliver us from the evil one,* as often translated.)

Pray for protection against any evil thing or influence that could harm your heart or mind or lead you into temptation. Ask for protection from the enemy and his demonic forces and influences in this world. Pray for protection for your family in the same way.

For Yours is the kingdom and the power and the glory forever. Amen.

Finally, close with the greatness of God and the fact that you will be with Him for eternity and receive the blessings of eternal life. Know that He will bring the whole earth to justice and that someday there will be no more pain and sorrow for those who are saved. Know that His kingdom will reign forever and ever through His power and might. Know that your life and everything you do should be for His glory.

WE SHOULD GO TO GOD IN PRAYER WHEN WE ARE SICK OR HAVE PROBLEMS.

God instructs us to receive prayer when we are sick. James 5:13-16 tells us that if anyone is sick, the elders should be called to anoint the sick person with oil and pray for healing for that person. God doesn't always choose to heal. Paul faced this fact when his thorn in his flesh stayed with him for life. We must remember that most of Paul's other prayers were answered as God did many miraculous events in order to save him from shipwrecks, storms, prison, many enemies, and even a deadly snake. God constantly came to Paul's rescue.

God uses the rough roads of life to draw us closer to Him and to develop our Christian character. When we run into those rough roads, sometimes all we can do is pray and ask others to pray. We must always pray in faith with full confidence that God can and will do what is in our best interests. Also, we always have a need to pray against temptation, so pray against temptation of all kinds (Luke 22:40).

DO NOT OVERLOOK THE IMPORTANCE OF FASTING.

Fasting, that is going without food or giving up something pleasurable for a period of time, was practiced regularly throughout the Old and New Testaments. We come closer to God through this sacrificial act. Fasting is the giving up of something in the flesh that we enjoy in order to obtain something of the spirit from our Father. Fasting always involves sacrifice. God calls on us to set aside times of fasting. Fasting should be a regular part of our Christian life. In the Bible there were different kinds of fasts. Fasting can be undertaken for a special purpose to ask God for a particular thing. Fasting can also be for a special season. The main purpose of fasting is to draw us into a closer place with Jesus. Jesus pointed out that fasting was needed in order to accomplish certain objectives such as the casting out of particular types of demons. Fasting makes us more humble as we recognize our total dependence on God for all things (Psalm 35:13), and fasting will bring us into a deeper level in our prayer lives.

Fasting may consist of going a day without food or going without a single meal. Fasting may last several days or a much longer period while limiting yourself to juice only. Fasting can be anything that involves a sacrifice on our part. When we are in need of food from fasting, we will turn our thoughts to God. Fasting makes us appreciative of a single piece of bread because we know that even that comes from God. When we understand what it is like to be hungry, our compassion for those in need will increase.

When we fast, we will be stretched in our faith. Our prayer life will become more effective as we seek Jesus more intensely. God commands us to fast, and we should do it. It is a sacrificial offering that pleases God. Jesus fasted. In fact, once Jesus fasted for 40 days as He prepared for His ministry and sought God's direction for His life (Matthew 4:2). Fasting has a spiritual intensity about it that draws us to the Lord and makes it more likely for us to hear His voice. When we fast though, we must not brag about it or go around looking grim (Matthew 6:16-18). We must make our sacrifice of fasting a joyous thing.

WITHOUT PRAYER, WE ARE SPIRITUALLY DRY. PRAYER TAKES US TO THE LIVING WELL TO BE FILLED BY GOD.

Many books have been written on the power of prayer. This is just a short chapter that covers only the fundamentals on a very important subject. As our car can only run with gas, our lives can only run with prayer. Prayer is the way we go to the well to become filled by the Holy Spirit. It is an essential ingredient in the life of every believer. We should not look on it as an unwelcome chore, but rather we should pray with great joy and expectation. Prayer is our invitation for the Holy Spirit to empower us to reach out with the love of Jesus for others in this troubled world.

FOLLOW THESE IMPORTANT INSTRUCTIONS ON HOW TO PRAY.

Do not pray to show off like the Pharisees that Jesus described as hypocrites. Prayer outside a church or small group should be a private matter in a private place. Jesus also warns against meaningless repetitions and pagan babble (Matthew 6:5-6).

We should pray with faith and fervently as James 5 tells us. Mark 11:23-24 also tells us that a prayer with faith can move a mountain. Anything is possible with God. To pray fervently means to really put your heart into your prayer to God.

There is power anytime two or more gather together to pray in agreement and unity. Jesus tells us that when two are more are gathered in His name, what they ask will be granted. This is true with family prayers or small group prayers or simply prayer with a prayer partner.

Pray for your enemies and those who persecute you (Matthew 5:44). This will soften your heart and guard you against bitterness and unforgiveness. Remember that even though a person has treated you unjustly or unfairly, God still loves that person and wants to save him or her. Your prayer may be instrumental in God's changing that person's heart.

Pray before undertaking anything of importance or when you might be facing danger. Whenever Jesus faced a crisis, He went off to be alone and to pray. Jesus' prayer in the Garden of Gethsemane before His crucifixion shows the importance of prayer prior to facing extreme adversity (Matthew 26:36).

Remember that God describes His church as a house of prayer. Your congregation should be devoted to prayer. Your individual life, your family, and your church family should all be built around prayer (Matthew 21:13).

Be an intercessor for others. We are all called to be intercessors for others. Praying for the needs of others or for your city, your church, or your country is called intercession. You actually stand in for the other person as you pray. You stand between that person and the Father. To this day, Jesus is an intercessor for each of us and prays for us (Romans 8:34). You are called to be an intercessor and to pray fervently for those whom God puts on your heart.

Pray daily that God will draw you closer to Him and change your life. Pray that God will always be at work in your life. Pray that the Holy Spirit will enable you to love Him more. Pray for the strength to be more obedient to Jesus and to follow Him more closely. Pray daily for the things you need from Jesus to grow in the Christian faith.

Use a prayer journal or list and also write down the results of your prayers.

The enemy will do all within his power to distract you. Also, your own mind may wander, and you may have problems concentrating. That is why you sometimes need to get in your special prayer place and whisper out loud and follow a list. You can keep your list in your Bible and change it from time to time. But use a method for your prayers while at the same time being flexible by listening to the Lord and adding those things He reminds you to pray for.

Be so committed that nothing keeps you from pursuing your daily prayers. Make your prayer life the highest of priorities and never let any excuse get in your way. Make a concerted effort to develop good habits of having an uninterrupted prayer time that you honor daily. The better your prayer habit, the more enriched your prayer life will be.

"Confess your trespasses to one another, and pray for one another, that you may be healed. The effective, fervent prayer of a righteous man avails much" (James 5:16).

DISCUSSION QUESTIONS

1. Discuss what your prayer life consists of on a day-to-day basis right now.

2. Now discuss those things that you want your prayer life to consist of from now on.

3. Get a separate notebook and begin to keep a prayer journal. Write down the people and situations you need to remember in prayer. Have a section for recording significant spiritual events in your life and God's answers to your prayers. Share your progress with the group.

4. Discuss some significant times when God answered your prayers.

8

PRAISING GOD WITH A PASSION

"Bless the Lord, O my soul; and all that is within me bless His holy name! (Psalm 103:1)

PRAISE AND WORSHIP SHOULD COME FROM DEEP WITHIN OUR SOULS. WE SHOULD YEARN TO PRAISE GOD.

There is a beautiful passage of Scripture beginning at Luke 19:37. As Jesus made His final triumphant march into Jerusalem just prior to the Crucifixion, the whole crowd of disciples began to praise God in loud voices for all of the miracles they had seen. When the Pharisees asked Jesus to rebuke His disciples for such conduct, Jesus replied, "If these should keep quiet, the stones will immediately cry out" (Luke 19:40). Jesus' point was that everything and everyone should passionately praise the Lord. If people don't praise Him, creation will! Psalm 148 commands the angels, the sun and moon, the heavens, and all of creation to praise the Lord.

Praise, adoration, and worship are often neglected areas in our own lives and in our congregations. Yet, God calls us to praise and worship Him constantly. We are to do this privately, and we are to do this publicly within the church body. Praise and worship should be a part of our prayer life, but we should also make time to focus on God alone through praise and worship. The difference between prayer and worship is that in worship, our focus is on the majesty and the greatness of God. Our focus is on the living Jesus who saved us through His amazing grace. Most of the 150 psalms are filled with praise, worship, and thanksgiving. Read Psalms 145–150 to get a feeling for the many passionate ways that our God can be praised.

Praise and worship mean going to God with no agenda except to concentrate on Him, His love, His mercy, His greatness, His holiness, and those attributes that make Him God. To praise and worship God is also to express our deep love for our Lord and Savior, Jesus Christ.

God commands us to praise and worship Him. I will repeat that. God demands that we praise and worship Him. He does not need our praise and worship. It does not add a single thing to His greatness or glory; however, God knows we need to worship Him. The Bible contains some 350 references about the praise and worship of God. There are as many passages about worship as there are about prayer, exceeded only by passages about love.

The truth is that God has created us with a deep need to worship Him. That is the way we are made whether or not we realize it. When we behold the reality of His love and grace and mercy, our hearts are compelled to praise Him. Then nothing can hold us back from worshiping our Lord. When we become aware of our own weaknesses, our own sinful nature, and our own insufficiency, we will feel a passion to adore the Father and the Son who saved us. If we choose not to express this great need from our heart to worship the living God, our lives will not be complete. How much we desire to praise God from our hearts is a clear indicator of just how much we love Him.

Worship transforms us.

The dictionary says that praise is "a word pointing out the value or worth of someone or something." Praise is also defined as "words or song setting forth the glory and goodness of God." God will work on the transformation of our lives when we come to Him in praise. The fact that God works through the praise of His people is a reality and one of His truths. Through praise we can reach out and touch Him like at no other time. The joy and peace that come from such praise is indescribable, drawing us closer to the living God.

To precisely define praise and worship of God is beyond human capacity. The dictionary uses such definitions as "to show great honor and respect"; "great love, admiration, and adoration"; "devotion and reverence"; "to hold very dear and consider extremely precious."

Praising God from the heart brings on mysterious riches. We cannot fully appreciate how it works, only that it does work. People involved in times of true worship to the Lord will need no further encouragement. They will sense a great blessing and will simply want to worship the Lord.

Authentic praise brings forth a greater presence of the Lord through His Holy Spirit. David, who wrote most of the psalms, put great emphasis on praise and worship. With a heart for God like no other person in the Bible except Jesus,

David said: "As the deer pants for water brooks, so pants my soul for You, O God" (Psalm 42:1). When we enter into true worship, our souls will cry out even as David's did. David worshiped God with a passion. If you do not enjoy the passion for worship like David, examine your heart. Worship and a heart for God are closely related. Obviously, you are missing out on a real joy that God wants to put into your life.

When a congregation is focused on worship alone, everyone is brought closer to God. Every believer will be affected as the Holy Spirit comes in power and truth and love. Some may shed tears of joy and compassion while others may be overtaken with a wonderful sense of peace.

God inhabits the praises of His people (Psalm 22:3). This means that during worship we will feel God's presence. That is also one of the blessings that instills in us a yearning to worship. The great commandment says we should love our God with all of our heart and soul and strength and mind. We obey this commandment through acts of compassion and through obedience to God. We also follow this commandment through worship. Worship expresses our love to God from the bottom of our hearts.

OUR JOY IN THE LORD IS MADE COMPLETE THROUGH PRAISE AND WORSHIP.

Through worship we should expect great joy and pleasure simply by being in God's holy presence and focusing solely upon God and Jesus (Psalm 16:11). During engagement a man and a woman usually have a strong outpouring of adoration toward each other. When we worship God, we should have that same degree of passion (1 Peter 1:8).

Praise makes the enjoyable even more enjoyable. That is why husbands and wives who are in love keep expressing their love for one another. Think about why spectators enjoy cheering for their favorite sports team. Thousands will yell out their approval at a score or goal. In a concert hall we stand and applaud at length for an excellent piano recital. Most of us have a strong emotional desire to shout praise for the athlete or musician who does well. We have a deep need to praise spontaneously that which we highly value; therefore, we should never be reluctant or self-conscious in our praise of the Lord. In this we should take great delight. If we enthusiastically praise people but hold back our praise for our Lord, we may need to question our priorities.

God demands that we praise Him with a passion. God tells us to raise our hands to the sky (Psalm 63:4); to fall on our knees (Acts 7:60;) to fall down on our faces before Him (Revelation 4:10); to praise Him with song and sing to Him a new song (Psalms 33:3; 40:3); and to dance with joy as David did (2 Samuel 6:14-16). The Bible speaks of all kinds of musical instruments being used to praise the Lord. There were cymbals, tambourines, trumpets, rams horns, flutes, and all of the instruments of that day (Psalm 150). People of the Bible also praised the Lord with shouting and raising of hands (Psalms 66:1). We can praise the Lord with a shout or with a quiet reverence. The main thing is not how we worship the Lord, but that we do worship Him from our souls.

The praise of God's people can take many forms. Our individual praise takes on different forms as the Spirit of God leads us. God has given us so many wonderful ways to praise Him. Through true praise, our spirit connects directly to the Spirit of God, our Father and the Creator of the universe. If we cheer enthusiastically over a mere sporting event, how can we keep from worshiping the God who gave us life and snatched us from the jaws of hell? In Luke 17:11-19, Jesus recounts a parable about the ten lepers whom He healed and saved from much pain and probably an early death. Of the ten lepers who were healed, only one came back to give the glory and praise to Jesus. You must ask yourself: am I like the nine who forgot all that Jesus had done or am I like the one who praised and thanked Jesus for new life?

WE SHOULD FIND GREAT DELIGHT AND JOY IN PRAISING THE LORD.

The Bible tells us in Revelation about the angels who stand around and simply praise and worship the Father and Son. One passage speaks of 100 million angels praising the Lord (Revelation 5:11). Keep in mind that angels are extremely intelligent creatures, and that they take great joy and pleasure in simply worshiping God. If praise and worship sounds boring to us, we should look at our relationship with God. Our desire to worship may be a good measuring stick of how much we love Jesus. The more we love Him and the more we desire Him, the more we will want to praise Him. And as we praise Him, our praise is a great weapon of spiritual warfare against our enemy, the devil, because we declare our faith and God gets all the glory.

We should praise God in the church. The church family should take great joy and delight in coming together to praise God corporately. Hopefully, every church will place a high priority on worshiping together, providing special times just to praise God.

Praise should also be an experience that can happen anywhere. You can praise the Lord by singing along with a praise tape when driving down the highway. Praise can be a family event too as your family or a group of Christian friends gather together to praise the Lord. Praise can be a private experience when you shut everything out of your life at home except focusing in on God—maybe with praise music and maybe without. Praise can simply be telling Jesus how much you love Him. Your praise is a vital part of your relationship with the living God.

There is a great old hymn that says in the chorus, "This is my story. This is my song. Praising my Savior all the day long." Praise should become an automatic part of our being and an integral part of our relationship with God. To praise God is to declare the victory of Jesus on the cross and to identify ourselves with our Father who loves us. Praise helps usher in the Holy Spirit and brings a joy and a peace to our innermost being as we connect to the God of our salvation. The Bible speaks of the passion we should have within our heart and soul: "My soul longs, yes, even faints for the courts of the Lord; my heart and my flesh cry out for the living God" (Psalm 84:2).

As we close this chapter, make a commitment that before the day is out you will go before the Lord in praise and worship. In doing so you are to have no other agenda than to focus in on your loving Father and His Son. Find a relatively quiet place and simply praise the Lord. Add some praise music if you like. Nothing takes you into the presence of God more than praise and worship. Just as you enter into times of prayer and Bible reading, enter into frequent times of praise.

"Alleluia! For the Lord God omnipotent reigns! Let us be glad and rejoice and give Him glory" (Revelation 19:6-7).

Discussion Questions

1. What do you enjoy the most about worshiping and praising God?

2. Discuss the benefits that you receive when you fervently praise and worship the Lord.

3. How can you improve your praise life? Discuss several specific ideas.

9
TWO KINGDOMS AT WAR AND OUR OLD ENEMY

*"For we do not wrestle against flesh and blood, but against princi-
palities, against powers, against the rulers of the darkness of this
age, against spiritual hosts of wickedness in the heavenly places"
(Ephesians 6:12).*

GOD HAS A KINGDOM, SATAN HAS A KINGDOM, AND THE TWO
KINGDOMS ARE AT WAR.

The next two chapters will focus on two kingdoms which are at war. There
is a great battle going on right now on this earth and in the heavenly places. This
is a spiritual battle in which the souls of many people hang in the balance. As
believers, we are part of God's army and called to take our stand for Jesus in this
battle. All people, believers and unbelievers alike, are part of the battle whether or
not they want to be.

This chapter will focus on the two kingdoms which are at war and in deadly
opposition to each other. Then this chapter and the next chapter will discuss our
three mortal enemies: the devil, the flesh (that is our sinful nature), and the world
and its ways. These three enemies work in concert to keep us from salvation and
to render even the saved person an ineffectual warrior in God's kingdom. We
must know our enemies, and we must also know how to appropriate God's
strength to overcome these foes. These chapters contain essential spiritual principles from the Word of God that will help you do just that.

The first kingdom—the good kingdom—is God's kingdom. This kingdom
is also known as the kingdom of heaven. This is where Jesus rules as King. The
second kingdom is the kingdom of darkness over which Satan rules. In fact, the

Bible says that Satan is the prince of this world (John 12:31). We all have our citizenship in one kingdom or another. When we accept Jesus Christ as our Lord and Savior, our citizenship is transferred to God's kingdom (Colossians 1:13 and Ephesians 2:19). But until we know Jesus, our citizenship is in this world, the kingdom of darkness. What a privilege and glorious thing it is to be part of God's kingdom and a citizen of heaven. As Paul said in Philippians 3:20-21, "For our citizenship is in heaven, from which we also eagerly wait for the Savior, the Lord Jesus Christ, who will transform our lowly body that it may be conformed to His glorious body." That is good news to know we will live forever as citizens of heaven. Unfortunately, while on this earth, we are part of an eternal battle with the other kingdom.

The two kingdoms are engaged in mortal combat over the souls of men. The stakes are high. War does not get any more serious than this. The forces of God's kingdom include the good angels that do exactly as Jesus commands and the church, that is all of us who believe in Jesus. On the other side are Satan and the demonic forces, about whom the Bible gives us detailed instruction.

Christians need to face the reality that the unseen spiritual forces are real and can have a big impact on our families, our cities, our nation, and our well-being. The Bible gives us a road map describing our enemy, his demons, and the forces of evil. Our principal battle is with Satan and his army: "For we do not wrestle against flesh and blood, but against principalities, against powers, against the rulers of the darkness of this age, against spiritual hosts of wickedness in the heavenly places" (Ephesians 6:12). This passage directly refers to Satan and his demonic forces who are highly organized and have power and strongholds throughout the world. Satan's goal is simple. He wants to destroy people, families, communities, cities, nations, and the church. Satan's first priority is to keep everyone he can from believing in Jesus so that people will go to hell and be under his control. If that fails, then his second priority is to neutralize and render impotent as many believers as possible so that they will not take the Gospel message and the love of Christ to a lost and hurting world.

Satan not only exists, but he possesses great power and intelligence. Jesus spent a lot of His time on earth confronting Satan, who was trying to stop Jesus at every turn. Jesus was well aware of Satan's power. Jesus told us to pray for protection from the enemy. In fact, the Lord's Prayer in some translations says we should pray "deliver us from the evil one," which refers to Satan. God wants us to pray for protection from this enemy just as we pray for other needs. God will answer our prayer and deliver us from the enemy.

After the Leap

JESUS HAS WON THE WAR, BUT THE BIBLE TEACHES WE MUST
STILL BE ON GUARD AGAINST THE ENEMY.

The first basic principle we must understand is that God has already won the war. God always wins and is in total control of everything that occurs. God defeated Satan once and for all when Jesus died for our sins on the cross. Through Jesus' death on the cross and His resurrection, the power of sin was broken for those who believe in Jesus Christ. No longer are believers blinded and enslaved to sin. As the memory verse at the end of this chapter says, "He [Jesus] who is in you is stronger than he [Satan] who is in the world" (1 John 4:4). The Bible tells us that someday Jesus will return to judge Satan and send him to the pit of hell, but in the meantime, God, for reasons we may not understand, permits Satan to enjoy his limited but very destructive power. Yet Jesus also promised us in Luke 4:18 that He came to set the prisoners free. What Jesus meant by this is that He can and will free us from the power of sin and the power of the devil if we will let Him.

Jesus understood Satan and knew of his crafty schemes. Satan tried to destroy Jesus' ministry on earth. At the beginning of Jesus' ministry, Jesus went into the desert and fasted and prayed for 40 days to prepare Himself for His mission here on earth and to strengthen Himself against any attack (Matthew 4:1-11). The devil came to Jesus and offered Him all the kingdoms of the world if Jesus would just worship him, Satan. Jesus resisted and won that great battle. Jesus rebuked Satan, and throughout Jesus' ministry He warned His disciples to pray and be watchful about resisting the devil. Without God, Jesus knew that none of His disciples, or any believer, was a match for Satan.

On our own, we are easy targets for Satan. But with God on our side we should not fear Satan. We should fear only God. We should have no respect for Satan's character, but we should recognize Satan's power to harm us in the absence of God's protection. We must never be fascinated or drawn to Satan or demonic power, but we should focus instead on Jesus and work at being obedient to Him. That will be our best weapon.

God wants us to know about Satan so we can defend ourselves against him. That is why the Bible exposes our enemy and his ways. The Bible says Satan prowls like a lion looking for someone to devour (1 Peter 5:8). Satan wants to bring us to total destruction. As prince of this world, Satan not only preys on the world, but he also intelligently carries out his strategy to enslave all people, in all nations. To accomplish his mission, he invades the lives of evil rulers in order to bring cities and even countries into darkness, greed, and corruption.

SATAN IS A REAL PERSON AND HAS MANY DEMONS IN HIS ARMY.

Satan is not alone in his battle; indeed, he has millions of demonic beings on his side (Revelation 12:9). The Bible tells us about the strong influences these demonic beings can have on human beings. Seldom do we see them, but they are real. We know this because Jesus confronted demons and cast them out. Jesus said they exist. Jesus recognized that demons were a real problem. Any of us who have lived very long have witnessed evidence of demonic influences in the lives of others.

The Bible doesn't give us all the details about Satan and his army, but the Bible tells us all we need to know. The Bible tells us how Satan became the enemy of God. It tells us that Satan at one time was a very powerful and important angel in heaven, but he rebelled against God and was disobedient. When that event occurred, God expelled Satan, and millions of other angels who followed Satan, from heaven (Ezekiel 28:11-19). From that time on Satan and his demons have brought people misery (Isaiah 14:12-15). Satan hates God and wants to keep all humans separated from God through sin. Satan began his work on this earth in the Garden of Eden, when he led both Adam and Eve into sin soon after they were created.

Demons do exist, are plentiful, and cause a variety of pain and trouble. Open doors of sin appear to be the most common way they find their way into human beings. Demons are often referred to as unclean spirits. Demons have distinct personalities and character types as they often specialize in causing problems in a particular area of a person's life. Demons have emotions (Luke 8:28). Demons are capable of promoting lust, anger, idolatry, and all forms of sin. Demons have also been known to cause disabling problems such as dumbness (Matthew 9:32); blindness (Matthew 12:22); deformities (Luke 13:11-17); and insanity (Luke 8:27-29).

Demons can get inside a person and affect the way that person thinks and acts. Demons who are in a person need to be cast out. Jesus cast demons out of many people when He was on earth (Mark 9:14-29). When Jesus departed, He commanded His believers to continue to cast out demons in His name (Mark 16:17). Whether a demon comes in to possess a person or whether the demon simply exercises influence over that person's life, we do not want the demon around. As Christians we need to be able to discern when demons are a problem and know how to seek help from the church. Praying for deliverance should normally be done under the authority of a church and by those who are prepared to engage in this kind of spiritual warfare. Deliverance was a normal part of Jesus'

After the Leap

ministry (Luke 4:31-36). Based on what Jesus commanded His disciples, deliverance should also be a ministry within the church today by those who are equipped (Matthew 10:8).

THE BIBLE SAYS SATAN IS A LIAR AND A MURDERER WHO WANTS TO DESTROY US.

The devil has a simple strategy for trying to destroy us—he uses blatant lies. Jesus gives us a clear picture of Satan's character. In John 8:44, Jesus said of the sinners who did not believe in Jesus, "You are of your father, the devil, and the desires of your father you want to do. He [Satan] was a murderer from the beginning, and does not stand in the truth, because there is no truth in him. When he speaks a lie, he speaks from his own resources, for he is a liar and the father of it." Jesus just described the two most basic character traits of the enemy: Satan likes to lie and kill. He did this from the beginning with Adam and Eve when he enticed them to disobey God. Satan played on the pride of Adam and Eve by convincing them they could be more like God if they ate from the tree of the knowledge of good and evil. Satan's goal with each of us is the same as it was with Adam and Eve. By appealing to our pride and our desire to be independent of God, Satan tries to convince us that we do not need God.

Satan appeals to our basic desire to exalt ourselves. Satan's goal is to keep us from putting our faith and trust in Jesus, which is necessary for eternal life. Then, after we become believers, Satan's goal is to divide and conquer. If he can't keep us from salvation, then he wants to weaken us so we will be incapable of doing the work God has called us to do, reaching the lost with the good news about Jesus. One of Satan's biggest lies is that he does not exist and is just a myth. Satan knows if people do not think he is real, then they will not take him seriously. Also, they will not be on guard against his schemes. Another lie Satan tells us is that demons do not exist. This goes along with Satan's strategy to keep us from taking demons or spiritual warfare seriously.

Satan is the master of lies. Satan is tricky. The Bible says that Satan can even disguise himself as an angel of light. Some of the common lies and trickery are listed below. Do any of these lies surface in your world today or in your mind?

"Neither Satan nor demons really exist, and there is no hell or eternal punishment either." Obviously, if we buy into these lies, there is no reason to be saved and no reason to fear God because we can believe whatever we want and do whatever we want without any fear of punishment or consequence.

"Go ahead and commit a little sin. It won't harm you." If we fall for this trap and do sin, then the next sin and the next will come more easily. Before we know it, we will be knee-deep in sin and will have given the enemy an open invitation to come in.

"Live it up today because you will always have time to get right with God." If we fall for this lie, we will grow farther and farther from God and not even desire to get right with Him. Besides we never know the day or the hour of our earthly death so we must first put our faith in Jesus.

"You are so good and so much better than those around you." If Satan convinces us that we can make it on our own and are better than others, then he has filled us with pride and thus, rendered us of little use for God's kingdom. The fact is we should always recognize that we are sinners. Anytime we see another person sinning, we should humbly admit that "there but for the grace of God go I." Satan appeals to our pride, but God wants us humble.

"If you just live a good life, you will go to heaven." This is a terrible deception because Jesus is the only way to heaven. Tragically, many who call themselves Christians fall for this lie, do not put their personal trust in Jesus, and still believe they will make it to heaven on their own good works. Beware of this deadly snare.

"You are so bad and have committed so many terrible sins that God will never forgive you." If you have bought into this falsehood, reread the prom-ises of God and Jesus as stated in the second chapter of this book. God for-gave Paul, who was among the worst of sinners, and He will forgive all our sins of any kind if we repent, believe in Jesus, and confess our sins.

"You are so unworthy, imperfect, and insignificant that God could never care about you." If the enemy can get us to believe this lie, we will be defeat-ed before we get started. The devil likes to keep us feeling sorry for ourselves and without hope. We must always know exactly who we are in Christ. The fact He loves us so much that He died for us gives us great worth.

Satan is smart and will use every lie he can to lead us down the path of destruction. Always be alert. Test all of your thoughts with the Word of God.

In addition to being a liar and a murderer, Satan has other characteristics for which we must be on guard. Satan is a tempter (Matthew 4:3); an accuser (Revelation 12:10); a sinner (1 John 3:8); and a slanderer (Revelation 12:10). Satan has many tricks in his bag. His methodology of deception includes posing as an angel of light (2 Corinthians 11:14). He attracts people into false religions (1 Timothy 4:1-3); seduces people into sinful lifestyles (Ephesians 2:1-3); sends false teachers (2 Corinthians 11:13-15); and likes to show off his magic (2 Thessalonians 2:9). Satan can cause a multitude of problems for believers. That is why Jesus prayed that His believers would be kept from Satan's power (John 17:15).

WORSHIP OF ANYTHING EXCEPT GOD GIVES A STRONGHOLD TO SATAN AND HIS DEMONIC ARMY.

Satan desires to be worshiped. Worship of anything except God gives a stronghold to the enemy and is an open invitation for satanic and demonic control in our lives; therefore, we must avoid any form of worship other than that focused on God. We must not belong to any religious cult, practice any idolatry, or worship any idol or false gods. Such practices are an abomination to God and empower the enemy to come into our lives.

Our God is a jealous God and demands that we worship Him alone. He demands it because He alone is worthy. He also demands this for our own good. If we worship false gods, any occult or satanic thing, Satan will be in position to harm us. Never consult, give credit to, praise, or make any sacrifice to any demonic spirit (1 Corinthians 10:20). God does not want us to fool around with divination, sorcery, voodoo, witches and witchcraft, fortune tellers, astrology, magic card reading, necromancy (talking to the dead), black magic, or any other supernatural kind of thing. Avoid Ouija boards and games like Dungeons and Dragons, which are a part of Satan's world. Do not play around in the area of the supernatural. God hates such practices (Deuteronomy 18:10-13). Do not even read the horoscopes in the local newspaper. This supernatural practice of predicting the future is not innocent child's play but a form of witchcraft—an abomination to God.

GOD WILL PROTECT US FROM THE ENEMY, AND GOD HAS AN ARMY OF ANGELS TO HELP HIM.

God will protect us from our enemies, including Satan, the world, and our own flesh if we will be obedient and come to Him for help. Our strength is in

Jesus and our citizenship is in heaven. As Philippians 3:20 puts it, "For our citizenship is in heaven, from which we also eagerly wait for the Savior, the Lord Jesus Christ."

God gives us another weapon to fight this mighty battle and that is the church, the bride of Christ. Standing united in the faith, we are fellow soldiers in this eternal battle for the souls of men and women everywhere. We are to proceed as children of the living God and conquerors in Christ even against our strongest and most ancient foe.

God has an army of angels in His kingdom. God's angels are wonderful beings whom God sends to assist us, often in answer to prayer. Angels watch over and protect God's people more than we will ever know. Normally angels are unseen although many Christians have reported seeing angels. The Bible has numerous stories concerning the many times angels have rescued people in perilous situations. Angels of God have also brought judgment and destruction to evil forces. Angels have announced good news such as the birth of Jesus. Angels have given direction and protection to those in trouble and have ministered to those who are hurting. God uses His angels as He pleases. We do not pray to angels. We pray to God who often uses His angels in answer to prayer. Angels are real. God uses them to serve us in many ways. Thank God for His angels.

As citizens of heaven and as part of the church, we are called to join forces in a mighty battle in which God has already won the victory. This battle is not ours to win, but the battle belongs to the Lord. God always wins. Thus, with God at our side, we will truly be conquerors in Christ Jesus. The Bible says that someday Satan will be a mere footstool for King Jesus (Hebrews 10:12-13). And our hope and our faith for all things is in Jesus who promised us in Matthew 28:20: "I am with you always, even to the end of the age."

In the next chapter we will talk about the flesh and the world and examine more specifically how to defend ourselves against all three enemies—Satan, the world, and our own flesh through the power of Jesus Christ.

"He [Jesus] who is in you is greater than he [Satan] who is in the world" (1 John 4:4).

Discussion Questions

1. What does it mean to you to have to be either a citizen of heaven or a citizen of this world?

After the Leap

2. What ways is Satan using to lead you into sin or separate you from God? Discuss the weapons of spiritual warfare you should employ against each of Satan's tactics.

3. Look at the list, earlier in this chapter, of the lies Satan spreads. Do you ever believe any of these? To which ones are you most vulnerable? How can you best combat these lies?

10

OVERCOMING THE WORLD AND THE FLESH

[Jesus said]: "Watch and pray, lest you enter into temptation. The spirit indeed is willing, but the flesh is weak" (Matthew 26:41).

WE BATTLE TWO OTHER ANCIENT FOES BESIDE SATAN. THESE ARE OUR FLESH AND THE WORLD.

The Bible teaches that we are born in the flesh with a basic nature to sin, and that there are no exceptions. It is this sin nature that Satan preys on. Ephesians 2:1-9 describes the basic universal predicament:

> And you He made alive, who were dead in trespasses and sins, in which you once walked according to the course of this world, according to the prince of the power of the air [Satan], the spirit who now works in the sons of disobedience, among whom also we all once conducted ourselves in the lusts of our flesh, fulfilling the desires of the flesh and of the mind, and were by nature children of wrath, just as the others.

This was our state until God saved us through the death of Jesus on the cross because of His amazing grace.

Thus, the flesh is a powerful force, and we only have victory over the flesh through Jesus and not by any works of our own (Ephesians 2:8-9). Add to Satan and the flesh a third enemy which is the "world" and its ways and systems, and we have insurmountable problems without Jesus.

This chapter will discuss the basic problems of the flesh and the world. As we begin, Christians must realize that they cannot compartmentalize these three ancient enemies. All three of these enemies work together in close harmony and with a deadly conspiracy to keep us either unsaved or ineffective in God's kingdom if we are saved.

Simply stated, our flesh consists of all of those natural and carnal desires that we have within us apart from God. If we did not have Jesus, then everything that we had a desire to do would be born of the flesh. Fleshly desires do not just include those from birth but also all those desires that the world and its ways have put in our heart. Satan, knowing the particular weaknesses of our flesh, sets up his specific schemes, temptations, and traps to ensnare us. Even after we are saved, there is a constant tension between the desires of our flesh and the desires of the Holy Spirit within us.

At the heart of our flesh, we want to satisfy our own lusts and find our significance apart from God. To live in the flesh is to desire to satisfy our own ego irrespective of God's will for our lives. Living in the flesh and living under the direction of the Spirit of God are total opposites. Our lifetime battle is to overcome our own flesh and to walk according to the Spirit of God.

As we explained at the beginning of the book, God finds us in our flesh and draws us to Himself through the power of His Holy Spirit. Then, when we accept Jesus as our Lord and Savior, the Spirit gives us true life for the first time. The Bible teaches we are dead to our sins in our flesh but alive in the Spirit. The Christian life then becomes a pilgrimage of trying to put our flesh behind us and focus more on Jesus, loving and serving Him more each day.

The world, which we will look at next, has a strong influence over our flesh as the world panders to our most base and evil desires. When the world says: "You are number one!" and "You are all that matters," this is tempting stuff. Then Satan comes along and throws out his hook to influence us to give in to our carnal desires. The end result can be a sin that grows like a cancer unless Jesus intervenes; therefore, the Bible says we are to be wise about our enemies so that we can avoid the pitfalls that come our way. If we recognize the truth about ourselves and know ourselves, then we are better positioned to call on our Lord for help.

How does the world influence us and shape our desires, our thoughts, and our lives?

The next enemy we'll discuss is the world. When we speak of "the world," we are talking about the way the godless world operates. The world system is the prevailing system around us. It is born out of Satan's lies. The world system, which refers to the influence and practices of the world, is a powerful influence that draws godless people into its clutches. The world system is a powerful force that keeps us away from God (Matthew 18:7). Jesus said time and time again that we will belong either to the world or to Him.

All of us are subject to being influenced by the world's viewpoint and by popular opinion. We do not have to look far to see the influence that the world has over people, nations, leaders, customs, and habits. The world tells us if it feels good, do it. The world tells us it is all right to pursue sinful ways as long as everyone else is doing it. The world tells us to look out for ourselves first, last, and always. The world says eat, drink, and be merry for tomorrow we may die. The world promotes and appeals to man's most base desires.

The committed Christian must go up against the world every day, and face criticism and persecution for being different. The truth is that there is a world system, which the enemy has played a major role in creating. We must recognize this system for exactly what it is and understand how with God's help we can overcome it (John 16:33).

The world's system stands in direct opposition to God's ways because it exists to glorify human beings and not God. The world system exists so we can seek our selfish pleasures. The world's standards are at odds with God's perfect standards. The world condemns some terrible sins, but not others. For example, the world condemned Hitler for attacking innocent nations and killing 6 million Jews; however, the same world says that it is permissible to kill several million little babies per year by legal abortion. The world simply does what it does to please the flesh.

The world could care less about God's eternal truths and His standards for how we should live. World systems pass laws that are harmful to everyone such as legalized gambling, legalized pornography, or whatever else serves the pleasure of people. God's laws are based on truth and what is good for people. The world's laws are based on what is popular with people.

The world has an entirely different set of priorities and standards than God has. Most people, including many Christians, are unaware that the world's standards are different from God's. When we see "everybody" doing a sinful act, we can easily be swayed into thinking that such conduct is permissible. Before long our conscience, which God put in us to warn us that certain acts are wrong, becomes numbed from the constant bombardment of the world.

The world invades our homes with ungodly music and television, which glamorize illicit sex, violence, corruption, and greed. People in the United States

After the Leap

watch television an average of 30 hours a week, thus becoming numb to the prevalent themes of murder, adultery, and greed. The end result is that the world preaches a powerful message: such immoral behavior is fun and acceptable. When was the last time on television that you saw a normal Christian family praying over a meal or going to church or having devotions at home? When was the last time you saw a normal family with one father and one mother living a good and decent life? When did you last see an evening show or daytime serial present God or His commandments in a positive way? The truth is seldom if ever do we see any positive Christians values displayed through the entertainment media.

In reality, the world's major institutions often poke fun at God's truths and His laws. Three of our powerful influences—the media, the entertainment industry, and the academic community—often attack the basic premise of the Christian life: that moral absolutes do exist. The world's view is to poke fun at any leader who claims God created absolute laws and standards by which we are to live. Unlike generations past, many today consider the Ten Commandments to be a useless relic of the past. Even though the United States was founded on a belief in God and on God's laws, the growing consensus in the U.S. is that people, not God, should decide the law. This is a blatant lie from the enemy who seeks to destroy us. Right and wrong do not depend on the opinions of people. They depend on the laws of God. Sadly, surveys have shown that even many evangelical Christians do not believe that laws are absolute. The eternal truth is that God created the law, and His law is just as good and true today as it was the day He declared it.

As has always been the case, the world is at odds with God's truths. The underlying thought is that the world and not God has the answers to all problems. To know what a terrible lie this is, all we have to do is look around and see the tragic consequences. People continue to slaughter and mistreat others with little regard for life, liberty, or justice. Nevertheless, God is considered irrelevant to our culture according to the new world order. It does not seem to matter that every great nation, which has pursued its own way instead of God's way, has ended in total destruction. The immorality of a nation will bring it to destruction just as individual immorality will destroy the individual. Although the Bible warns us of the disastrous consequences of not following God's law, the world does not listen.

We must stand firm against the world and its system.

The world and its standards are in basic conflict with Jesus' standards. We must be aware of the evil worldly influences on our lives, our families, and our friends. We must be vigilant not to succumb to the ways of the world. Only through the love of Jesus and the power of the Holy Spirit can we overcome the world. Otherwise, it will simply be too much for us. Jesus says we cannot serve two masters, for we will love the one and hate the other. Jesus also says we cannot serve both mammon and Him (Matthew 6:24). Mammon represents all the things of the world. Jesus has given us a conscious choice to make. If we choose Jesus over the world, we do not battle alone. Jesus is by our side enabling and empowering us to overcome the world, our flesh, and Satan.

It is not easy to stand up against popular opinion and the accepted standards of the world. This is particularly difficult for young people, who see their friends having "fun" by doing evil. It is not easy to swim against the tide, but we must. God did not call us to this earth to be politically correct or to agree with popular opinion. God called us to stand firm for Him and to follow Him. Christians must stand apart. Christians must stand for what is right. To do so in the face of a prevailing world philosophy that declares there is no such thing as real truth is difficult. But Jesus died so we would worship Him and not the world. The world will not save us. It will only bury us. Jesus says, "I am the Truth," and there is only one truth—God's truth. Now each of us must choose for ourselves—either Jesus or the world. We cannot have it both ways. Are you ready to follow Jesus and not the world?

The world will always be in conflict with God's ways and God's plan. That is one reason the Bible is so important—it tells us the truth about how to live. The Bible is God's standard for our lives. All Christians have an obligation and duty to do it God's way and not the world's way. A commitment to God's truths protects us from the world's insidious influence on our lives. Our best weapon, of course, is to focus not on the things of this world but on Jesus, developing a strong personal relationship with Him. When we do this, the things of God will increase in our lives and the temptations of this world will decrease. If we seek first the kingdom of God, all of the things we need will be added to us (Matthew 6:33). This is what the Bible promises; therefore, the primary weapon of spiritual warfare is to love God and Jesus with all of our heart, soul, mind, and strength and to obey God's law. Our most powerful weapons are prayer, worship, the Word, and the church.

WE MUST PUT ON THE FULL ARMOR OF GOD.

Now that we have discussed the world and the flesh, we will look at the basic weapons we have to fight the devil. Ephesians 6 tells us how to put on the full armor of God so that the enemy cannot harm us. We will examine how to put on this armor. The armor we are speaking of contains those basic character traits that God wants us to have and that flow from the heart. With these worn to perfection, the enemy will not harm us. Turn now to Ephesians 6:10-20 and read it, thinking carefully about the importance of each of these pieces of armor for our protection.

The Apostle Paul compares the effective Christian soldier to the well-armed Roman soldier of that day. At that time, there was no greater warrior than the well-armed and fully equipped Roman soldier. From a spiritual standpoint we have to put on our armor to battle Satan, the world, and the flesh just as the Roman soldier did prior to battling his enemies.

Paul starts by telling us to put on the **belt of truth**. The warrior's belt held everything in place. For us the truth about God and Jesus and who we are in Christ holds everything together. Jesus is the Truth as well as the Way and the Life as John 14:6 tells us. We must cling to Jesus and His truth.

Next, Paul says to put on the **breastplate of righteousness**. Righteousness, that is pursuing holiness and not sin, will protect our hearts from the evil one. When we fail to pursue righteousness in our lives, we leave our hearts unprotected and the enemy can do damage. We have no righteousness on our own power but only because of what Jesus did for us on the cross. Because Jesus died for our sins, we can be forgiven. He made His righteousness available to us. Satan will always tell us we are unrighteous and unworthy, and he will try to overwhelm us with feelings of guilt and insignificance. This is not true because the Bible promises we can claim our righteousness through what Jesus did for us on the cross. Obedience to God and getting right with God through confession and repentance when we slip keep us strong in the righteousness of Jesus.

Our feet must be shod with the **gospel of peace**. We stand on that firm foundation of the peace that only Jesus can bring. Also, we use those same feet to carry the good news to the lost. This peace protects us from the enemy knocking our legs out from under us. When we are at peace, we have neither anxiety nor fear of the enemy. Jesus came to give us that peace which is a mighty protection against the enemy (Philippians 4:7).

Next, we are to take up the **shield of faith**. Our faith in Jesus is what saves us. Faith is knowing that God is with us. Our faith keeps us pressing onward and fighting the good fight. Satan wants to take away our faith by planting doubt and unbelief, but it is that very faith that is our shield of protection against his attacks. The more we step out in faith to serve Jesus, the stronger we become in Christ. As we grow in faith in Christ, the influence of the enemy diminishes.

Next, we put on the **helmet of salvation**. We know in our minds that we are saved through Jesus. This fact should give each of us great peace of mind and comfort. Being secure in Jesus will protect our minds from the constant lies the enemy tells us. Salvation gives us permanent security, something the enemy cannot steal. We are to guard our minds by resting in our salvation (Romans 12:2).

Lastly, we are to take the **sword of the Spirit**, which is the Word of God. This sword is both an offensive and a defensive weapon. The Holy Spirit wrote the Bible. The sword of the Spirit is the Bible. If we stay in the Bible and digest it and apply it daily, we have a powerful weapon to use against the enemy. The Word of God is a two-edged sword that cuts sharply. Jesus used the Word against the devil in Luke 4:1-13. And we know that the Word of God is also our strength. In obedience to the Word, that is God's law, we find protection from the enemy.

All six pieces of armor are prescribed by Paul for the victorious Christian life. We would be wise to put on this armor daily, asking God for more faith, more truth, more righteousness, more of the Word, more of the peace of Jesus, and a greater realization of our salvation. These essential traits are foundational to our walk in Christ and will give us what we need to fight against our ancient foe.

WE MUST FLEE FROM THE DEVIL AND RESIST TEMPTATION. WE MUST ALSO BE HUMBLE, SELF-CONTROLLED, AND ALERT.

"Resist the devil and he will flee from you," the Bible tells us in James 4:7. We are called to be firm, to stand up, and to resist. We resist by fleeing from the temptation that is before us. We also resist by removing ourselves from any tempting circumstance. The Apostle Peter has some good advice about the enemy: "Humble yourselves, therefore, under God's mighty hand, that He may lift you up in due time" (1 Peter 5:6, NIV). Humility is a powerful weapon against the enemy. Humility is the opposite of pride. Satan likes for us to be prideful, and he appeals to our prideful flesh. Our pride gets us in trouble. Humility keeps us close to God.

Peter goes on to say that we should be "self-controlled and alert. Your enemy the devil prowls around like a roaring lion looking for someone to devour. Resist him, standing firm in the faith, because you know your brothers throughout the world are going through the same kind of sufferings" (1 Peter 5:8-9, NIV). The devil wants to devour our flesh. He wants to do this by gaining a stronghold in us through our sin. But we are called to resist the devil and stand firm.

The Bible says that the God of all grace will restore us and make us strong, firm, and steadfast.

Know your weaknesses and pray continually for God's help.

Finally, you must do your part. You must know yourself, your own weaknesses, and you must be willing to change. You must realize those areas in your life in which you are most vulnerable to attack by the enemy. Make a list of those weaknesses in your flesh. Then confess these weaknesses to God and ask Him to begin to change you and strengthen you in each of these areas. Ask Him to show you what you must do to overcome these specific temptations. Ask God to change your heart so that you will love Jesus more each day and the pleasures of this world less. Remember, Jesus did not come to leave you in your helpless state of sin. He came to set you free. Always keep your eyes on Jesus as you increase your love, your faith, and your obedience to Him. Fear not because God is on your side. Live like it.

"Do not love the world or the things in the world. If anyone loves the world, the love of the Father is not in him" (1 John 2:15).

Discussion Questions

1. What are the things of this world to which you are most attracted? Make a list, and then analyze each of these things. Are they good or bad? What would Jesus say?

2. What are the two or three things that are hardest to deal with concerning your own personal fleshly desires? How can you best protect yourself from your own weakness?

3. How do you protect your family or friends from the bad influences of the world?

II

THE GREAT COMMANDMENT

[Jesus said] "You shall love the Lord your God with all your heart, with all your soul, and with all your mind. This is the first and greatest commandment. And the second is like it: 'You shall love your neighbor as yourself.' On these two commandments hang all the Law and the Prophets" (Matthew 22:37-40).

WHAT THE COMMANDMENTS ARE ALL ABOUT.

Obedience to God's commandments is the key to the good life here on earth. The entire Bible emphasizes the blessings of obedience and the curse of disobedience. Learn these commandments with your mind and plant them in your heart.

God gave Moses the Ten Commandments, which are the basic laws for God's people. Jesus, when asked which commandment was the greatest, gave us The Great Commandment, set forth above. He said all the other commandments hang on this one.

God's commandments are also a love letter to His people. God knew that if His people followed His commandments, they would be blessed in every part of their lives. God also knew that disobedience to His law would bring about curses, that is tragedy and heartache.

Our God is a perfect God. He is a holy God and a God of perfect righteousness and justice. He sent His commandments for us to follow. These commandments are as applicable today as they were some 4,000 years ago when God gave them to Moses. Our job is to follow these commandments and have such a love of God that we will delight in His law.

Many people have the wrong idea about the Ten Commandments. Many people believe that God's laws are outdated and serve no useful purpose in today's modern world. Nothing could be further from the truth. Jesus told us that lov-

After the Leap

ing God and loving others was so important that all the other commandments were covered by this Great Commandment. If we will learn God's commandments are for our personal welfare, then we will be more inclined to obey them.

All of God's commandments were created so we can live in joy and peace. God instructed us to obey His law. Jesus, of course, also said the same thing. Jesus said, "If you want to enter into life, keep the commandments" (Matthew 19:17). Jesus knows what is best for us. God's law was created so we could live together in love and without chaos. God's laws are a precious gift to each of us because they are designed to protect us from the destruction and heartbreak that flow from disobedience.

Jesus always upheld God's commandments. In Matthew 5:17, Jesus said, "Do not think I came to destroy the Law or the Prophets. I did not come to destroy but to fulfill." Jesus went on to say, "Whoever therefore breaks one of the least of these commandments, and teaches men so, shall be called least in the kingdom of heaven; but whoever does and teaches them, he shall be called great in the kingdom of heaven" (Matthew 5:19).

In the final analysis, all of God's law is about love. When Jesus was asked by the lawyer which commandment was the most important, Jesus told him, "You shall love the Lord your God with all your heart, with all your soul, and with all your mind. This is the first and great commandment. And the second is like it: "You shall love your neighbor as yourself. On these two commandments hang all of the Law and the Prophets" (Matthew 22:37-40). If we loved God with all our hearts, we would never consider hurting other people, stealing their property, or coveting what they own. If we love God that much, we also would not consider worshiping any idol or false god.

God's laws are extremely important to Him, but He is most interested in our hearts.

God is interested in our hearts more than anything else. Jesus told us that if we look at another woman adulterously, then we have committed adultery (Matthew 5:28). He said the same thing about having any anger in our hearts toward anyone (Matthew 5:22). Jesus knew that if our hearts were pure, we would not proceed to the next step, which is committing the sin (Mark 7:21-23). If someone acted nice around a neighbor, but when alone cursed that neighbor under his breath or deep down inside, what is it that God sees? God sees the heart, of course. God sees the hatred that arises from deep within. Our hearts determine how we really feel about someone. God focuses on the heart, and God desires a clean heart. As we study the commandments of God, keep in mind that the heart is what matters most. Psalm 139:23 gives us profound advice for all times when it says, "Search me, O God, and know my heart."

The problem with our natures is that our hearts are not pure. From impure hearts come sinful desires. Once the desire surfaces, it often turns into a sinful action. God does not like any sinful conduct because it causes harm to the sinner and the person sinned against. Sin always tears down relationships between the one who sins and the victim of that sin, not to mention the terrible precedent-setting witness to children in future generations. God wants us to seek passionately after His holiness and His righteousness. There is no happiness without holiness. Jesus said, "Blessed are those who hunger and thirst for righteousness, for they shall be filled" (Matthew 5:6). Remember, peace follows purity for there is no stricken conscience with purity. Seek to lead a life of obedience. Seek first the kingdom of God, and blessings will follow.

God's Ten Commandments are just as applicable today as ever. We must live by them.

The Ten Commandments clearly tell us what God wants us to do. He wants us to obey these commandments. When we fail to obey them, there are serious consequences for our own lives. God will forgive us when we fail, but God commands us not to sin in the first place. It is important to understand God's principles about obedience and disobedience to His commandments. God says that there will be strong consequences for those who disobey. Turn to Deuteronomy 28 and read about the great blessings that come from obeying God's commands. Then study the last part of that chapter to understand the curses that flow from disobedience. Finally, know that if you have sinned, there is hope. Read Deuteronomy 30 to understand the wonderful blessings that come to God's wayward child who repents and is brought back into a loving and obedient relationship with the Father. The classic case is the story of the "Lost Son," which you should read in Luke 15:11-32.

God will forgive us and let us start afresh when we repent, confess, and ask His forgiveness. Even so, the consequences of sin remain. There are normally at least two victims for every violation of the Ten Commandments—the person sinning and the person sinned against. There are other unintended victims such as family members or friends we disappoint. The Bible says the sins of the fathers carry down to the children of the third and fourth generation (Exodus 20:5). Alcoholism, sexual sins, and other addictions are prime examples of areas where we frequently see children following in the parent's footsteps.

Our God is a Holy God. He gives us clear and specific standards to follow. God wants us to be pure and righteous (Isaiah 3:10). God does not want us to inflict unnecessary wounds and heartbreak on anyone, including ourselves. The Ten Commandments are simple to understand and cover basic human behavior. Governments may enact thousands of laws, rules, and regulations that we are to obey, but these commandments are the bedrock foundation of all good laws. These ten laws are foundational to the Christian life. Because God loves us, He wrote His commandments on stone, showing that they are for all time. They are absolute truths to be applied to everyday living.

WE SHOULD OBEY GOD'S COMMANDMENTS BECAUSE WE LOVE HIM.

God wants us to know His law, obey His law, and take His law into our hearts. As the psalmist said, we should meditate on His law day and night (Psalm 119:97). We should take these laws into our hearts and souls and minds. Our obedience to His law is an expression of our love for God (John 14:15). We love Him because He first loved us.

As you read the next several chapters, you should understand more fully why each and every commandment is absolutely necessary for living. Memorize the Ten Commandments. Be able to recite each commandment and understand why disobedience to God's law will bring separation from God and harm to your life.

One of the main ways we express our love for the Father is to obey His commands. Our love of God and our love of Jesus should be our first priority. Then comes love of our neighbor. The Bible says in 1 Peter 4:8 that love covers a multitude of sins. This does not mean we are free to sin. Peter is expressing the truth that the love of Christ stands above everything else. With such a love in our hearts, we are far much less likely to sin.

OUR LOVE FOR THE FATHER AND JESUS IS FOUNDATIONAL FOR ALL OF LIFE.

According to the Great Commandment, God says we must love Him with all of our hearts. He doesn't say just a little of our love or most of our love. He says with "all" of our hearts. This means we must love God and Jesus with a passion. We must love Him from early in the morning until we go to bed at night. Our love for Him must be all-consuming, burning within our souls. Also, we must love Him not with mere words but also by reaching out to others in need. Love is an emotional heartfelt thing, but love is also an action thing.

We express our love to God when we go to Him in prayer. When we worship Him from the bottom of our hearts, we show our love. When we cry out to Him from our pain or hurts, we show our love. When we enthusiastically sing to Him or praise Him in joy, this is an act of love. When we unselfishly sacrifice for others without any expectation of anything in return, we express our greatest love. Jesus said what greater love can a person show than to lay down his life for a friend (John 15:13). Jesus did that for us. Jesus' extreme example of love was His dying on the cross so we might live. First John 4:17 tells us that love has been perfected among us, so that we might be bold and love others in this world. Verses 18-19 go on to say that "There is no fear in love; but perfect love casts out fear. . . . He who fears has not been made perfect in love. We love Him because He first loved us."

Love such as Jesus has comes only through the power of the Holy Spirit. As Paul said so beautifully in 1 Corinthians 13, if we have not love we are nothing. Also, Paul reminds us in this wonderful chapter that love never fails, but hopes and perseveres no matter what. Above all things, God commands us to love. Love of the Father and love for each other is the Great Commandment. Keep the Father and the Son foremost within your heart and mind and soul. Please read and ponder those attributes of love as described in 1 Corinthians 13.

WE SHOULD LOVE OUR NEIGHBORS AS OURSELVES.

Jesus wants us to love everyone with the same kind of love He showed for us. Jesus doesn't merely desire that we love everyone, He commands us to love everyone. The term *neighbor* is not limited to our next-door neighbor, but includes everyone we know. God commands us to love believers and unbelievers alike. Keep in mind that God loved unbelievers so much that He sent His Son to die for them.

To love some people is really tough—particularly if they smell bad, lie or cheat, or are obnoxious. It is also tough to love those who have wronged us. The truth of the matter is that without the work of the Holy Spirit in us, we do not have the ability to love our enemies, particularly those who are unlovable. We cannot love our enemies unselfishly in our own strength. Jesus wants us to see other people through His loving eyes. Jesus wants us to have compassion for the unlikable and the ugly.

It is easy to love our friends and our relatives. Almost everyone, including

After the Leap

sinners, does that. Jesus said in Luke 6:32, "If you love those who love you, what credit is that to you? For even sinners love those who love them." Then, Jesus went on to say, "Love your enemies, do good and lend hoping for nothing in return; and your reward will be great and you will be sons of the Most High" (Luke 6:35).

Jesus has unlimited love for all sinners no matter what they have done in the past. Jesus wants to reach out to the unsaved and bring them to salvation. Jesus loved sinners when He fed the hungry, visited the prisoners, healed the sick, and reached out to the "least of these" (Matthew 25). Now Jesus commands us to bring His love to these lost and hurting people. To love others is the most basic command of all. Paul tells us in Romans 13:8, "Owe no one anything except to love one another, for he who loves another has fulfilled the law."

JESUS CALLS US TO LOVE EVERYONE—NO MATTER WHAT THE CIRCUMSTANCE.

Jesus commands us to love our brothers and sisters in Christ. In John 15:12 Jesus said, "Love one another as I have loved you." In fact, 1 John 3:10 reminds us that anyone who does not love his brother is not a child of God, but a child of the devil. Read 1 John 3 carefully, and you will discover that one who does not love his brother is not born of God. We are to love everyone as He loved everyone.

John tells us that anyone who loves his brother lives in the light, but he who hates his brother walks in darkness (1 John 2:10-11). You cannot love God and hate your brother. John also says that anyone who says he loves God but hates his brother is a liar (1 John 4:20).

Our love for others should include people of all races, all religions, all church denominations and, of course, people of both sexes. God has no place for racial prejudice or any other kind of prejudice in His kingdom. We are called to love, not hate. To believers, Paul says, "There is neither Jew nor Greek, there is neither slave nor free, there is neither male nor female; for you are all one in Christ Jesus" (Galatians 3:28). No one person is better than another—all are equal in the sight of God. As for nonbelievers, Christians are commanded to love them too even though they may look different, speak a different language, or belong to a different religion. Remember, Christ came to die for the lost. We are called to love the lost and to tell them about Jesus. No man or woman should look down on or feel superior to any other man or woman. If you have any prejudice against anyone because of race or religion, confess it as a sin and ask Jesus to work on your heart by replacing your hate with His love.

Jesus calls on us to love everyone under all kinds of circumstances. This does not mean we have to approve of what another person does. We are called to hate the sin, but to love the sinner.

What is agape love? What is that truly unselfish love that Jesus had?

There are probably more references to the word *love* in the Bible than any other word. What is meant by love? Let's look at the word *agape*, which is the special kind of love Jesus has for all of us.

The word *agape* is the Greek word that Jesus used to describe unselfish love. There are many kinds of love. The Greeks had several different words for love. *Eros* meant a love of the thing itself such as a beautiful woman, a great painting, or a lovely landscape. Another Greek word for love was *phileo*, which meant a brotherly kind of a love. This is the kind of love we have for someone we care for and whom we expect to love us in return. It is easy to love someone who loves us. Christians and non-Christians love their children and their friends. This is a natural kind of love of which even our fleshy nature is capable.

The word *agape* describes the kind of love Jesus always has for everyone. Agape love is totally unselfish. That is the word Jesus used when He called us to love one another. Agape love is when we love someone and do not expect a thing in return. Agape love is when we love someone who, from the world's standards, does not deserve to be loved. Agape love means to pour out your life and energy to help someone else when there is not a single logical reason to do so except for the love of Jesus.

Agape love is doing what is in the best interest of another person. It is listening to another person and not making judgments against him. Agape is being a friend in time of trouble. It is forgiving that person who has wronged us and letting that person know that she is forgiven. Agape is not gossiping or saying bad things about another person. It includes one friend going to another friend in love to tell the truth even when the truth will hurt. Agape love is the practice of being patient and never giving up on another person no matter what.

Love can be having a warm feeling for someone, but that is a small part of love. Unfortunately, the world teaches that all that there is to love are the romantic or emotional feelings we have for someone else. Real love, that is agape love, is much more than that, as Paul described it in 1 Corinthians 13. Love is an action when we sacrifice and do something for someone else. Love is being available when the other person needs you. Love is acting out of compassion for the person being loved. Love is treating the other person the way that you would wish for that person to treat you. Love is getting up and feeding someone who is hungry.

Love often means taking risks and doing things out of our comfort zone. The key is to be led by the Holy Spirit in the way we love others. Love is taking the effort to become a friend in order to earn the right to be heard so we can share the good news of Jesus Christ. Love is setting a good example for those around us to follow. Love is not letting someone down because of our sin. Love is sometimes just accepting that other person for who he is.

To love is to encourage another person and to be supportive. To love is to serve and have a servant's heart. Jesus came to serve, and this is one of the main ways that He showed His love. Jesus' ministry was one of serving others in order to make broken lives whole. No person was ever the same after meeting Jesus. That person may have rejected Jesus, but that person was still touched by His love. Jesus loved when He reached out to the woman at the well even though she was a notorious sinner who had many husbands (John 4:6-42). Jesus was doing an act of love when He chastised the Pharisees and Sadducees in the most critical sermon He ever gave (Matthew 23). Sometimes the most difficult act of love is to go to a friend in love and tell that friend that she is doing something sinful. There will be times this will be our responsibility if we truly love that other person.

Jesus gave us the ultimate example of love when He died on the cross for us so we might be saved. Always remember that when we love sacrificially as Jesus showed us, the people we love will see Jesus in us and know that it is Jesus who makes the difference. We witness for Jesus by and through the power of His love. And when we love Jesus with all our hearts, we will see others through the eyes of Jesus, and we will not be able to hold back from loving them.

"By this all will know you are My disciples, if you have love for one another" (John 13:35).

Discussion Questions

1. How are you reaching out in love to those from whom you expect nothing in return?

2. If you had a friend living in sin, what would you do?

3. Write down at least three specific things that you can do and will do in the near future to love someone else with the love of Jesus. It may be as simple as writing a letter to someone or making an effort to visit someone who is hurting to offer encouragement.

After the Leap

12

PUTTING GOD FIRST
(COMMANDMENTS 1–4)

(These are the first four of the Ten Commandments.)

1. "You shall have no other gods before Me."

2. "You shall not make for yourself any carved image. . . . You shall not bow down to them, nor serve them."

3. "You shall not take the name of the Lord your God in vain."

4. "Remember the Sabbath day, to keep it holy."

(Exodus 20:3-8)

"You shall have no other gods before Me." (The First Commandment)

These first four commandments instruct us to put God first and worship Him alone. Jesus tells us, "No one can serve two masters; for either he will hate the one and love the other, or else he will be loyal to the one and despise the other. You cannot serve God and mammon" (Matthew 6:24).

Thus, the first commandment is the most fundamental. God said, "You shall have no other gods before Me." That is so simple, but so difficult for us to follow. Our God is a jealous God (Exodus 34:14). He knows that He is the only God worthy to be worshiped. God knows that any time we worship a false god we are turning our love away from Him and entering into a dangerous relationship.

We have proven throughout history that we have a great desire to worship other gods. The Old Testament contains many stories of people building idols and worshiping them as gods. This practice makes no sense and serves no worthwhile purpose. In the days of the Old Testament, people were always going up to high places to build altars or to set out a bunch of rocks to worship. At one point, the Israelites built a golden calf to worship (Exodus 32). Christians today can get off track too. Paul, in 1 Corinthians 10:20, warned the Gentiles in the church at Corinth not to make sacrifices to demons or to have fellowship with them. These practices, which are demonic in origin, still go on today in many different ways. The very act of sacrifice to idols or idol worship is an open invitation to Satan and the demonic forces.

Why do people engage in such a ridiculous activity that God detests? There are two reasons. The first reason is that we have been deceived by Satan, who hates our worship of the true God. Satan and his demons like to put these ideas into our heads. The second reason is that we want to be like God and assume His role. Thus, we create our own gods so we can feel powerful and believe we can control our own destiny. The only problem with this idea is that is God is in control of everything. We are not God, and we cannot control the events around us. Our choice is to worship and obey God or to rebel and do our own thing. When we choose to rebel and seek anything other than God to worship, that is idolatry.

The only difference in yesterday's idolatry and today's idolatry is in what we worship. Some of the things like witchcraft, satanism, and fortune-telling are just the same today as they were centuries ago. For the most part, however, man has turned from worshiping piles of rocks to worshiping things that bring pleasure or power. Whatever consumes our minds and hearts that is not of God becomes an idol for us, and we fall into idolatry. We must keep this fact in mind as we learn about this commandment.

Obedience to God begins with worshiping God because He demands it for our own good. If we truly worship Him in spirit and in truth, we will not get sidetracked into worshiping or following other gods. God demands our loyalty. We are to worship Him alone (Revelation 15:4).

"You shall not make for yourself any carved image." (The Second Commandment)

Idolatry occurs when we put anything above God. When we put our own pleasure or our own ambitions or anything else above God, that is idolatry. Whenever our attention is primarily focused on alcohol, drugs, sex, power, or greed, we are practicing idolatry.

After the Leap

Some people still follow the abominable practice of worshiping false gods by dabbling in the supernatural world in violation of God's law. This form of idolatry gives the enemy a stronghold. The enemy's goal is to kill us by getting us to worship him instead of God. One of the ways Satan accomplishes his goal is by deceiving us into the practices of witchcraft, astrology, fortune-telling, talking to the dead, Satan worship, and other cultist practices. Everyone who engaged in these practices in the Bible drew a curse and suffered great tragedy. King Saul is just one example (1 Samuel 15:22-23; 1 Chronicles 10:13-14). Through such practices, we reject God and consent to the devil's ways, giving the enemy legal ground to harm us (Leviticus 17:7-9; Deuteronomy 32:16-17).

God wants us to remain pure in our practice of worshiping Him alone. God does not want us to mix the true faith with another faith or any other form of religious practice. Deuteronomy 18:9-12 (NIV) issues a strong warning: "When you enter the land the Lord your God is giving you, do not learn to imitate the detestable ways of the nations there. Let no one be found among you who sacrifices his son or daughter in the fire, who practices divination or sorcery, interprets omens, engages in witchcraft, or casts spells, or who is a medium or spiritist or who consults the dead. Anyone who does these things is detestable to the Lord."

Beware of the New Age practices of meditation in which you empty your mind. God does not want us to engage in anything spiritual that is not of Him. Guard your mind. Any worship or practice that is not of God is of the enemy. Paul warns us in 1 Timothy 1:3-5 not to teach or practice any doctrine but that of Jesus Christ. He tells us not to "give heed to fables and endless genealogies" but to "love from a pure heart, from a good conscience, and from sincere faith." Paul goes on to tell us in 1 Timothy 4:7 to "reject profane and old wives' fables." Man-made religions and beliefs are nothing but fables. Paul tells us, "For the time will come when they will not endure sound doctrine, but according to their own desires . . . they will heap up for themselves teachers; and they will turn their ears away from the truth, and be turned aside to fables. . . . But be watchful in all things" (2 Timothy 4:3-5). By definition a fable is any fiction, invention of man, or falsehood. A fable includes any religious, theological, or philosophical belief that does not come from God.

Avoid any worship of Satan. Today, Satan has followers who worship him directly and engage in terrible deeds, including the sacrifice of children and animals in secret ceremonies. Fortune-tellers make a living by using demonic power in order to make their clients believe they can predict the future. This is not some kind of harmless fun. It is serious business. Any power from the spirit world other than the Holy Spirit is evil. Avoid it. In Galatians 5:19-20, Paul again denounces idolatry and witchcraft. Paul calls on the church to rebuke some members sharply so "they may be sound in the faith, not giving heed to Jewish fables and commandments of men who turn from the truth" (Titus 1:13-14). Remember, our God is a jealous God.

Have nothing to do with any game or any activity that tries to invoke a supernatural power. Do not join any cult or organization which is religious in nature or which has religious ceremonies or rituals. We have a propensity to create secret organizations with religious overtones that require some form of allegiance. Only God through His Bible defines who God is. Have nothing to do with any doctrine or religious system that originates anywhere other than the Word of God. Do not get involved with anything that tries to substitute its beliefs for the Bible and the basic truths of the Christian faith. God does not want our minds polluted even a little. You can have a jug of pure water from a well, but if you put a drop of poison in it, that water is unfit. God demands His well be clean and pure.

These first two commandments are foundational to our faith.

"You shall not take the name of the Lord your God in vain." (The Third Commandment)

The third commandment tells us not to take the name of the Lord in vain. God's name is very important to Him and should be very important to us. God is known by many names throughout the Bible. Each name describes who He is. God is very jealous of His name and has commanded that it not be misused in any way. The same holds true for the name of Jesus.

Anyone who maliciously or without thinking misuses the name of the Lord commits a sin. God wants His name to be treated with the deepest respect (Hosea 12:5). Calling the Father a bad name or using His name as a swear word is a serious thing. Such practices show our thoughtlessness, rebellion, and total lack of understanding about who God is. None of us would go before a judge, who was getting ready to sentence us, and call him a bad name or insult him to his face. It is far worse to insult God. God hears all that we say. When we misuse His name, we insult Him to His face. His name must be honored above all names.

To use God's name in vain is the height of arrogance, pride, and thoughtlessness. We must hold God's name in fear and awe and the highest respect. His name is so important that He created a commandment concerning this one thing.

Of course, if we love Him even a little bit, we will never misuse His holy name—not if we know anything at all about God.

"Remember the Sabbath day, to keep it holy." (The Fourth Commandment)

God worked for six days to create the earth and everything on it. Then, on the seventh day God rested. Now God commands that we set aside one day a week for rest and worship. God desires that we treat the Sabbath as a very special day in which we focus on the Lord, worship Him, and set our hearts on the things of God and not of the world.

God tells us two other important things about this very special day. First, He blessed the Sabbath Day, and second, He made it a holy day. Thus, God has told us that we can expect something special, that is His blessing, when we keep this day holy (Isaiah 58:13-14).

When Jesus came, we learned more about the Sabbath. The religious Jews, such as the Pharisees and Sadducees, had applied rigid rules to practices on the Sabbath. Some of the Jewish people still follow these rules today and will not undertake any activity on the Sabbath. Every time Jesus healed anyone on the Sabbath, the religious Jews criticized Him. Jesus responded by saying, "Therefore it is lawful to do good on the Sabbath" (Matthew 12:12). In this same chapter of Matthew Jesus reminded these Jews that if one of their sheep fell in a pit on the Sabbath, surely they would rescue it.

In Matthew 12, Jesus said that He, Jesus Christ, was Lord of the Sabbath. In explaining the Sabbath, Jesus told the story about how David and his friends entered the temple and ate the consecrated bread when they were hungry. Jesus also said He desired mercy over sacrifice. In other words, what David did was good because loving others was a greater thing under God's law. In fact, Jesus saw that it was honoring to the Sabbath to extend His love to the hungry. To work on the Sabbath, when working on the Sabbath is not a necessity or an emergency, is something we should avoid. One principle reason is that we will miss the blessing God has in store for us by not using this time to worship and rest in the Lord.

The Sabbath was made for man to renew His relationship with God and to rest. Many men and women, however, want to work at their jobs continuously. The Sabbath was meant for us to take our hearts and minds off work and worldly things so we can focus on Jesus. Try to set aside this day for worship and refreshment from the Lord. You will be blessed when you use this day for renewal of your body, mind, and spirit.

After the resurrection of Jesus on Sunday, Christians have celebrated their Sabbath on Sunday, which is the first day of the week. Sunday is the day Jesus had victory over the grave so Christians have rejoiced on this day ever since. This special day gives us a weekly opportunity to come and be filled with the Bread of Life and the Living Water of which Jesus spoke. Often Communion, taking the wine and the bread as Jesus commanded, is an additional blessing on this day. This day is a glorious time to be refilled by the Holy Spirit. Receive the joy and peace and blessing the Father wants you to have by keeping this day holy.

ALWAYS PUT GOD FIRST, LAST, AND FOREMOST. HE WILL HAVE IT
NO OTHER WAY.

Jesus made it clear in Luke 16:13 that man cannot worship both God and mammon. Mammon refers to things or money. Jesus said, "No servant can serve two masters; for either he will hate the one and love the other, or else he will be loyal to the one and despise the other. You cannot serve God and mammon."

You cannot worship both God and the world. Jesus prayed that His disciples would not be of this world, and thus, not open to the influence of the evil one. In John 17:15 (NIV), Jesus said, "My prayer is not that you take them [the disciples] out of the world but that you protect them from the evil one. They are not of the world, even as I am not of it." When we are of the world, we will worship the things of this world. God says worship Him and Him alone.

You should memorize all Ten Commandments. This week memorize the first four, which are at the start of the chapter. The other six follow in the next several chapters. Every Christian should know all Ten Commandments.

DISCUSSION QUESTIONS

1. What does your heart desire the most on a day-to-day basis? Do you idolize anything other than God? What is it and what do you plan to do about it?

2. Do you have any ties to any occult or non-Christian organization that makes any religious statements that you are supposed to follow? Do you engage in any activities such as astrology or fortune-telling or New Age practices such as meditation? What do you plan to do about your involvement in any of these practices?

After the Leap

3. Do you ever misuse God's or Jesus' name? If so, what do you plan to do about this? How do you think it makes God feel when you misuse His name?

4. Write down the various blessings, the good things that you will receive, from honoring the Sabbath. Now look at the things you do on the Sabbath. What adjustments in your life are you willing to make concerning the Sabbath?

13

THE HOME—PARENTS AND CHILDREN (5TH COMMANDMENT)

"Honor your father and your mother, that your days may be long upon the land which the Lord your God is giving you"(Exodus 20:12).

GOD CREATED THE HOME, AND GOD WANTS TO PRESERVE THE HOME THROUGH CHILDREN HONORING THEIR PARENTS.

The fifth commandment, listed above, centers around parents and the home. This chapter will focus on how children should treat their parents and how parents should treat their children. The next chapter will focus on the Christian marriage, which is the basic foundation of a good home.

Keep in mind that these two chapters on the home are only short summaries of basic biblical principles. Anyone becoming a parent, husband, or wife needs to spend considerable time learning how to go about these serious Christian responsibilities. Anyone preparing for parenthood or marriage should attend Christian seminars, read Christian books, talk with experienced Christian friends, and use all the resources of the church.

First and foremost, keep in mind that God created the home as His most basic institution. The home is a very special place. The home is where children learn about Jesus and the importance of obeying God's laws. The home is a place where family members should become close and bond intimately. The parents are meant to be a blessing to the children and the children to the parents.

The Bible says, "As for me and my house, we will serve the Lord" (Joshua 24:15). The home is the first place where we learn about God and about Jesus and the Holy Spirit. The home is a mini-church. The family collectively, that is the home, should take on the attributes of Jesus. The home should be a house of prayer, a place where the Word is taught and honored, where God is praised, and where Jesus reigns. The home should be a joyful place where family members grow together in Christ as they share good times and hardships.

The home is to be a special place. It should be a haven and refuge from the outside world—a place of safety and security from outside attacks. God intends for the home to be a place of peace and love. Certainly, there will be disagreements and differences of opinion, but in a godly home, members discuss issues in love, seeking God's direction. In the healthy home there will be encouragement. Every member exhorts others to do well the task at hand. The family is meant to operate as a team that, with God's help, overcomes the enemy and the obstacles the world puts before it. The family that follows Jesus is a winning team because Jesus always prevails.

Today the home is under attack. More homes are breaking up through divorce than ever before. Today more children are born to unmarried parents than ever before. In today's world, it is considered normal to have homes where the parents are not married. The institution of the home is frequently ridiculed on television programs and in the movies. A few decades ago, television series revolved around good traditional homes, but today anything goes. Today, one seldom sees a program about a home with a father and mother who have been married once and have children that belong to both parents.

Christian parents must stand firm and resist the ways of the world. They must prepare themselves to assume an important leadership role concerning the many crucial issues that will confront their children—premarital sex, anger, violence, bad company, drugs, alcohol, and the media. Christian parents cannot afford to have the world's culture raise their children. Children whose precious and tender minds are not protected from the constant onslaught of sex and sin will pay a heavy price. Satan is trying to destroy the home, and the world's ways are his ways of trying to accomplish that goal. That is why God calls for our homes to be built on a rock and not on sand. God is that rock.

Who will rule in your house? Whom do you serve? "As for me and my house, we will serve the Lord" (Joshua 24:15).

GOD HAS GOOD REASONS FOR TELLING US TO HONOR OUR PARENTS.

Authority in the home resides with the parents. That is the way God designed it. Without this principle in operation, the home would be full of chaos and confusion. Chaos would then lead to lawlessness. God has set out a certain order in the family that He expects us to follow for our own good and for our own peace and prosperity.

The good home is a place where the husband and wife set a godly example, and the children want to honor their parents. Unfortunately, many parents are far from perfect. Some parents never live up to the standards that God has imposed. Many homes are disorganized and dysfunctional because of confusion, lack of discipline, or addictive behavior on the part of the parents. Sin and disobedience take a terrible toll as many parents are so far removed from God that they do not have a clue of what to do. Little children suffer and often grow up to be like those parents. Crime rises and the prison population grows as the world's ways erode the home.

When things break down in the home, the children have a choice. The choice is to honor the parents as God commanded or to become bitter, resentful, or angry. God wants children to honor parents in order to prevent the formation of any roots of resentment or bitterness. God commands children to honor parents even if the parents do not deserve it.

"Honor your father and mother that your days may be long upon the land which the Lord your God is giving you" is the fifth commandment. God wants children to love, to respect, and to honor their mothers and fathers. Honor means to respect and to hold in high esteem. When children honor parents, God promises His blessing to the children. This includes the blessing of long life (Exodus 20:12).

When children do not honor parents, division and dissension result. Such constant bickering, complaining, and dissension eat away at any home's foundation. Disrespect of parents, in whatever form, fosters rebellion. Children are to obey their parents just as adults are to obey their Heavenly Father.

Obviously, no child should be expected to undergo physical abuse from a parent. Such crimes should be reported to someone in the church body or to the proper governmental authority. God's command to honor one's parents is not about condoning harmful criminal conduct. God is talking about a normal relationship that should exist within all homes, in which children submit to the authority of their parents and honor them.

EVEN THOUGH PARENTS MAKE MISTAKES, PARENTS SHOULD BE HELD IN HIGH ESTEEM.

To honor one's parents means to speak well of one's parents. Children should not go through life blaming parents for their problems even if the parents have let the children down. A parent may have sinned against a child. That parent should seek forgiveness. If the parent does not seek forgiveness, the child should still forgive the parent. Under God's plan for the family, God knows that it is unhealthy for a child to go through life with resentment or anger toward a parent. This is true even if the parent seems to deserve such treatment. The consequences of a broken relationship within the family run deep and can leave lasting scars. God wants families to live together in unity and constant reconciliation.

Children, love your parents and hold them in a special place regardless of the past. If there is any unforgiveness to be dealt with, go to your parents and tell them that they are forgiven. Tell them you love them. Mean it from the heart. God will honor such unselfish love with blessings beyond understanding. Further, He will give you His peace and His joy because you have obeyed Him.

Children are a gift from God, and parents are a gift to children. The family is a holy institution in which spiritual training and growing in the ways of the Lord should be the highest priorities. The support and safety that the family provides to children is essential to their spiritual, mental, and physical growth. If the family is not united under the headship of Christ, the children are at risk.

BEING A PARENT IS A GIFT OF GOD AND A SERIOUS OBLIGATION AND TRUST.

There is no more important ministry than being a godly parent. Children are sensitive, delicate, and easily influenced by parents. The way parents exercise their duties will largely determine the children's future and their ideas about God. God wants parenting to be done with great wisdom.

The father and mother have equal responsibilities in the raising of children. The roles are sometimes different, but parents should work together in raising children. One important role falls to the father as the head of the home. The father is to be the spiritual leader in the home. The father has a crucial role to lead by a Christlike example and to have a game plan for the family to mature spiritually. The father should assume his role with the heart of a servant and with the love of Jesus. As the spiritual leader, it is up to the father to know the home's spiritual condition. A crucial role of the mother is to nurture and raise the children in the faith. This is as important as any ministry in the kingdom of God. The father and mother form a team in this process. The parents should teach the Bible and the importance of prayer. With unity and commitment to Christ, parents can fulfill their God-given role.

Parents must prepare themselves for undertaking the challenge of raising children. This chapter only touches on a few of the important principles that every Christian, parent or not, should know about the home. The parent of any child should invest a great deal of time and energy in understanding how to raise children in a Christian home. Many good Christian books have been written about parenting. Parents also need continuous help from their church and sound advice from discerning Christian friends. Parenting seminars are most helpful. Parents must learn how to be effective Christian parents.

Parents must also realize that children are likely to pick up the character traits of their parents. Sons often follow in a father's footsteps. The example a mother sets for a daughter has more influence than any words. History seems to repeat itself from one generation to the next. The alcoholic father is much more likely than a sober father to have an alcoholic son. The father who abuses a child physically sets in motion an example that is often repeated. Most inmates in prison, who have abused or assaulted others, experienced the same sort of treatment during their childhood. What parents do is more important than what they preach.

All experts agree that the early years are the most important in the development of the child. God wants children to be obedient and to be able to love others and to receive love. When children sees parents do immoral things, they learn to live that way. Such children often grow up with strong feelings of guilt and low self-esteem. Often children will believe they contributed to the parents' bad behavior and will carry a sense of shame for life. On the other hand, when children are loved by parents, then they learn how to love others.

In a healthy Christian home, children need to learn that it is all right to express their feelings. Healthy families talk about their problems and do not hide sinful behavior. Healthy families correct bad situations by talking things through and seeking God's help.

THE BEST THING ANY PARENT CAN DO IS TO HAVE A CLOSE AND LOVING RELATIONSHIP WITH JESUS.

The most basic thing that all children need to know is that God loves them and that their parents love them too. Children need to know that their parents love them unconditionally—that is even when they are bad or disobedient. Children's self-worth and self-esteem depend from infancy on that agape-like parental love, that same unselfish love that Jesus demonstrated to all of us. Without parental love, children will not have much self-worth or hope for the future. Such a feeling of insignificance will likely drive them into alcoholism or drugs to escape the pain or in the other direction of seeking money, power, or popularity in order to be somebody. The love of parents is essential. Love, and particularly the love of Jesus, is the foundation for good parenting. For parents to have that kind of love for their children, they need to have a close personal relationship with Jesus. If parents have that unselfish love of Jesus, children will see that joy and want to know Jesus too. Children do not inherit eternal life. Putting one's faith and trust in Jesus is not something that is passed down from a parent to a child. Each person must make a commitment to Christ to be saved. In the Christian home, of course, there is a much greater likelihood that children will trust in Jesus when they observe believing parents.

Our homes should be built on a rock. They must rest on that firm foundation over which God reigns (Matthew 7:21-29). Children need to be taught the basics of the faith, including the importance of prayer, worship, reading the Bible, and regular church attendance. Children should witness their parents reaching out to the sick and the poor, showing what love is all about. The family needs to have times of prayer and Bible reading together. Prayer at each meal and at bedtime should be a habit.

Parents should also let their children see that their faith is important. Parents should teach that God is a holy God who hates sin and at the same time is an intimate Daddy who cares about all our needs. Children's image of God is critical. Usually they will view God in the same light as the father or the authority figure in the home. If the father is cruel or not caring, then children's perception of God is likely to be the same.

Parents should pray for their children. Parents should pray for their children to come to know Jesus Christ as Lord and Savior. Parents should pray for protection of their children. Parents should pray for all the important decisions that children will make in life, including a marriage partner and a vocational calling. These prayers should start while the child is still in the womb or very young. Little is more important than the prayers of the father and the mother for their children.

THE RIGHT KIND OF TRAINING AND DISCIPLINE IS AN EXPRESSION OF LOVE.

The Book of Proverbs gives good advice for children and parents alike. Proverbs 13:24 tells us that parents who love their children will be careful to discipline them. Proper discipline is an expression of love. The fourth chapter of Deuteronomy discusses in detail the importance of teaching the Ten

Commandments and the law of God to our children and to our children's children. Ephesians 6:1 tells children to obey their parents in the Lord. This implies that parents have a duty to teach, and children have a duty to obey. Ephesians 6:4 instructs parents not to exasperate their children, but instead to bring them up in the training and instruction of the Lord. Children also must learn there are boundaries that govern their actions. The normal child wants to know the rules and that the rules will be enforced fairly and consistently. The healthy child realizes that parental discipline is a form of love and essential to the peace of the home. "Train a child in the way he should go, and when he is old he will not turn from it" (Proverbs 22:6, NIV).

Godly discipline does not call for hurting a child or yelling or screaming at a child. A parent should never abuse a child, and even a spanking should be administered by the parent under control. Violence and verbal abuse have no place in the Christian home.

Jesus knew how to treat little children. He loved them and loved their simple faith. He took them in His arms and gave them comfort. Jesus said, "Let the little children come to Me, and do not forbid them; for of such is the kingdom of heaven" (Matthew 19:14). He set the perfect example of loving children. Even when Jesus was busy and His disciples wanted Him to stay on schedule, Jesus took time to love the children. Parents should follow Jesus' example.

Children are the most precious gift that parents will ever have, yet parents do not own children. Children belong to God. Parents are blessed with children for a limited time. God gives parents a few precious years to make an indelible impression on the character of their children. God's goal for all children is that they grow up to be the people that God intended them to be.

Parents must take control of the home. Parents must know what their children are doing at all times, protecting them from bad books, bad activities, and bad company. Do you know your children's friends? Parents must know the television programs their children are watching and limit the hours and the kinds of programs they are allowed to watch. Parents should be attentive to the kinds of music their children are listening to. Music can have a strong influence. Music with words full of sadism, sex, and violence will take its toll on the life of the child. Is the music your children listening to uplifting to the soul? Does it lift up Jesus? Is it satanic or demonic in nature? What kind of life do the words and the music promote? It is not easy to keep up with children and their friends and their activities. But parents must know what is going on and always be ready to step in and take corrective action.

Parenting is the most challenging job that any person ever undertakes.

Parenting is tough and frustrating at times and requires much patience and the help of the Holy Spirit. Parenting is also most rewarding and a great privilege given to us by our loving Father.

We all need to be involved in teaching the Bible to children, and this needs to start at an early age. Memory verses and songs about Jesus are important too. In 2 Timothy 3:15, Paul reminded Timothy that his learning of Scripture from infancy was what led him to salvation. In other words, the salvation of your children may rest upon how well you teach the Word to them when they are young.

The most important thing you can ever do is to teach and show children just how much God loves them and to what extremes God will go to take care of them.

All human beings, including children, have a great yearning to be loved and to feel significant. These needs must be met if a person is to have a healthy and whole life. The truth is that only Jesus can perfectly meet these two great, basic needs. Foundational to meeting both of these needs is for children to realize the following truths deep down in their hearts. Parents who impart these truths to their children are doing the most important thing they can do for them. For real security and a sense of peace, children must take the following eternal truths into their hearts.

God loves you and will always love you no matter what (Psalm 118:1, 29).

God will never ever leave you or desert you (Hebrews 13:5).

God loves you the way you are (Psalm 139:13-16).

God loves you when you sin or do stupid things (Psalm 103:8-14).

God wants you to obey Him because God knows what is best (John 15:14).

God always hears you (Psalm 138:3), and He will never disappoint you (Psalm 27:10).

God will always be there for you and will never give up (2 Timothy 2:13).

If children know these truths in their hearts, they will find their security in God and not drugs, alcohol, sex, wealth, popularity, or anything else that is of the world. The greatest heritage you, as a parent, can leave with your children is to be like Jesus—that is show them the same kind of love that the Father shows. In other words, will you love your children always? Will you love your children when they let you down, or sin, or are intentionally disobedient? Will you always be there for your children? Will you always be there to listen and respond with love and to provide godly instruction and encouragement? No matter what happens, will you never, never, never give up on your children? If you answered "yes" to all of these questions, then you are well on your way to witnessing the love of Jesus to your children.

Remember, parents should be strong disciplers of their children by doing whatever they can to lead their children to salvation and on to the joyous and victorious Christian life.

"And you, fathers, do not provoke your children to wrath, but bring them up in the training and admonition of the Lord"
(Ephesians 6:4).

Discussion Questions

1. Describe the prayer life and the spiritual life of your family.

2. If you have children, what specific things are you doing to bring them up to know Jesus and to serve Him? Write out each thing you are doing in the home to help develop your children's spiritual growth.

3. What are the main worldly problems or bad influences your children or anyone else in your family face? What can you do to deal specifically with these problems?

4. Are you holding on to any unforgiveness or resentment or bitterness against your parents? If so, how do you plan to get rid of it, and how do you plan to reconcile with your parents to the best of your ability? Write out a plan.

After the Leap

14
THE HOME AND
THE CHRISTIAN MARRIAGE

"Husbands, love your wives, just as Christ also loved the church and gave Himself for it" (Ephesians 5:25).

"Let each one of you . . . love his wife as himself, and let the wife see that she respects her husband" (Ephesians 5:33).

GOD'S FIRST AND MOST BASIC INSTITUTION IS MARRIAGE. MARRIAGE IS SACRED AND REQUIRES PREPARATION.

Marriage is ordained by God, not by human beings. Marriage vows are made to God. Marriage is God's basic institution and was created before the church. Because marriage is something God designs, we should take it as seriously, if not more seriously, than any other decision in life.

No one should enter into marriage lightly. Preparation for marriage is essential. Preparation for the Christian marriage should begin with the Christian role modeling of parents. Parents should let their lives teach their children the basics of a good marriage. Witnessing a strong Christian marriage and the love of a husband and wife for each other is the best marriage training for children because they have a tendency to follow the parent's example.

Christian parents must instruct their children never to marry an unbeliever. A person considering marriage should not think that the other partner will be converted after the marriage. If anyone is going to be converted, the time for that to happen is before marriage. Second Corinthians 6:14-16 (NIV) reminds us, "Do not be yoked together with unbelievers. For what do righteousness and wickedness have in common? . . . What does a believer have in common with an unbeliever? What agreement is there between the temple of God and idols?"

Paul uses some strong language to show the great differences between a believer and an unbeliever. The basic reason a Christian should not marry an unbeliever is that they are not on the same page as to what is important in life. They will be at odds concerning God, Jesus, moral values, the Bible, and life's most crucial issues. One partner will believe Jesus is the only way to heaven, and the other will believe that Jesus is irrelevant and that there is little or no reason to listen to or follow Him. The two extreme positions are incompatible and invite constant conflict. This tension and dissension will spill over to children and be harmful to their physical and spiritual lives. And, of course, the children of such a marriage may well take after the unbeliever. God desires both peace and salvation for the family. Starting a marriage poles apart goes against God's infinite wisdom and His instruction to us.

Should a believer already be married to a nonbeliever, the believer should honor the marriage commitment. Marriage is for life. That believer should also pray continuously for the salvation of the nonbelieving spouse and show the love of Christ throughout the marriage.

Prior to marriage, the bride and groom must prepare themselves. A great change is in store for both parties as two people who previously managed their own time are now going to become one, live together, and be responsible to each other. This in and of itself is a radical change. Christian premarital counseling and other assistance from the church is a must to make sure that the two people understand the obligations of marriage and the permanence of their vows to God. The man and woman who marry must also understand basic things about each other. In the first place, God made man and woman different. A man needs to understand that women are usually more relational and more sensitive to another's feelings. A woman needs to understand that many men have problems expressing their true feelings and entering into deep relationships. The best time to learn about the other sex is before marriage, not after.

No two people ever come to the marriage table with the same expectations. Often, the expectations are poles apart. The couple needs to know in advance what issues they face. If the issues are basic, then they need resolution before marriage. For minor issues and future issues that will arise, each partner needs to make a strong commitment to the other to seek unselfishly God's solution. Differences will always exist, and approaching conflicts in marriage with the love of Jesus is always the best solution. Also, in order to prevent any startling surprises, all basic issues should be brought to light, discussed, and resolved in advance. A couple needs help in going through this essential premarital process.

The couple needs to spend quality time in good Christian counseling in order to prepare to build a godly home. Time spent in preparation for a lifetime of marriage is far more important than preparation for the ceremony itself. Unfortunately, young couples and their families often spend more time planning the ceremony and the reception than preparing for marriage.

MARRIAGE IS BUILT ON THE LOVE OF JESUS AND IS MEANT TO LAST FOR A LIFETIME.

Any marriage should be based on the love of Jesus Christ. The love that comes from our flesh is not sufficient to sustain a long-term relationship when trouble strikes. A husband and wife, who through marriage become one flesh, are called to love each other unselfishly with the love of Jesus. That kind of unselfish love, which flows both ways, insures the marriage will be joyous and last a lifetime.

Jesus does not like divorce. Marriage is something that God wants to last. Although the Bible permits divorce under limited circumstances, God intended marriage for life. God takes marriage so seriously that He requires a lifetime commitment by those who marry. This covenant is as serious a commitment as anyone can make. It is a promise to God Almighty as well as to the marriage partner. By this promise to God, each partner gives his or her word to stand by each other and be supportive of each other until death. That is why potential brides and grooms should know what marriage is all about before any ceremony takes place.

Jesus emphasized the closeness of the union that forms at marriage. In this spiritual and mysterious relationship, the two become one flesh. Jesus, in repeating what God said about marriage in Genesis, declared in Matthew 19:5-6: "For this reason a man shall leave his father and mother and be joined to his wife and the two shall become one flesh. So then they are no longer two, but one flesh. Therefore what God has joined together, let not man separate." Remember, marriage is from God and not human beings. Becoming one flesh with another human being is sacred and serious.

THE BIBLE HAS WONDERFUL INSTRUCTIONS FOR MARRIAGE.

Once married, couples should continue to turn to the Bible for basic instruction. In Ephesians 5, the Bible says that wives are to submit to their husbands and husbands are to love their wives as Jesus loved the church. How did Jesus love the church? He sacrificed His life for the church, His bride. Husbands are called on to show that same love for their wives.

The husband is the head of the house as Jesus is the head of the church. Jesus came as a servant and spent His lifetime in service to others. Husbands are not called to act like some dictator or to be controlling of their wives. Jesus is not talking about a master and slave when He says the husband is the head of the home. Rather, Jesus is talking about sacrificial love and servanthood. The analogy Jesus makes is the church. Jesus heads the church. Yet, Jesus sacrificed all. Jesus came to serve, and He paid the ultimate price. The husband is to serve his wife and family sacrificially as well.

As the leader of the home, the husband must also lead spiritually. When decisions are to be made, the husband should call his wife and himself to prayer, seeking God's will. A husband and wife should discuss important matters freely. They should honestly share feelings and opinions. The two should listen to God's voice and reach a decision based on God's will. Again, both parties need to reach out to each other sacrificially, based on their love for each other.

A good marriage is built on love. The main instruction the Bible gives the husband is to love his wife (Ephesians 5:25). This passage is very strong and specific because it says husbands should love their wives as Jesus loved the church. Love goes far beyond the expression of feelings. Love involves sacrificing for the other person. Also, a husband ought to love his wife as he loves his own body (Ephesians 5:28). Paul also told the wives to love their husbands (Titus 2:4) and to submit to their husbands (Colossians 3:18). Paul said the older women in the church should train the younger women to love their husbands. Paul instructed the wives to respect their husbands (Ephesians 5:33); and the husbands to respect their wives and to be considerate of them (1 Peter 3:7). Husbands should not be harsh with their wives (Colossians 3:19). Turn to 1 Corinthians 13 once again and read it to understand love in the context of marriage.

If the love of Jesus is present, the Christian marriage will grow stronger as husband and wife work together to overcome conflict and adversity. There is power in that kind of love that comes only from the Holy Spirit. This kind of love will produce joy and peace and the complete union that God intended. Marriage is not a fifty-fifty proposition. Marriage means each partner gives his or her all.

HERE ARE SOME ARE FUNDAMENTAL WAYS TO PROMOTE A HEALTHY CHRISTIAN MARRIAGE. HOW ARE YOU DOING IN EACH OF THESE AREAS OF YOUR MARRIAGE?

Seek God together. Pray together often and pray out loud together. Be in agreement in prayer. There is power in the prayer of a husband and wife praying in unity for their family. Worship together and read the Bible together. Pray for the children together. Discuss spiritual issues and things of the faith together. Know each other from a spiritual standpoint. Seek God's voice together. Be one in Christ together. Work toward godly goals as a team, and establish a home where Jesus is Lord.

Communicate openly with each other. Honest and full communication is an expression of love. Spouses need to share the things on their hearts. Often men and women have different interests and speak different languages. Often men do not like expressing feelings or speaking any language at all. That is not good. The husband and wife become one in marriage and need to share their feelings, problems, goals, desires, and everything in life. If something is important to one spouse, the other needs to listen. To listen is an expression of love. Talk about any and every issue that either spouse believes needs resolving.

Yield to one another. Neither the husband nor the wife will have all the right answers. Both husband and wife should yield to each other's desires. Mutual respect of ideas and submission to each other in love is essential. Flexibly submitting to each other and putting the other person first is an expression of sacrificial love.

The husband and wife should bond together and enjoy the sexual relationship as God intended. God made the sexual relationship for the husband and wife to enjoy and reserved sex for marriage only. A healthy relationship enhances the sexual intimacy of the marriage. The sexual union is a celebration and renewal of the marriage as it unites the two as one. It is also a blessed event because of God's order of procreation. Paul knew sex in marriage was essential because Paul called for special times of abstinence in order to pray together. Read the Song of Solomon to get a glimpse of the beauty of sexual love.

Spend time together and enjoy each other. Husbands and wives need to work on their relationship with each other constantly because that is one way they grow in their love for one another. This requires time. The husband who gives all of his time to his work neglects his wife. Likewise, the wife who is a mother should not neglect the husband because of the pressures of child rearing. Husbands and wives must carve out time to be alone together for the good of the whole family.

Be united and support and encourage each other. Bickering, arguing, and belittling each other tear down the relationship. A husband and wife need to build each other up and encourage each other. In a good marriage, the couple is a team trying to achieve agreed-on Christian objectives. Supporting each other as much as possible is an act of kindness and love. Look for the good and not the bad in each other.

Be quick to forgive and to forget. Read the chapter on forgiving others and apply it to the marriage. Husbands and wives must forgive each other constantly in order to be in a perpetual state of reconciliation through the forgiveness process. Be quick to forgive and do what God does—forget.

Remember marriage takes a lot of hard work and a strong commitment. Each marriage partner needs to be so encouraging, so lovable, and so supportive that the other partner will never have any desire to be married to someone else. Spouses should live so unselfishly within the marriage that life without each other would be intolerable. Love is just that strong. Unselfish love, that is the kind of love Jesus had, is the true cement that binds the marriage together for a lifetime.

BE ON YOUR GUARD AGAINST POTENTIAL PROBLEMS.

Even if you have a strong marriage, avoid temptation. Most affairs begin innocently and grow out of friendships through social situations among friends or at the workplace. Avoid any opportunity for a relationship outside of marriage to begin in the first place. Avoid any unnecessary opportunity to be alone with someone of the opposite sex. Do not get emotionally involved with a member of the opposite sex who is not your wife or husband. Be aware of your circumstances. Be alert.

A second major problem within marriages is money. The husband and wife both need to understand how the money is being spent in the household. Each needs a say in how that money is spent. It should be spent wisely and in agreement. The husband and wife need to discuss expenditures and give each other some latitude. If there are monetary problems, Christian financial counseling is a good idea. If one spouse believes he or she is being treated unfairly, this can cause serious problems in the marital relationship. Be fair and open with each other about money and about how it is being allocated and used.

A third probelm in many marriages is verbal or physical abuse. A husband should not lose his temper, scream at, or strike his wife, and vice versa. Problems must be discussed in a rational, sensible way and with loving care.

The seeds of divorce or separation can grow out of numerous causes. Perhaps the most common cause is a failure of commitment from a lack of love. If you get in any kind of trouble within your marriage, go to the church or a to professional Christian counselor for help. A husband and wife need to work continuously on their marriage. Do not be afraid to seek counseling or assistance from the church. All marriages have conflicts and disagreements. That is to be expected. So be realistic and expect problems to arise. The secret to the good marriage is found in how these conflicts are handled. In our flesh, we will always want to try to get our spouse to change and be more like we are. The spouse who tries to control his mate will be the source of many problems. Remember, when you put your spouse first and your self second, then good things begin to happen. Problems in marriage should be seen as a blessing because working through problems with the love of Jesus will strengthen the home.

The honeymoon may change but should never end. Marriage should improve with age. Love should grow stronger, not weaker. It is the love of Jesus that makes this possible, not the romantic emotions of the world. Talk to any married couple who is sold out to Jesus, and you will find a couple more in love today than the day they married. That is what God desires.

"As for me and my house, we will serve the Lord" (Joshua 24:15).

Discussion Questions for the Married

1. What areas of your marriage are you the weakest in when it comes to loving your spouse?

2. What can you do to strengthen your marriage from a spiritual standpoint? Make a list of things you and your spouse can do together to strengthen your faith.

3. How do you and your spouse resolve disputes or differences of opinion in your marriage?

4. What are you doing to insure fair distribution of money? How do you and your spouse budget and deal with monetary issues?

Discussion Questions for the Unmarried

1. Do you think God has any special assignments for you since you do not have the usual family responsibilities?

2. If you desire to be married, what are you doing and what are you praying about so the right person that God has in mind may come along?

3. As a single person, what specific things can you do to assist and support other family members in a spiritual way?

15

MURDER, ANGER, AND LOVING YOUR ENEMIES (6TH COMMANDMENT)

"You shall not murder" (Exodus 20:13).

"Get rid of all bitterness, rage and anger, brawling and slander, along with every form of malice. Be kind and compassionate to one another, forgiving each other, just as in Christ God forgave you"
(Ephesians 4:31, NIV).

WE SHOULD NOT MURDER.
WE SHOULD NOT HATE ANYONE EITHER.

"You shall not murder" is the sixth commandment that God gave to His people. Jesus not only recognized this as an important commandment, but He also took this commandment to a new and higher level. Jesus was concerned not only with our physical acts, but also our hearts. Jesus said that hatred or malice within the heart can be as serious of a sin as murder (Matthew 5:21-22). In this chapter we will study the sixth commandment and then study what Jesus says to our hearts.

"You shall not murder" in the Hebrew reads "thou shall do no murder." This is not a commandment about either the death penalty imposed by the state, an accidental killing, killing in self-defense, or killing during war. This commandment is about murder. We know murder is a terrible sin. Murder is the unlawful taking of another's life. Suffice it to say, abortion, genocide, and assisted suicides violate this commandment. The fact that governments may condone these types of killing does not make them right in God's eyes. Murder is always wrong, and no human reasoning will make it right. Murder is a serious sin because the life that God gives is a precious thing.

Jesus not only said we should not murder, but He also said we should not be angry or hate anyone. Jesus spoke to the condition of our hearts and our state of mind. Jesus knew that if we never got angry with anyone or never hated anyone, we would not then commit murder. From hatred in our hearts develops the desire to harm. Out of this desire comes the harmful act. Jesus wants us to have a clean heart—a heart of love and not hate. The question we must ask ourselves is: are we filled with love or hate?

Jesus came to bring the perfect and unselfish love of God to this earth. His act of love on the cross was the extreme example of love. Jesus now commands us to love one another. This includes our enemies (Matthew 5:44). Jesus loved the sinners. In fact, He loved those who sinned against Him. Even on the cross Jesus asked the Father to forgive those who were killing Him (Luke 23:34). Could we think of a greater example of love than that? Jesus asks us to have the same love for others that He demonstrated to everyone He touched here on earth. When we understand something about the depth of Jesus' love, then we can better understand what Jesus expects of us. Jesus said, "Love one another; as I have loved you" (John 13:34).

JESUS WANTS US TO DEAL WITH OUR ANGER. WE ARE CALLED TO HATE SIN BUT TO LOVE THE SINNER.

Jesus told us to turn the other cheek to our enemies and to go the second mile with our brothers and our enemies. Jesus also told us that an eye for an eye and a tooth for a tooth is no longer the standard (Matthew 5:38-48). Jesus said even the pagans love those who love them first. Jesus calls us to love even those who persecute us. That is a radical concept, but Jesus wants us to have a new heart.

Anger is a normal human emotion. All of us have this emotion to one extent or another. Anger is not bad. Jesus expressed anger at sin when He overturned the tables of the money changers and drove them from the temple, which was God's holy place (Matthew 21:12). God hates sin and so should we. Throughout the Bible, God expressed His anger over sin. Of course, He was slow to anger. We can be assured, therefore, that our anger is a normal reaction to some events. Anger at sin is to be expected. For example, sometimes we get angry when we see someone sinning and hurting another. Our main concern should not be whether or not we will get angry but how we will let anger go so that it does not turn into hate or bitterness. We must learn how to deal with our anger, how to turn it into love, and how always to have self-control. Ephesians 4:26 warns us not to let the sun go down on our wrath. In other words, we should deal with anger quickly and decisively and deal with it from the heart. Confess anger toward anyone else as a sin and release it to Jesus. Ephesians 4:27 goes on to say that anger gives a foothold to the devil. All sin opens us up to the schemes of the enemy, and anger is no exception.

Like unforgiveness, anger can be a destructive emotion. Anger can be destructive to the recipient, and anger can also do great harm to the person who is angry. Uncontrolled anger can be deadly. Controlling anger is not good enough. We need to do more than suppress it. Suppressed anger is still anger and will arise later. We must deal with it in a Christlike way so that we glorify Jesus and do not yield to our own flesh. We must learn to see our enemy through God's eyes and the love of Jesus. Through His eyes that person is no longer the enemy, but one to be loved.

Let's look at what anger really is and how God directs us to deal with it. The Latin root for *anger* means "to strangle." Anger, as defined in English, means an emotional reaction or antagonism, an inner frustration, an impulse to retaliate, punish, or seek revenge. Anger can range from harsh words to an act of murder. In an instant, anger can cause us to lose our temper and engage in destructive behavior. In an instant, we can speak out of anger and lose a lifetime friend. In an instant, our Christian witness to another can be destroyed because we appear to be just another fleshly person. Out of such a loss of self-control can come fights and ugly behavior (Psalm 37:8). An angry person is often like a disaster waiting to happen as a result of some small event. The Bible instructs us that God is slow to anger (Psalm 86:15). Jesus was slow to anger. We are to follow Their example.

We must recognize that anger can be a strong emotion. If you are dealing with an anger problem, you need help from good Christian counsel whether it is from within the church or from a Christian counselor outside your church. To squelch or suppress anger without dealing with the problem is not the answer because the anger will build up and is likely to explode later. There are many good Christian books on anger, and reading a book on the subject is a good starting place; but if you have a problem, get the help you need. You need to be in touch with your feelings and understand what is going on inside in order to deal with the problem. In addition, commit any problem with anger to serious prayer so God can lead you to the right answers and healing.

When you feel anger coming on, Jesus wants you to stop and think about what you are doing. We are told in Galatians 5 that part of the fruit of the Spirit is self-control. Pray for self-control. When a policeman sees a heinous crime being committed, unless a life is in danger, the good policeman does not pull out his gun and start shooting. The good policeman calmly arrests the man and does not lose his temper. He has the right reaction because he is under control. He would have the wrong reaction if he lost his head and started shooting. Regardless of circumstances, we must never lose control and seek to destroy whatever or whomever is in our path. If you become angry, remove yourself from the situation. Cool off. Pray. Do not stand there and vent your anger. Then as soon as you have calmed down, take the appropriate steps to deal with the problem. The Bible teaches us to deal with our anger as soon as possible.

Anger is a major problem with many people—particularly young, immature males. As a result, acts of anger take a deadly toll each year. Most murders are committed out of anger, and an increasing number of deaths on our highways are caused by angry drivers. Anger breaks up homes, causes violence in the family, and leaves little children terrorized and afraid. If a parent has an anger problem, chances are the children in that home will grow up with an anger problem too.

Many individuals suppress their anger only to find that it erupts and explodes at a later time. That is why anger must not be buried but dealt with by getting it out on the table and seeking God's help. Christians must know how to deal with their own anger and how to minister to others who need help dealing with anger. Anger is a major problem in the lives of Christians and non-Christians alike. Just as a person getting married needs counseling, the person with an anger problem needs to seek help to find ways to get rid of anger before it turns into a more serious problem.

We must recognize that anger can be a destructive personality trait and open us up to attack by the enemy. Ephesians 4:31 tells us to get rid of all bitterness, rage, anger, brawling, slander, and malice. All of these characteristics are related. When one or more of these traits come into our lives, we must seek help from God through the church and through prayer and through a real commitment to change.

WE MUST SEE OUR ENEMIES THROUGH THE EYES OF JESUS AND NOT THROUGH OUR OWN EYES.

Jesus does not want us harboring ill will or malice toward another, even if we do not intend to harm that person. In the Sermon on the Mount, Matthew 5:21, Jesus equated anger against another brother with murder. After saying that anyone who murders will be subject to judgment, Jesus said, "But I tell you that anyone who is angry with his brother will be subject to judgment" (Matthew 5:22, NIV).

This type of anger was such an important topic with Jesus that He did not want someone to make an offering to the Lord without first being reconciled to his brother (Matthew 5:23-25). Jesus went on to say in the same passage that we should settle matters quickly with our adversaries.

Jesus said, "Love your enemies, bless those who curse you, do good to those who hate you, and pray for those who spitefully use you and persecute you" (Matthew 5:44). We are to "abound in love to one another" (1 Thessalonians 3:12). Jesus does not draw a distinction between our family members, our fellow church members, and the pagan who has done a bad thing. His instruction is clear. We are to love our neighbors as ourselves (Matthew 22:39). Remember, anger can be destructive to a long-term friendship. James 1:20 says, "The wrath of man does not produce the righteousness of God."

Anger is a foolish thing for us to be caught up in. Ecclesiastes 7:9 says, "Do not hasten in your spirit to be angry, for anger rests in the bosom of fools." Think about how many times you have seen someone who was angry and that person looked just like a fool. Proverbs 22:24-25 tells us, "Make no friendship with an angry man . . . lest you learn his ways and set a snare for your soul." Setting a snare for our souls is serious. Proverbs also tells us that a quick-tempered person acts foolishly (Proverbs 14:17).

Anger is tied closely to wrath and malice, which are destructive states of mind. Colossians 3:8 tells us to "put off all of these: anger wrath, malice, blasphemy, filthy language out of your mouth." What good can possibly come from being angry at another person, at yourself, or at your circumstances in life? Lay your anger, hate, and malice at the cross of Jesus. Then take the love of Jesus to friends and enemies alike.

Jesus said: "But I say to you, love your enemies, bless those who curse you, do good to those who hate you, and pray for those who spitefully use you and persecute you" (Matthew 5:44).

DISCUSSION QUESTIONS

1. List any people with whom you are angry right now.

2. What does God want you to do about this anger that you have for these people?

3. How has anger affected your life? What do you need to do about this?

4. Is there anyone you need to seek out and ask for forgiveness? Is there anyone to whom you need to offer forgiveness? If so, write down names and what you plan to do about forgiveness.

16

YOUR BODY IS A HOLY TEMPLE (7TH COMMANDMENT)

"You shall not commit adultery" (Exodus 20:14).

Jesus said: "But I say to you that whoever looks at a woman to lust for her has already committed adultery with her in his heart" (Matthew 5:28).

GOD LIMITS SEXUAL RELATIONSHIPS TO MARRIAGE ONLY, AND THERE ARE NO EXCEPTIONS.

The Bible has a simple message concerning sexual relationships. Sex is a good thing, but sexual relationships are reserved for marriage in order to provide the blessings God intended. All other forms and kinds of sexual unions are forbidden by God.

God created everything. He created marriage, He created sex, and He created the ability for a man and a woman to have children. All of these things are good, or God would not have created them. God set up an important principle and law that He commands us to follow. God commands us to limit sex to the marriage relationship. Limited to marriage, sex is a blessing that brings joy, contentment, intimacy, and children, which are all good things. Sex is intended to be practiced frequently in marriage because it brings a husband and wife closer together in one flesh and creates a mystical bonding that undergirds the marriage. Sex among unmarried Christians brings with it guilt and shame as well as lasting emotional scars; therefore, it should be avoided.

Most men are born with strong sexual desires. Some women have strong desires and others moderate desires. One reason Paul encouraged marriage was so that men and women would not commit sexual sins. If God had not created the sexual desire between man and woman, the world would not be populated as God intended. God told His people to be fruitful and multiply, but within the confines of marriage.

God prohibited many different kinds of sex, including sex with animals, sex between two males or between two females, sex among those who are related, and sex between any male and female who are not married (Leviticus 20:10-20). We are called to follow God's standards and not those of the world. The world's philosophy is "if it feels good do it," and "anything goes if it is between consenting adults. " These are lies of the enemy. Broken homes, disease, and heartache are direct results of illicit sexual relationships. Sex between one husband and one wife for a lifetime does not produce bad results, only the joy that God intended.

Sexual sins are easy to fall into. This is because the world, through magazines, television, and movies, bombards us with the message that consensual sex is appropriate and normal conduct. Just because a majority of the population may violate God's commandments does not make it right. When you stop and think about it, adultery or fornication is a very selfish act. It robs the husband or wife (or the future husband or wife) of the purity of the marriage relationship. It is a betrayal of the marriage vows and a poor example for the children. A few moments of physical pleasure are not worth the long-term results of guilt and alienation that is bound to flow from such an irresponsible act. Such a way of life opens the door to the enemy for an obsession or addiction to sex. So-called one-time sexual encounters can escalate into a lifestyle that is difficult to overcome. Believers must avoid compromising situations and pray against falling into sexual immorality (Acts 15:20).

One reason we obey God and do what He says is because He is God and He said it. This should be reason enough. Also, God said that sin leads to death. "The wages of sin is death" is the way Paul put it in Romans 6:23. God had something else to say about the consequences of disobedience to His commandments. In Deuteronomy 11:26-28 (NIV), God spoke clearly of the consequences of sin:

> See, I am setting before you today a blessing and a curse—
> the blessing if you obey the commands of the Lord your God
> that I am giving you today; the curse if you disobey the com-
> mands of the Lord your God and turn from the way that I
> command you today by following other gods, which you may
> not have known.

God makes it clear that to live for Him in obedience to His Word brings forth His blessing. The Bible says this in many ways over and over again.

Sexual sins open the doorway for the enemy to have a stronghold over us and do damage to our character and our innermost being. Most discerning Christians believe that constant and deliberate sin is an open invitation for the enemy to have influence over their lives. People who are obsessed with alcohol, drugs, or sexual addictions often struggle with demonic influences, which are extremely difficult to overcome. That is why sexual sins need to be dealt with as soon as possible before this pattern of conduct gets beyond control and becomes habitual.

THE CHURCH SHOULD PLAY A MAJOR ROLE IN ENCOURAGING SEXUAL PURITY AND IN PROVIDING HEALING TO THOSE TRAPPED BY SEXUAL SIN.

Jesus wants to free us from bondage to sin. When someone suffers with sexual addictions, the church should provide opportunities for healing. Often, the problem is one that goes back to childhood. Regardless of how long the problem has lasted or how severe it may be, Jesus stands ready to heal and deliver anyone taken in sin. The church needs to step in and be equipped to minister to those in need so that through the power of the Holy Spirit, the person may be healed.

God prefers we never get into sexual sins whether it be an affair or a "casual" sexual encounter. Sexual sins have caused many deaths and much suffering. Millions of people around the world are dying as the result of AIDS. Venereal diseases take many lives and cause grief, pain, and permanent illness to millions more. Sex outside of marriage risks deadly diseases whether or not precautions are taken. Sex outside marriage risks unwanted children, who often are killed through the additional sin of abortion. Sex outside marriage brings guilt and shame to those involved because that is the way God made us. Sex outside of marriage affects our mental health as well as our physical well-being. Illicit sex robs a married partner of the loyalty and faithfulness promised at the time of the marriage. Turn to Proverbs 7 and read about how the seduction of the adulteress leads to the grave.

Jesus wants our hearts to be pure. That is why Jesus said in Matthew 5:28: "Whoever looks at a woman to lust for her has already committed adultery with her in his heart." This form of sin begins in the mind. The mind fuels the desire, and the desire brings about the act. That is why we must keep our thoughts pure

After the Leap

in sexual areas. Pornography and sexually stimulating images are dangerous. Our minds will feed off these things and create its own much greater desire for sexual pleasure. Before too long our sexual habits and desires may well be out of control. We are to keep our minds pure. We are to seek the mind of Christ. In Romans 1:24-32 Paul spoke strong words regarding God's stance on the issues of sexual lust and depravity:

> Therefore God also gave them up to uncleanness, in the lusts of their hearts, to dishonor their bodies among themselves, who exchanged the truth of God for the lie, and worshiped and served the creature rather than the Creator, who is blessed forever. Amen. For this reason God gave them up to vile passions. For even their women exchanged the natural use for what is against nature. Likewise also the men, leaving the natural use of the woman, burned in their lust for one another, men with men committing what is shameful, and receiving in themselves the penalty of their error which was due. And even as they did not like to retain God in their knowledge, God gave them over to a debased mind, to do those things which are not fitting; being filled with all unrighteousness, sexual immorality, wickedness, covetousness, maliciousness; full of envy, murder, strife, deceit, evil-mindedness; they are whisperers, backbiters, haters of God, violent, proud, boasters, inventors of evil things, disobedient to parents, undiscerning, untrustworthy, unloving, unforgiving, unmerciful; who, knowing the righteous judgment of God, that those who practice such things are worthy of death, not only do the same but also approve of those who practice them.

OUR BODIES ARE A HOLY TEMPLE BECAUSE JESUS RESIDES THERE. THUS, WE ARE TO KEEP THEM PURE.

There is one more reason for purity in our lives. Romans 12:1 tells us that our bodies are living sacrifices to the Lord. Certainly, we do not want to offer to God an impure body. First Corinthians 6:13-20 speaks forcefully to this issue.

> Now the body is not for sexual immorality, but for the Lord and the Lord for the body.... Do you not know that your bodies are members of Christ? Shall I then take the members of

Christ and make them members with a harlot? Certainly not! Or do you not know that he who is joined with a harlot is one body with her? For "the two," He says, "shall become one flesh." But he who is joined to the Lord is one spirit with Him. Flee sexual immorality. Every sin that a man does is outside the body, but he who commits sexual immorality sins against his own body. Or do you not know that your body is a temple of the Holy Spirit who is in you, whom you have from God, and you are not your own. For you were bought at a price; therefore, glorify God in your body and in your spirit which are God's.

Keep your body pure. Remember Jesus resides there. When we fall into sexual sin, we must repent and receive God's forgiveness. Like Mary Magdalene, who experienced the forgiveness of God, we too can become new and pure people. After Mary Magdalene was forgiven, Jesus saw her as a virgin. She had a new and fresh start, and she also knew she had a special reason to remain pure. Jesus had not only forgiven her, but He had also forgotten her sin. Of course, the consequences of the sin may remain, but those who have received God's forgiveness start anew, perfectly cleansed by the sacrifice of Jesus on the cross. They now stand blameless in God's sight with a new beginning. This should be an encouragement to all who have gone astray but have since come to God in repentance and forgiveness. With this new beginning, that person is now called to live a life of purity.

IT IS ESSENTIAL TO MAINTAIN SEXUAL PURITY AND TO AVOID TEMPTATION.

Proverbs 4:23 (NIV) puts it so well: "Above all else, guard your heart, for it is the wellspring of life." Guard your heart and mind against thoughts of sexual sin. Do not fantasize about sexual thoughts because this is the seed for illicit sex. Watch your eyes as well as your thoughts. Avoid lusting after another even if just for a brief mental encounter. Make a commitment to God to remain sexually pure from now on even if you were not pure in the past. Ask God to provide you the strength to live up to that commitment each day. Then do your part by avoiding either people or situations that could lead you to impure actions, including sex outside marriage. Remember, your body is a holy temple in which the Spirit of God resides. Keep your body pure so the Holy Spirit will be honored as a welcome Guest.

"Do you not know that your body is the temple of the Holy Spirit, who is in you, whom you have received from God, and you are not your own? For you were bought at a price; therefore glorify God in your body and in your spirit, which are God's" (1 Corinthians 6:19-20).

Discussion Questions

1. When you begin to have a lustful thought, what can you do to guard your mind? How should you avoid lustful thoughts before they begin?

2. Why are sexual sins so important to God even if the people involved are consenting adults?

3. Why do sexual sins tear away or destroy the marital relationship?

4. What sexual sins are confronting you today, and what do you need to do about them?

17

HONESTY, INTEGRITY, AND YOUR TONGUE (COMMANDMENTS 8–9)

"You shall not steal. You shall not bear false witness against your neighbor" (Exodus 20:15-16).

GOD WANTS US TO BE PEOPLE OF INTEGRITY.

John 14:6 describes Jesus as the way, the truth, and the life. God is truth and Jesus is truth. The Holy Spirit is described as the Spirit of Truth. In fact, all truth comes from God. God wants us to follow Jesus and be people of truth. Truth is an integral part of God's character. Therefore, God wants us to be a people of truth, people of integrity who serve Him in His kingdom. God is simply not going to use a double minded or dishonest person to do His work.

The Bible is clear about stealing and telling lies. We should not do it. We sin whenever we do anything that is dishonest. The eighth and ninth commandments deal with issues of integrity. Our word should be our bond. We should always speak in truth. We should live every facet of our lives in truth. Ephesians 4:25 instructs us, "Therefore, putting away lying, each one speak truth with his neighbor, for we are members of one another."

Just like murder and adultery, which start in the mind, dishonesty has its roots in the mind. God wants us to have clean minds and pure hearts. True integrity is devoid of deception in any form. Jesus calls us to have integrity in every part of our lives. He calls for us to have integrity in our personal lives, in our financial dealings, in our work, in our homes, and in all our relationships. Proverbs 19:9 (NIV) says, "A false witness will not go unpunished, and he who pours out his lies will perish." What a warning God has given us.

DO NOT BE A HYPOCRITE OR DOUBLE MINDED. IN ALL THINGS BE HONEST.

Jesus hates the sin of hypocrisy. In Matthew 23, Jesus, in very strong language, told the Jewish religious leaders what He thought about being double minded. These particular Jews led a double life because on the outside they appeared to be pure and holy and just. On the inside, their hearts were corrupted by pride, and they had no compassion or love for anyone. Jesus referred to these Jewish leaders, who were called the Pharisees, as "hypocrites, blind guides, serpents, a brood of vipers, and fools." Jesus condemned this hypocrisy. Jesus knew these Pharisees cared only about looking good before other men. Jesus said these men did not practice what they preached. The Pharisees told others to be holy and merciful when they themselves were full of greed. Jesus explained, "For you are like whitewashed tombs which indeed appear beautiful outwardly, but inside are full of dead men's bones and all uncleanness."

People of integrity are the same on the outside as they are on the inside. They are what they appear to be—nothing more and nothing less. They are transparent and do not fear their innermost thoughts being held up to the light. They are vulnerable and do not fear saying exactly what is on their hearts.

Jesus wants us to live like we preach. Jesus doesn't want us to be one thing for the world to see and something different in our hearts. He doesn't want us to make a big deal over how honest we are. Jesus said simply, "Let your 'yes' be 'yes' and your 'no' be 'no.' For whatever is more than these is from the evil one" (Matthew 5:37). Jesus said do not swear at all by heaven or by earth. We are to have simplicity in character. We are to be plain spoken. We should say what we mean and mean what we say. And say it simply. We must not be double minded.

DO NOT STEAL, LIE, OR CHEAT.

Theft and being dishonest are closely related. Both are sneaky and deceitful. Theft is when we take something that belongs to someone else without that person's permission. Theft is a very serious crime, which can land a person in jail or in the penitentiary. It can be committed in many different ways. We can steal from the government if we cheat on our income taxes. We can steal from a neighbor in the middle of the night. We can steal from the person for whom we work when we take home tools or company property. Jesus said lying and stealing are serious sins; but Jesus calls us to an even higher standard. Jesus says honesty and integrity start in the mind. Ephesians 4:28 says, "Let him who stole steal no longer, but rather let him labor, working with his hands what is good, that he may have something to give him who has need." Honest work, not theft, is God's way to prosper.

When we speak, we should not exaggerate or leave false impressions. We should avoid boasting. We should disclose all the facts anytime the other person is relying on what we are saying. Our speech and actions should not be done to build up ourselves, but to bring glory to Jesus. We should be honest in all things.

Not only does all truth come from God, but it is through the power of the Holy Spirit that God speaks to us in truth. When the Holy Spirit convicts us or calls to our attention any dishonest or misleading acts, we have a duty to take corrective action, confess our sins to the person we have wronged, and as best we can make the matter right.

TO BE A PERSON OF INTEGRITY, YOU MUST BE WILLING TO BE HELD ACCOUNTABLE.

Constantly check yourself to see if there is any part of your life that lacks integrity. Is there anything that you are doing that you would not want exposed to the light? If there is, you have a problem. God sees everything you think and do. All is exposed to God. He knows your every thought and your every act. Will your thoughts and acts withstand the light of God?

We all need to be held accountable—usually by those who know us best and love us most. We need a close friend or small group to hold us accountable. Husbands and wives need to hold each other accountable.

Is what you say you do reflected by what you actually do? Are you totally honest when you are alone and no one is looking? Are you honest in all your business transactions? If someone in a store undercharges you for an item, do you correct the mistake and make it right? Will all your words and all your actions pass God's standard of being totally honest? If you walk in truth, you will never have to cover anything up. You will never have to look over your shoulder. You will never have the fear or apprehension of being caught in a lie. The enemy, who is described as a liar and a murderer, will have no entryway into your life because of deception. Always be in position to hold your head up straight and look anyone in the eye.

Colossians 3:9-10 (NIV) says, "Do not lie to each other since you have taken off your old self with its practices and have put on the new self, which is being

After the Leap

renewed in knowledge in the image of its Creator." Our lives cannot testify to Jesus unless they are lived in integrity and truth.

How do you use your tongue? Does it glorify God or tear others down?

Your tongue should be an instrument of truth and should be used to carry out God's purposes for your life; therefore, always be aware of what you say, how you say it, and the impact what you say will have on others. Jesus said, "For every idle word men may speak, they will give account of it in the day of judgment. For by your words you will be justified, and by your words you will be condemned" (Matthew 12:36-37). If these words won't make people think about the importance of everything they say, then no warning will ever be sufficient.

The tongue is a powerful thing. The words we say bring a blessing or a curse. Our words build others up or tear them down. Our tongue can speak love or encouragement or hurt others deeply. The tongue can bring unity or dissension to the body of Christ. As Proverbs 21:23 says, "Whoever guards his mouth and tongue keeps his soul from troubles." The Bible has much to say about how we are to use our tongues.

A great Bible passage about the tongue is James 3. Please turn to this chapter and read it slowly. In these 18 verses is excellent advice about how the tongue can be a godly instrument or a tool producing disaster like a match that sets a deadly forest fire.

James 3 contains four more basic principles about the tongue: (1) the tongue should not be used to criticize and judge other people, (2) the tongue should not be used for slander or gossip, (3) the tongue should not be used to brag about oneself, and (4) the tongue must be kept under firm control.

The tongue should not be used to criticize others or to judge other people.

As James starts out this chapter, he makes the point that those of us who judge others and tell others how to live their lives will be held to a higher standard. When we criticize or condemn others, we bring condemnation on ourselves. Unless we are acting in a court of law or as part of the government or the church, we have no right to judge others. We do have the obligation to speak out against sin, but we are not called to judge the sinner. There is a time for correction and discipline within the family, the workplace, the government, and the church. That kind of correction must always be done in love. That is not what we are speaking of here. We are talking here about the practice of using the tongue to heap criticism, curses, belittlement, or condemnation on another person. Jesus teaches that to the extent we judge others, we open ourselves up to judgment. It is like forgiveness. We learned in the chapter on forgiveness how Jesus will not forgive us when we refuse to forgive others.

Let's look at Jesus' teaching on judging others. Jesus said, "Judge not, that you be not be judged. For with what judgment you judge, you will be judged; and with the same measure you use, it will be measured back to you" (Matthew 7:1-2). Jesus goes on in Matthew 7 to say that we should not criticize the speck in our brother's eye, when we have a log in our own eye. When we criticize another person, such as saying that Jim will never amount to anything, we are making a judgment. When we say that Sally is hateful or mean, we are making a judgment. When we say that Richard is not as good as we are, we are making a judgment. Every time we attack someone's character, we are making a judgment. Be careful about using your tongue to put others down. Do not pronounce judgments on other people with a loose tongue.

This is not to say we never make judgments. We make judgments in the home when we discipline a child, at work when we must deal with problems, and in other situations. When you have to confront another, do so in love—not condemnation.

This does not mean that a Christian brother or sister should avoid going to someone in love and confronting that individual with a sin. The Bible sets forth a procedure for that. First, you go to the person who has wronged you and in love seek reconciliation and justice. If that does not work, the Bible says you next take a Christian friend with you to confront the individual. Then, if that doesn't work, you turn the matter over to the church. Matthew 18:15 and 1 Corinthians 5 explain the principles involved, including how churches ought to deal with ongoing sin. The law permits an individual to go to courts for justice, but Christians are instructed to try to resolve differences through the church. The point is that there are times when we must speak in truth, and what we say may hurt the other person. Nevertheless, we misuse the tongue when we criticize, condemn, or judge without serving a Christlike purpose. Don't do it.

DO NOT TALK ABOUT PEOPLE BEHIND THEIR BACKS. THAT IS GOSSIP.

Gossip is closely related to judgment or criticism. The Bible condemns gossip. Proverbs 11:13 says that "a talebearer reveals secrets, but he who is of a faith-

After the Leap

ful spirit conceals a matter." When a friend tells you something, whether in confidence or not, do not repeat the information if it will harm someone. Do not repeat what has been told you in confidence. Proverbs 16:28 (NIV) tells us "a gossip separates close friendships." How sad it is to think of the many fallen friendships that are caused by one friend talking about another friend. If you constantly criticize your friends or acquaintances in another person's presence, that person is unlikely to want you for a friend. The reason is that he will feel as if you will be critical of his every act too. God wants us to promote intimacy and honesty. Gossip destroys both. Gossip is deadly and divides friends and destroys unity in the body of Christ. Proverbs 20:19 warns us about those who gossip by saying that we should avoid a man who talks too much. If people refused to gossip, then past wounds and sins against each other could more easily be healed. Proverbs 26:20 says that without wood a fire goes out and without gossip a quarrel dies down. Remember, Satan loves gossip because it promotes hate and disunity among believers and damages the effectiveness of the church.

The basic problem with gossip is that it is meanspirited, intended to do evil, and harm the person being talked about. Jesus said, "For from within, out of the heart of men, proceed evil thoughts, adulteries, fornications, murders, thefts, covetousness, wickedness, deceit, licentiousness, an evil eye, blasphemy, pride, foolishness" (Mark 7:21-22). When we gossip about another human being, we need to examine our hearts. God sees our hearts and will hold us accountable. Remember, when we gossip, we defile ourselves.

In 2 Corinthians 12:20, Paul warned the church at Corinth against quarreling, gossiping, slandering one another, jealousy, and dividing the church by factions. A faction is when one group of people gets together to either run the church or to take control over others in order to get their own way. Don't be part of any faction because factions are divisive to the body of Christ.

DO NOT USE YOUR TONGUE TO BRAG ABOUT YOURSELF OR TO BUILD YOURSELF UP.

The Bible says we should not to brag (James 3:5). Some of us boast or brag in subtle ways to call attention to our own importance. God calls us to be servants and to act in humility, not in conceit or arrogance. In fact, Jesus tells us not to seek greatness: "For he who is least among you all will be great" (Luke 9:48). Are you using your tongue with a spirit of humility? Also, we should have a godly purpose in those things that we say. Ephesians 4:29 says, "Let no corrupt communication proceed out of your mouth, but what is good for necessary edification, that it may impart grace to the hearers." The question is: are your words imparting evil or good, condemnation or grace?

Be wise and cautious in how much you talk about yourself. Some people seem to have a bad habit of focusing on themselves all the time. Some people seem to be able only to talk about their own problems and experiences and nothing else. Constantly talking about oneself is selfish, prideful, and boring. Remember, it is only when you focus on someone else that you can bring the love of Christ to that person. There are times we should share our personal experiences in order to pass on information and to witness about the Lord. But we should have a good purpose for that other than promoting our own egos. We must always ask ourselves the question: does what I say have a real purpose? There are times when we need to talk about ourselves—particularly when we are seeking prayer, advice, or some form of ministry. When we have a need, we should take that need to a Christian brother or sister we trust or to the church. That is different from the egotistical habit of boasting about ourselves.

GOD CALLS ON US TO CONTROL OUR TONGUES, BUT IN OUR FLESHLY STATE THIS IS NOT POSSIBLE.

Are you in control of your tongue and every word you say? Do you ever break out with curse words to make a point or to condemn someone or something? Most curse in order to look big, feel important, or to get rid of hidden anger. Regardless of the reason, the foul language is offensive and creates a negative atmosphere. Certainly, Jesus would say, "Let every word of your mouth be acceptable in My sight" (Psalm 19:14).

The true solution to controlling our tongues lies in who we are in Christ and our relationship with God. As we grow in the Spirit and as we walk closer with Jesus, then we get that fruit of the Spirit, spoken of in Galatians 5:22-23. That fruit is love, joy, peace, long-suffering, kindness, goodness, faithfulness, gentleness, self-control. This is a gift that comes only from God. It gives us the power of the Spirit to control the tongue. Yes, we should cooperate and work hard on our own to control our temper and control what we say. If, however, we grow in Christ and take on the fruit of the Holy Spirit, we will not have to work so hard at controlling our tongue. Our very being will undergo a basic change. The new self will be more thoughtful and loving and under control. When we do speak from love with the listeners' best interest in mind, others will look forward to hearing our words. We must have faith that if we really want to change our

After the Leap

speech, we need more of Jesus in us. The key to change is having a deeper and more intimate relationship with Jesus.

The tongue can be a wonderful instrument to bring glory to God and can be used in His service.

The tongue and even our choice of words can be a wonderful blessing and encouragement to others. God wants us to speak those words that God, not our flesh, wants that other person to hear. Always be aware of the power of the tongue and how it can bring healing and encouragement to everyone—particularly to those who are hurting.

Proverbs 22:11 says, "He who loves purity of heart and has grace on his lips, the king will be his friend." This does not mean we should insincerely flatter someone. It means we should speak from a loving heart with God's grace. The word *gracious* comes from grace, and only God can give real grace. Paul in Colossians 4:6 instructs us, "Let your speech always be with grace, seasoned with salt, that you may know how you ought to answer each one."

The next time you get together with your spouse, your children, your parents, a friend, or a casual acquaintance, make a practice of speaking encouraging or healing words that meet their needs. Ask God to help you use that time as a blessing. Ask that the Holy Spirit guide you in all you say. Think about the ways you can use your time together to bring that other person closer to Jesus. Think about the problems that person may be going through, and how you might respond in love. The key to using your tongue is having the mind of Christ.

"Reckless words pierce like a sword, but the tongue of the wise brings healing. Truthful lips endure forever, but a lying tongue lasts only a moment" (Proverbs 12:18-19, NIV).

Discussion Questions

1. Do you ever engage in gossip? How? What steps you are going to take to correct this?

2. When some other Christian starts gossiping about someone else, how should you respond?

3. Do you have a tendency to criticize other people? If so, what would Jesus advise you to do?

4. Are you willing to be a Christian who encourages others? Make a list of people who have been a positive influence in your life, and make a point to write or talk to one of these individuals each week, telling that person what he or she has meant to you.

5. Make a short list of people around you and each day figure out how to express one encouraging thought to one of these individuals.

After the Leap

18

DO NOT COVET—GOD'S GRACE IS SUFFICIENT (10TH COMMANDMENT)

"You shall not covet your neighbor's house . . . your neighbor's wife, nor his manservant, nor his maidservant, nor his ox, nor his donkey, nor anything that is your neighbor's" (Exodus 20:17).

GOD DOES NOT WANT US TO YEARN FOR WHAT OTHERS HAVE.

This chapter will discuss two things. The first is what it means to covet, and the second is God's amazing grace. Coveting refers to that strong natural desire on the part of most of us to want something that someone else has. It may be material goods or wealth, but it also could be power or position or popularity. To covet is to believe we need whatever we are coveting in order to be happy. God commands us not to "covet" what others have. The secret to avoiding coveting is to understand about God's grace. This mysterious thing called grace is something that we are freely given the moment we are saved. We do not earn it. It is there for us if we will just accept it. We need to understand why this grace is sufficient and leads to true happiness, while coveting is a fake pathway to happiness and separates us from God.

What does it mean to covet? Basically, coveting is a sin of the heart because coveting shows a heart focused on the world instead of on God. We must realize the most precious treasure is in heaven and not on this earth. Jesus tells us in Matthew 6:19-20 (NIV): "Do not store up for yourselves treasures on earth where moth and rust destroy, and where thieves break in and steal. But store up for yourselves treasures in heaven, where moth and rust do not destroy, and where thieves do not break in and steal." Jesus in verse 21 tells us, "For where your treasure is, there your heart will be also." If our hearts are right, we will not covet. Jesus is concerned with our hearts. All the earthly treasures in the world and all the power and popularity in the world do not compare to that treasure of knowing Jesus. Loving Jesus through a strong and personal relationship is our best defense against the desire to covet.

God's grace is sufficient to meet our needs.

The problem with most of us is that we do not know what it is that gives real significance and meaning to life. Many things of this earth are important such as family, children, friends, and having food and shelter, but many other things that we desire in life are not important to our welfare or true happiness. When we desire things or a position in life in order to be important or significant, we practice idolatry (Colossians 3:5). In the end, our focus on these things will not bring us happiness or significance. Our identity and significance should be with Christ, and then we will treasure the love of good things like family and friends even more.

The worldly things we covet will never satisfy. Within our hearts all of us have a great desire to be loved and to be accepted. Material goods and fleshly passions will never satisfy our heartfelt need to be loved. Only the knowledge that we are important to the God who created us will satisfy that deep longing in our souls. Until we really understand that our true identity must be in Jesus, we will strive for cheap substitutes. We will never find true self-worth in either our earthly achievements or the toys we accumulate. Our worth as a human being lies in Jesus Christ and His love for us.

All of us face periodic temptation to covet what our "neighbor" has. As the commandment says, it may be his wife, his servant, or his car. Perhaps we want to be highly respected like that neighbor down the street or very popular like that fellow classmate. It is a lie of the devil that we need something our neighbor has in order to be happy. Many a person has worked a lifetime to make a fortune to keep up with his neighbor only to discover the emptiness of wealth or the power that comes with it. To work an entire lifetime to achieve a worldly fortune, only to find it does not truly satisfy, has led many men and women to serious depression or suicide.

Ungodly objectives never satisfy. If a person is focused on earthly goals such as obtaining wealth, taking drugs, or obtaining some exalted position, that person cannot ever get enough of whatever it is that he or she seeks. Solomon is the perfect example of this truth. King Solomon had everything. He had many wives and girlfriends (concubines), thousands of servants, enormous amounts of gold and precious jewels, huge herds of cattle, the finest in entertainment, and the best houses and chariots money could buy. He had all the power and things this earth has to offer. Solomon lacked for nothing. Was he happy? No, he was miserable. None of this brought him any satisfaction or happiness. Read Ecclesiastes 2 and you will see why Solomon said all of this was nothingness. Even Solomon, the wisest man of all, did not realize the vanity and the futility of chasing after the things of this world until it was too late.

WANTING WHAT OUR NEIGHBOR HAS SHOWS OUR RELATIONSHIP WITH GOD IS OUT OF WHACK.

When we covet, we show that our relationship with God is out of whack. God tells us "that His grace is sufficient." The knowledge that God's grace was sufficient made the Apostle Paul grateful for every little thing he had even when he was in jail. Before his conversion experience, Paul was a rising young star of Judaism and known for his dedication in persecuting the Christians, but he had no joy or peace. Until Jesus rescued Paul on the road to Damascus (Acts 9), Paul never knew he was chasing the wrong thing. Later, Paul discovered the astounding truth that God's grace is sufficient. After coming to know Jesus, even while imprisoned and chained in a damp cell, he sang hymns of joy and witnessed to the guards about Jesus. Paul loved Jesus and understood that the only thing he really needed was Jesus' amazing grace. This thing called grace led Paul to write, "We also rejoice in our sufferings, because we know that suffering produces perseverance; perseverance, character, and character, hope" (Romans 5:3-4). We now live with hope, which is essential to the human soul, because of God's grace.

This doesn't mean God is opposed to our having things or prospering financially. The Bible says it is good to earn a fair and just wage. We should have a desire to do good work. God will bless good and honest work. There is nothing wrong with being paid fairly for what we do. Even wealth can be a blessing if it is obtained and used according to the will of God. God pours out many blessings on His children, and these blessings take different forms because God knows what is good for each one of us. Wealth or any other thing becomes a problem when we believe it is necessary for our happiness (Luke 12:16-23). Wealth also becomes a problem when it gets in the way of worshiping God and becomes an idol, such as it was for the rich young ruler. See the story Jesus told, recorded in Luke 18:18-30.

GRACE, NOT GREED, IS THE ANSWER TO TRUE JOY AND HAPPINESS.

Jesus said, "Watch out! Be on your guard against all kinds of greed; a man's life does not consist in the abundance of his possessions" (Luke 12:15, NIV). Paul made the point that it is not earthly things that count but the things that Jesus does through us. As Paul said in Philippians 4:13 (NIV), "I can do everything through him who gives me strength." Paul did not say I can do all things because I am rich and powerful. Paul looked only to Jesus for his fulfillment in life. Paul summed it up in Philippians 3:8 when he said, "I also count all things loss for the excellence of the knowledge of Christ Jesus my Lord, for whom I have suffered the loss of all things, and count them as rubbish, that I may gain Christ."

Paul knew of what he spoke. Perhaps no one else in the entire Bible was more focused on earning his way to heaven than Paul. He was the Pharisee of Pharisees. Paul persecuted the Christians because he thought he was following the law. Before his conversion, Paul totally misunderstood why God had put him on this earth. Paul originally believed he would be rewarded with a special place in heaven for all of his many "good works" and for how well he followed the law. Paul mistakenly based his life on what Paul was doing for God and not on what God was doing for Paul. But when Paul met Jesus, he was blinded for three days. This was God's message to Paul that Paul had not been able to see the truth about Jesus. When Paul recovered his sight, he saw the truth about Jesus and His grace. From then on Paul was radically changed and could speak of little else.

From that new beginning, Paul became the most effective evangelist the world has ever known. Paul introduced Jesus to countless people and started churches all over the world. He took the Gospel to country after country and to the Gentiles on several continents. Now it was not a passion for the law but instead a passion for Jesus that gave Paul his meaning for living. Paul learned that this free gift of grace truly was sufficient to meet his every need. Paul wrote a book about salvation and works and grace. It is the letter to the Romans. When you understand the basics of the faith and want to get a handle on "grace," study the Book of Romans. None of us can really understand the fullness of God's grace, but the more we try to understand it and receive it, the more our faith in Jesus will grow.

HOW CAN WE DEFINE WHAT IS MEANT BY GRACE?

The word *grace* comes from the Greek word *charis*, which is the root word for charismatic. *Charis* refers to grace in all of its various forms and is a gift from

After the Leap

the Holy Spirit and by the power of the Holy Spirit. God's grace has been around forever. Noah experienced it in Genesis 6:8. Jesus received it in Luke 2:40. Through grace the early church was able to operate in a powerful way (Acts 4:33). That same grace is available to the church and to believers today. Our salvation comes to us by God's grace, but God's grace is so much more. We are called to receive God's grace so we can serve Him better (Hebrews 12:28). God's grace also provides that blessing of a deep peace in our innermost being so that we can undergo even tribulation and count it as joy. God promises us that He will show us "exceeding riches of His grace in His kindness toward us in Christ Jesus" (Ephesians 2:7).

Many great books have been written about God's grace. It is still a great mystery because God's grace brings endless depths and riches and blessings to the lives of all those who receive it in its unlimited forms. Grace does not lend itself to an easy definition. Grace means all of those free gifts from God that we do not deserve and that are such a blessing to us. Grace can only come from God and cannot be earned or deserved. Grace flows from the abundance of God's love and His mercy for each one of us. We are called to receive God's grace, which is limited only to the extent we know and love Jesus. God wants us to have all the grace that we can receive. Then God wants us to pass that grace on through our ministries and our love for one another (1 Peter 4:10). With grace comes the power of the Holy Spirit. Acts 4:33 says that "with great power the apostles gave witness to the resurrection of the Lord Jesus. And great grace was upon them all." As the memory verse in the next chapter says, "Each one should use whatever gift he has received to serve others, faithfully administering God's grace in its various forms" (1 Peter 4:10).

God's grace takes so many different forms that we could never include all of them, much less try to explain them in this short chapter. God's grace includes the fruit of the Spirit that God so generously bestows on us so that we might live a victorious life. God is generous with His grace (Romans 5:17). Ephesians 1:7 speaks of "the riches of His grace." God gives us what we need in order that we might grow closer to Him as we pass on His love to others. This is how we "faithfully minister God's grace in its various forms." Because it is His grace that fills the void in our souls and warms our hearts with His peace, truly God's grace is sufficient.

All of us receive God's grace: "To each one of us grace was given according to the measure of Christ's gift" (Ephesians 4:7). And grace will be with all of us who love the Lord Jesus (Ephesians 6:24). Are you receiving that bountiful and precious gift of grace in your life? If you are, are you passing it on? The more you pass it on, the more you receive of this precious gift. Remember, as the verse below states, nothing—no position nor possession—can ever satisfy like God's grace.

"And He [Jesus] said to me [Paul] 'My grace is sufficient for you, for My strength is made perfect in weakness'" (2 Corinthians 12:9).

DISCUSSION QUESTIONS

1. Are you ever jealous of anything that anyone else has? This would include his or her popularity, position, or personality. Make a list and then examine why you feel as you do.

2. Why do you think God's love and grace are sufficient to give you significance and joy and happiness in life? Do you have any trouble accepting His grace? If so, why?

3. Make a list of the three or four things you want most out of life. Now think about these desires in light of God's amazing grace. Do you need to change any of your priorities? How?

19
THE CHURCH IS THE BODY OF CHRIST

"Now you are the body of Christ, and each one of you is a part of it"
(1 Corinthians 12:27, NIV).

The church is not a building. The church consists of all people who believe in Jesus Christ.

First of all, we need a clear vision of what the church is. The church is the body of Christ. Jesus is the head of the church (Ephesians 5:23). The church consists of all believers who put their faith and trust in Jesus Christ for their salvation.

The church is not a building or the place where you go to worship. Before Jesus came to earth, the Jews believed that God showed up in the holy temple in Jerusalem only once a year. At that time the high priest of the Jews went into the presence of God behind a special curtain. No one else had direct access to God. The day Jesus was crucified that very curtain was ripped in two from top to bottom. Jesus has made it very clear that all believers now have direct access to God through the Holy Spirit. Jesus is now our one and only High Priest (Hebrews 4:14). After the time of Jesus on this earth, a new church was born. It is Jesus' church. Jesus is the Groom and this church is His bride. This bride, that is the church, is made up of all believers in Jesus throughout the world.

Today, Jesus lives in us through the power of the Holy Spirit. Because of this, our physical bodies have been described as holy temples of God. So today God's temple is not a collection of church buildings, rituals, theological statements, or anything else. Today, the temple is a collection of all believers, because that is where God is present through Christ in us. The Bible describes God's people as the stones in the church. We are bonded together and stand together because of Jesus who is described as the Cornerstone. Of course, a cornerstone of a building holds all the other stones in place (1 Peter 2:6). Without Jesus, the stones would come apart and become a pile of rubble. God is the rock and the foundation on which the church is built. The church belongs to Jesus as the bride of Christ. The church is of God and from God. Human beings have nothing to do with the creation of the church. Only Jesus builds His church.

Remember, in the church on fire for Christ, there is action. Jesus is always moving in the lives of believers in order to make them whole and attract others to Himself. The church is a hospital for sinners in order to patch them up and make them useful for spreading the Gospel and discipling others in the faith. The question is: what are you doing to set your church on fire for Christ?

We are called to be part of a family of believers, that is a local congregation. The Bible says our church should teach sound doctrine so that none of us will turn from the truth (2 Timothy 4:3-4). Make certain you join a church that teaches that the Bible is the Word of God and the source of truth. A Bible-believing church will hold to the essentials of the faith which are found in statements like the Apostles' Creed. These essentials include the total sovereignty of God; salvation by faith in Jesus alone, who died for our sins and was resurrected and is now King of Kings and Lord of Lords; and in the mighty Holy Spirit, who empowers us for living and every good work.

THE CHURCH IS THE BRIDE OF JESUS CHRIST. THAT IS HOW MUCH JESUS LOVES HIS CHURCH.

Jesus calls His church His bride. That is how much He loves His church. Jesus wants the same close intimate and loving relationship with His church that a husband should have with his bride. Jesus has called His church to be His unblemished and spotless bride (2 Corinthians 11:2). Sadly, the church today is fragmented and impure and not reaching the lost as it should. Too often the church reflects the flesh of people, who are walking on their own power and not by the Spirit of God. Too often, the church is weak and does not reflect the love of Christ. All congregations and denominations should constantly evaluate themselves to see that they are reaching out to save the lost and ministering to the poor as Jesus commanded. With all of its imperfections, the church is still the bride of Christ, although Jesus must weep over parts of the body. Jesus does not want His church to be a social organization, a political cause, or any man-made creation. Jesus wants a dynamic church to carry His name to a lost world. No church is perfect, but the difference in a godly church and a man-made church lies in the hearts of the members. Are their hearts focused on Jesus or some man-made institution?

In recent years, God appears to be raising up a new church that puts Jesus first and denominations and nonessential theological differences second. God is also empowering many Christ-centered ministries that are a crucial part of the church. The men and women in these organizations are called by God to carry out crucial assignments for the benefit of the church as a whole. These organizations include Prison Fellowship, Young Life, Promise Keepers, Campus Crusade, Youth for Christ, Focus on the Family, and literally thousands of other large and small ministries who are on the front line for God's kingdom. Although we refer to these organizations as the "parachurch," these men and women are as much a part of the church as those who are a part of a particular denomination.

We live in exciting times, and even in the face of the bride letting the Groom down, the Groom (Jesus) is calling His church to unity more than ever before. Christians throughout the world are uniting today to bring the Gospel of Jesus Christ to the lost. Through the efforts of the entire church, over 100,000 new converts are accepting Jesus every day. Nearly all people groups are being reached with the Gospel. Throughout the world, God is performing incredible and miraculous acts as He points the world to His Son as the answer for all of His children.

THE BASIC MISSION OF THE CHURCH IS TO SAVE THE LOST, THEN TO HEAL AND TO EQUIP ALL BELIEVERS SO THEY CAN SERVE JESUS.

After an individual is saved, Jesus wants to see that person set free of anything that would prevent him or her from doing His work. Next, Jesus wants that person to be equipped to serve Him in whatever ministries He has called that individual to. Every member of the church is part of the body of Christ, and God has called each member to specific work within the body.

The church needs more workers saving the lost. Jesus said, "The harvest truly is plentiful, but the laborers are few" (Matthew 9:37). Salvation of the lost is the first mission of the church. Jesus wants all of us to be equipped to share our faith to bring others to Christ. Jesus wants all of His believers to pray, worship Him, and know the Word of God. Jesus wants His church and each person in it to be empowered by the Holy Spirit to do great things for His kingdom.

Jesus commands believers to follow the commandments (Matthew 19:17). He wants believers who will spread the good news about Him in their workplace, neighborhood, city, nation, and world. He wants His believers to reach out in His name to minister in compassion to the sick, the hungry, and the prisoners. There is no more powerful tool of evangelism than for lost souls to see Jesus change the lives of men and women they know.

Jesus called all believers to be His church. He knew that acting together in unity, His believers could be effective. Jesus' church is called together in unity so that through the power of the Holy Spirit, God's kingdom will be established on this earth (Romans 15:5).

The church should be doing the work of Jesus. The best role model of the church is in the Book of Acts. The events in Book of Acts were not a one-time event in the history of Christianity. In the Book of Acts, people were saved, healed, and delivered from the enemy. Although the early Christians underwent persecution of the worst kind, they stepped out in faith. Through the power of the Holy Spirit, these early Christians did mighty works in the name of Jesus. Read the Book of Acts to understand the exciting history of the early church. These Christians set the example as to how we in the church today should follow Jesus.

God still does miracles today! Just as in the Book of Acts, God still heals, delivers persons from demonic influence, and does anything He pleases. We cannot limit God by the limitations of our own minds. The Bible says God will intervene to change lives through the church. The last thing that Jesus said in the Gospel of Mark was that all His believers should be involved in the healing of the sick and the casting out of demons in His name (Mark 16:15-18). This was a command, and Jesus will not leave us without means to carry out His commands. Jesus told us that when He left, the Holy Spirit would come in power to do mighty works. The Holy Spirit is alive today as Jesus performs miracles, saves the lost, and frees the oppressed.

When people rewrite the mission of the church, the church gets into trouble. The church can easily become too focused on rituals or tradition, be committee-driven rather than ministry-driven, be too concerned with its own growth rather than taking a city for Jesus, or be too exclusive to invite the poor within its doors. When the church is people-driven and not on fire for Jesus, it becomes an impotent institution. Some churches are not dead, but are just lukewarm like the church at Laodicea that Jesus condemned (Revelation 3:13-19). Each local church has a mission and an assignment from God. Each of us should be praying for our church and its mission daily. Because we are the church, the responsibility for the congregation and its mission falls on all of us and not just the paid pastor, the staff, or the church officers.

WHAT ARE YOUR GIFTS THAT NEED TO BE PUT TO WORK FOR JESUS, ESPECIALLY WITHIN YOUR CHURCH FAMILY?

Within our individual congregations, each believer has certain obligations. Each believer is part of the body of Christ. Just as an earthly body needs eyes to see, arms, a head, and so forth, the body of the church is the same. All of the parts of the body must work together to be effective (1 Corinthians 12:12). Each of us is a part of that body. To work as one body the church must act in unity according to the Holy Spirit. Paul said that the whole body needs to be "joined and knit together by what every joint supplies, according to the effective working by which every part does its share" thus, causing "growth of the body for the edifying of itself in love" (Ephesians 4:16).

God bestows His gifts on His believers. These gifts exist in order to further God's kingdom on earth. Paul tells us in 1 Corinthians 12:4 that there are different kinds of gifts, all working together for the common good. Among the gifts are the gifts of wisdom, knowledge, faith, healing, miraculous powers, prophecy, the ability to distinguish between spirits, tongues, teaching, helping others, and interpretation. God gives out numerous gifts to many in the church. These gifts come from the Holy Spirit, who empowers us for God's service. We need to understand our gifts, develop them, and use them for God's purposes. Read 1 Corinthians 12 to understand more about how these gifts of the Spirit function. Lastly, always remember this: to him that much is given, much is expected (Luke 12:48).

EACH CONGREGATION SHOULD HAVE A PLAN TO SAVE THE LOST AND TO REACH OUT TO THE HURTING.

Each congregation of the church should operate as a family of believers who love and care for each other as they reach out to the lost and hurting in the name of Jesus. The congregation is called to worship together, to pray together, to suffer and rejoice together, and to encourage and equip each other for God's kingdom purposes.

Jesus saved the lost by the method of reaching out to people to touch their deepest hurts and needs. He fed the hungry, healed the sick, cast out demons, and constantly showed His love and compassion for sinners. Jesus never once said to a sinner, "Go get cleaned up and then come back so I can save you." Jesus met that sinner right at the point of need. When that person had his or her deep heartfelt needs met, that person was then receptive to accepting Jesus as Lord and Savior. The church is called to follow Jesus and use His methods for reaching the lost. Is your church doing that? Remember that love and compassion go hand in hand with presenting the Gospel.

Churches should never compromise or change any biblical truth or the Gospel message. At the same time, the church should be very sensitive and flexible in figuring out the best way to present the Gospel to that particular audience at the time. It is not tradition or impressive church buildings that make their way into the hearts of men. It is the love of Jesus as reflected in a loving congregation that will attract the lost. The church family that has learned how to meet deep spiritual needs will reap the greatest harvest, and have the healthiest body. Creating effective opportunities for evangelism on the streets, in the neighborhoods, in the workplace, and among families should be a strong focus for the church. The church should consider different events to get the message out to the lost. The church must also make certain that each of its members is saved, discipled, equipped, and knowledgeable in the basics of the faith.

WE ARE CALLED TO BE JOYFUL AND GENEROUS GIVERS, AND TO TITHE.

In addition to using our spiritual gifts for the church's benefit, we are all called to give of our resources. As to our giving, God gives us specific instruction. We need to support the church financially through our tithe, which is generally understood to be giving at least one-tenth of the firstfruits of our labor. Tithing is a minimum that God requires, and we should give even more generously as the Lord puts it on our hearts. We should be cheerful givers because the Lord loves a cheerful giver (2 Corinthians 9:7). The Greek word used for cheerful was *hilaros,* from which the word *hilarious* comes. We should be hilarious givers. In other words, God likes a spontaneous giver who overflows with joy in the act of giving. "Remember the words of our Lord Jesus, that He said, 'It is more blessed to give than to receive'" (Acts 20:35).

We do not want to miss out on the joy of giving. We should never give begrudgingly or with a heavy heart. God has done everything for us, and God owns everything we possess anyway. We should not feel so tied to the things of this world that we are afraid to give in a hilarious and joyful way in celebration of Jesus. After all, only those things that we invest in spiritually will survive our life on this earth. We will only be able to take our relationship with God and our relationships with others into heaven. Giving to the things of God's kingdom is an expression of how much we love God. That is why we give. It should be out of a pure heart and a love of the Father. That is why giving is a joyful and hilarious act.

Keep in mind that we are the ones who receive the joy from giving and not God. There is nothing God needs from us, but God will give us His blessing when we obey. Often, those who give generously will be much better off financially as God does take care of the needs of His people. If we were to survey those in church who tithe and those who do not, we would find that those who tithe are much more likely to be out of debt and have their financial house in order. That is just the way God works. More important, God will surprise us and give different kinds of blessings to those who give sacrificially. We never know how God will bless us, but He will bless us when we give out of love in obedience to Him.

Nothing should ever rob us of the joy of giving. Some people will use any and every excuse not to give: "I have too much debt"; "I need to save for retirement"; "I need to send my kids off to college"; "That vacation comes first so I will give later." None of these reasons pleases God. The best reason a person could have not to give is that he or she is poor and without any resources. Jesus told a parable about the woman who had nothing but a couple of little coins, and she put both of them into the collection plate for the work of God's kingdom. Jesus praised her act of sacrificial giving because "she out of her poverty put in all that she had, her whole livelihood" (Mark 12:41-44). Jesus' point was that giving is a sacrificial act and the greater the sacrifice, the greater the blessing. Also, we learn that neither poverty nor riches are reasons not to give.

Our own church body should be a family that is dedicated to serving Jesus.

God says that His house is a house of prayer (Matthew 21:13). Our local church is called to be a place of prayer and worship. It should be a place where the Word is read, the Word is preached, and the Word is taught. It should be a place to come for healing and wholeness. The church should be a life-changing place where life is received through the power of the Holy Spirit. The church should be a place where Jesus reigns.

The church is a family, but it is a diverse family. In the church there is neither Greek nor Jew, male or female, nor any other divisions (Galatians 3:28). It takes all kinds of believers to make up the body. The church should be inclusive of all kinds of believers who are drawn together. This family comes together in love. The church family cries together and shares times of joy together. If one hurts, then all hurt. If one rejoices, then all rejoice. The church is a place where Christians minister to each other as well as to those outside the church.

God should direct each believer to a particular church. The believer should not just go where he is the most comfortable. The question is: what church family does God want you to be a part of, and what does He want you to do there?

One thing is certain. Wherever you go and whatever you do, Jesus said, "Let your light so shine before men, that they may see your good works and glorify your Father in heaven" (Matthew 5:16). Jesus said not to put our light "under a basket but on a lampstand" so it would bring light to all of those around us (Matthew 5:15).

If you are elected or appointed to a leadership position within the church, you need to know what the Bible requires of you. You must have a good working knowledge of the Bible, particularly the New Testament and life of Jesus. Know what Jesus expects of His people and His church. Know the qualifications to serve as an elder or deacon. Know the power of prayer, worship, and the Word. Leaders are called to lead by serving with love. Leaders must lead exemplary lives and be equipped to minister to the flock. Leaders, described in the Bible as elders (overseers) and deacons, should not think of themselves as rulers, although they must exercise authority in accordance with the Word. Just as Jesus thought of Himself as a servant, so must leaders think of themselves as servants. They are to serve in joy with the love and compassion of Jesus.

Remember, the church is not ours. The church belongs to Jesus and to Him alone. The purpose of the church is to glorify Jesus. Peter gave a beautiful description of the body of Christ when he said, "You also, as living stones, are being built up a spiritual house, a holy priesthood, to offer up spiritual sacrifices acceptable to God through Jesus Christ" (1 Peter 2:5). And the cornerstone of this building of living stones is Jesus whom Peter called "the chief cornerstone, elect, precious, and he who believes on Him will by no means be put to shame" (1 Peter 2:6)

"Each one should use whatever gift he has received to serve others, faithfully administering God's grace in its various forms"
(1 Peter 4:10, NIV).

Discussion Questions

1. What do you believe is your strongest gift for ministry within the body of Christ? Why? Are you using that gift? If not, what do you think you need to do in order to exercise that gift?

2. How are you purposefully demonstrating love to others within the body of your church?

3. What are you doing right now to build up the body of Christ within your own congregation?

4. Evaluate your giving to your church and the causes of Christ. Do you need to make any changes? If so, what?

20

GOD'S CALLING ON YOUR LIFE AND YOUR MINISTRY

Jesus said: "Therefore go and make disciples of all nations, baptizing them in the name of the Father and of the Son and of the Holy Spirit" (Matthew 28:19, NIV).

Do you realize that God has a plan for your life?

God has called all of His believers to do good works. Good works do not save us as we have already learned, but our purpose here on earth is to do "good works." The Bible says this in many different ways. We shall be known by our fruits. In other words, as the fruit tree produces good fruit, God has a plan for our lives to produce fruit. We can call this our ministry on this earth or our purpose for being here, but it does include good works.

"Good works" are not good works in the worldly sense of the word. When the Bible uses the term "good works," the Bible is speaking of those things we are called to do that further God's kingdom here on this earth and glorify Jesus. We do these kind of "good works" not to receive acclaim or to promote ourselves. We do these works out of sacrificial love just as Jesus taught us to do. We do these works out of that agape kind of love that the Holy Spirit has put within our hearts. These are the works that draw others to Jesus because of the power of His love. The extent to which we do those "good works" that God intended for each of us will depend on our love of Christ and our willingness to follow Him.

To put this another way, all of us have a ministry to which we are called. All of us have a destiny to fulfill. All of us must seek and find that plan that God has for our lives. No believer is exempt from service in the army of God; and just as in a good army, each one of us has a particular role to fill as a soldier in God's army and the church of Jesus Christ.

Please understand that you are not here by accident. God is concerned with how you live each day, but He also has a plan for your life. He has specific plans and specific tasks for each of us. He has short-range plans and long-range plans for us. All of us are called, and responding to that call leads to great joy and fulfillment even in life on this earth.

Some people are called to be full-time ministers of the Gospel. Most of us are not. Some people are called into a specific occupation such as being a physician. All of us are called to work, whether it is in the home or in the business world. The Bible has many passages and proverbs that praise hard work and good competent work. One way or another, we were born to work, and that is something God expects. God calls us to work in our family or wherever He has placed us. When we do a good honest job at the office or the plant or in the home and reflect the love of Jesus, we are doing God's work. We don't have to be inside a church or engaging in a full-time ministry to do God's work. For all of us, it is important that we be good and trusted workers wherever we are, and for all of us it is important that we also spread the Gospel and do those things for His kingdom to which He has called us.

Thus, we are called to advance God's kingdom both inside and outside the marketplace. All of us are called to respond with the love of Jesus and reach out to others. In other words, as part of our "good works" here on earth, we are all called to ministry in some way. God has things He wants us to do. We can't stay in Bible studies all our lives and never put what we have learned to good use. We study the Bible so we will know how to share Jesus with others and how to explain the Gospel and God's basic truths about life. Studying the Bible and doctrine is like going to school. We go to school so that we will be better equipped when we later go to work. Of course, we never quit studying, and we never quit working for God's kingdom either.

God does it all. God will provide the calling. God will provide us with opportunity to be equipped, and God will provide the opportunity to serve. We just need to get with it and obey. Further, God will use every life experience we have had to help us do a better job at whatever He has called us to do. The story of Moses is an example. Moses was one of the greatest characters in the Bible. He lived to be 120 years old. During his first 40 years, Moses grew up in Pharaoh's house and had a powerful position in Egypt. He spent those years thinking he was really somebody. Then for the next 40 years, God caused Moses to wander in the wilderness where he learned that he was a nobody apart from God. From this experience, Moses became the most humble man in the Bible and realized he could do nothing without God. At this point Moses was ready to serve and obey God. After 40 seemingly useless years in the desert, God used Moses mightily during the last 40 years of his life. God provided whatever it took for Moses to get the job done, including miracles such as the world had never seen. Moses answered God's call for his life, and no previous experience that Moses had went to waste. God accomplished many humanly impossible tasks because Moses was faithful, available, humble, and dependent on God. The point of the story is that God is also calling each of His believers today to service, and God will provide the means if we will respond as Moses did.

To know God's plan for our life, we must seek God and listen to His voice.

God still speaks to us today. Jesus, although He is the Son of God, took on a totally human nature during His stay on this earth. In His human form, Jesus relied on the Holy Spirit to guide and direct Him in everything He did. The Holy Spirit will also direct us if we let Him.

In John 7:16 (NIV), Jesus said, "My teaching is not my own. It comes from him [God] who sent me." Jesus said He could not do anything on His own without the Father showing Him. In John 5:19 (NIV), He said, "I tell you the truth, the Son can do nothing by himself; he can only do what he sees his Father doing, because whatever the Father does the Son does also." Again in John 8:28, Jesus expressed this truth another way. "I do nothing on My own but speak just what the Father has taught Me." Jesus said this so that His believers would know that this Counselor that Jesus promised would guide each of them like that too.

God will call His people to serve Him under the most unusual circumstances. For example, prison is not a place where anyone wants to go, but God has used many prisoners to further His kingdom. Many prisoners have been converted and turned their lives around in prison to become powerful witnesses for Jesus both in prison and out of prison, after being released. Often that prisoner is better suited to share Jesus with other prisoners because of his compassion and the fact that other prisoners can identify with him. Each one of us will have special missions we are called to do for God, and our past experiences will help equip us to do that "good work."

No matter what kind of work or profession we may end up in, rest assured that God has an important ministry plan for our lives. It may be feeding the poor, teaching the Bible, or setting up tables and chairs at the church. All ministries are important to God. God is not a respecter of persons, and doing the so-called little things is just as important to God as preaching to a coliseum of 10,000 people. So, no matter what you do for a living, God has a ministry for you. That ministry may be in the home, in the church, on the street, or on the mission field in Africa, but He *does* have work for you. Will you find out what it is and respond in love?

God has many ways to speak to us and direct us in our daily living.

How does God speak to us through the Holy Spirit? God speaks to us in so many different ways. Often, God speaks to us in the quietness of our souls. God usually gives us a sense of peace when we are lined up with the Father's will. God can speak to us through circumstances in life as one door opens and another shuts. We have to test these circumstances through prayer, the Word, and Christian friends so we are not deceived. We need discernment and confirmation to make sure what we have heard is from God. God speaks to us through His Word, the Bible. As you begin to read the Bible, ask God to speak to you. Ask God to reveal some truth that you need in your life that day. Ask God for special insights. As you read the Bible and take in His Word, God will put thoughts on your heart that are from Him.

Also, God can speak to us through other people. Often, we hear someone say, "When the pastor preached this morning, he really spoke to me about a certain thing in his sermon." God speaks to us through Christian friends, but again their advice must be tested carefully.

God speaks to us through prayer so we must know His voice and listen. God is not limited. He can even speak to us through dreams, but make certain that what you hear is from God before you act on the message. Remember, the enemy likes to deceive us and so does our flesh. The closer you walk with Jesus, the better you will be able to hear His voice. Finally, rest assured that God will never instruct you to do something that goes against His Word, the Bible, or that is inconsistent with His character.

As we listen to God's voice, we should be aware of what God is doing around us. Understanding how God is moving in your church, your city, or your family is important. We must have an awareness of what God's plans are for others with whom we are connected. We must be sensitive to what God is saying to our Christian brothers and sisters with whom we are associated in the church. Keep in mind that we are usually called to work as part of a team effort. God likes for His people to work together and always in unity. God does not have any super-stars out there. The church janitor is as important as the head pastor. All make up the body of Christ. Each one of us makes up a small part of body of Christ, and it takes a whole body to get the job done.

ALL OF US ARE CALLED AND NONE OF US IS ADEQUATE, SO JUST DO WHATEVER YOU DO IN LOVE WITH A SERVANT'S HEART.

Wherever and however we serve Jesus, the main thing is to bring His love to others. Don't hide your light under a basket as Jesus said. When we serve, we are to serve with a servant's heart. We are to serve with a spirit of humility as Jesus did. Jesus made a dramatic point of this principle when He, the Lord of the universe, washed the feet of His disciples. Then Jesus instructed His disciples to go and do likewise. Read John 13:1-17. All of us are in the foot-washing business. This is particularly true when we serve the least of these as Jesus commanded in Matthew 25:31-46. When we visit the sick or those in prison, or feed the hungry, we serve Jesus. What an honor that is. In fact, there is no greater honor or privilege or joy.

We do not have to be a full-time or paid minister of the Gospel. We do not have to be a gifted preacher or prophet. We might be like the deacons in the early church who were called to wait on tables so the elders could teach and pray for the sick. Whether we mop the floor or deliver food to the poor, all that we do in Jesus' name is a great honor.

Jesus told a very important story, which is called the Parable of the Talents. Talents were money, but for the purposes of this story, Jesus wants us to think of those talents as being that talent and ability that we have been given for God's kingdom work. In this story, which you can read in Matthew 25:14-30, a certain master left the country for a long time. When he left, he gave his three servants five, two, and one talents (valuable coins) respectively. The master expected that his servants were to invest this money wisely in his absence and make a good return. The two servants, who had five and two talents each, put their money to good use and earned a handsome profit. The servant who had only one talent did nothing with his talent. This servant said, "I was afraid, and went and hid your talent in the ground." Thus, this servant earned nothing for his master. The master was extremely upset and called this servant "wicked" and "lazy." Many of us are like the servant who buried his talent. We feel that we have such little talent or ability that we are afraid to step out and do something lest we fail.

After the Leap

Jesus' point in this parable is that He is the master and that He gives us all of our talent. First Corinthians 7:7 tells us that we each have our own gift. Some may have more gifts or talent than others, but all of us have something. Jesus commands us to use whatever talent we have for God's kingdom. Also, Jesus tells us that the better we use our talents, the more talents He will give us. When Jesus sees that He can trust us with a little, He will ask us to take on more responsibility in the work of His kingdom. First Corinthians 14:12 says we should try to excel in gifts that build up the body of Christ; therefore, we should practice our gifts and improve on our ability, but feeling inadequate in not an excuse. We all have at least one talent; and no matter how many we have, we are commanded to use them for God's kingdom.

WE MUST BECOME EQUIPPED FOR WHATEVER GOD HAS PUT ON OUR HEARTS TO DO.

The Bible speaks frequently of "gifts." A gift is like a talent. These gifts that the Bible speaks of are given to us by the Holy Spirit. God gives us the gifts as He desires, and He gives His gifts to all His people to be used. First Corinthians 12 lists these gifts from the Holy Spirit as: words of wisdom (usually when one person is given insight by the Lord about another person so appropriate prayer and action can follow); words of knowledge (again when God gives special insights into situations for use within the body); gifts of faith; gifts of healing (when a person has a special calling to pray for healing); working of miracles; prophecy (this is not only God revealing a future happening, but is any truth God gives to edify and help the body); discerning of spirits (used for the ministry of deliverance and the right kind of prayer to cast out demons); and the gift of tongues (both in speaking in tongues and interpretation of tongues).

This chapter cannot go into any detail about these precious gifts, but the church should do what it can to develop the gifts of its members through teaching, practical hands-on training and mentoring. The best training, of course, is just to get in there and do it. It's like jumping in the water to learn how to swim. You can listen to the instruction and that is good; but at some point you just have to step out in faith and get involved. One of the reasons the church exists is to disciple others, which includes spiritual training and preparation for service. If we are working within the church, then we must submit to the authority of the church. The church is not a place for Lone Rangers—that is people who do their own thing without regard to what the church is doing. Members of the body of Christ support each other as they carry out their mission in unity.

One way to discover your gift is to look at your own heart and see what God seems to be calling you to do. You may need training because few people have it all together at the outset; but if you have a compassion for a particular ministry, probably you should be serving there. Having a passion for your ministry is important but not essential. Sometimes God calls us to something, and when we respond in faith, He creates a passion and a joy that is beyond belief. Don't miss out, as Jesus may be calling you right now.

WE ARE ALL CALLED TO SPREAD THE GOOD NEWS ABOUT JESUS AND TO MINISTER WITHIN THE CHURCH BODY.

No matter what our ministry may be, there are certain things to which we are all called. One of these is knowing how to share the Gospel. Paul said, "For I am not ashamed of the gospel of Christ, for it is the power of God to salvation for everyone who believes" (Romans 1:16). We should be fearless and eager to spread the Gospel to any lost soul. The more we have the love and the passion of Jesus for the lost, the more passion we will have in our heart to spread the good news.

The Bible teaches that spreading the news about the saving grace of Jesus is the first mission of the church. The "Great Commission" at the close of the Gospel of Matthew refers to Jesus' command that we tell people at home and abroad about His saving grace. Jesus puts the highest priority on our participation with Him in saving the lost. Jesus does the saving, but He calls on us to do the presenting. Also, Jesus wants His disciples to boldly declare that Jesus is Lord and the only way to salvation. Jesus said, "Therefore whoever confesses Me before men, him I will also confess before My Father who is in heaven. But whoever denies Me before men, him I will also deny before My Father who is in heaven" (Matthew 10:32-33).

Every Christian should feel comfortable telling a stranger or a friend about Jesus. The church should train its members in evangelism. Members should also feel free to share the Gospel in the way the Spirit leads them. Our presentation of Jesus should not be a canned sales talk or a presentation of dry information. We should show our great love for Jesus with enthusiasm and do so in a natural way. We should just be ourselves and be sincere. One great saint once said when spreading the Gospel, "If necessary use words." His point was that our lives should be living testimonies so that people will see Jesus in us. When an unbeliever sees joy, peace, or life in the believer, this can be a more powerful testimony than words. When an unbeliever can see how Jesus has radically changed

After the Leap

the life of a friend, this is a powerful witness.

Jesus had such a heart for one lost soul that he told a beautiful parable in Matthew 18:12 about how a shepherd walked away from ninety-nine of his sheep just to go find one. Jesus wants each of us to have that same compassion for each individual we know who is not saved.

When we share the Gospel with someone and nothing happens, we should not be discouraged. Our role is to do our best to introduce Jesus to that other person. Only God can draw people to Himself for salvation. Salvation is a work of the Holy Spirit. People will not be drawn to Jesus through their own wisdom (1 Corinthians 1:21-25). If we are faithful to do our part, then that is all we can do. Simple presentations often work best. Our job is to be prepared and ready to give the basic facts of salvation along with our individual testimony about Jesus.

WE SHOULD KNOW HOW TO LEAD SOMEONE TO CHRIST ONCE THAT PERSON SAYS YES TO THE GOSPEL MESSAGE.

If you share the good news with an unbeliever who then says she wants to believe in Jesus, encourage that person to repeat the prayer of salvation. Boldly ask if you could lead the unbeliever in the sinner's prayer. There are no set words to the prayer, but you need to know the essentials so you can lead the person properly.

The request should go something like this—"Why don't you pray along with me so we can be certain you have asked Jesus to come into your heart?" When the person says yes, then just say, "Repeat this prayer after me." You can ask the person to pray silently or out loud. The prayer should go like this: "Dear Jesus: I know that I am a sinner. I am truly sorry for all my sins. I repent of my sins and my past and ask that You forgive me. Jesus, I want to put all of my faith and trust in You as my personal Savior. I want You to come into my heart and take over my life. Please come into my heart, dear Jesus. I accept You as my Savior. Thank You, Jesus, for dying for my sins on the cross. Thank You for saving me and giving me eternal life. Amen."

Jesus doesn't care about specific wording. He does care about that new Christian's heart. What He wants is for the person to repent, confess that he is a sinner, and trust in Jesus for salvation. When that happens, the person is saved even if he can't compose a beautiful prayer. Going through the prayer of salvation with someone lets that person know a definite transaction with God has taken place. Also, this declaration will help wash away future doubt that the enemy will try to plant. The person coming to Jesus needs to have that assurance that she was born again and is saved. Warn the person that the devil will try to convince her this salvation experience was not real. Encourage the person to stand firm in the faith. Also, explain that the act of receiving Jesus may not be an emotional experience. With many it is, and with many it is not. The amount of emotional feeling is not what matters. The honest transaction between God and that individual is what matters.

Now this new Christian needs to be discipled. Emphasize the need for the new believer to have someone disciple him during this early growth as a Christian. Emphasize the need to begin to study the Bible daily, to pray daily, and to find a church home. If you can, give him a Bible and offer to explain the basics of the faith. Meet with or call that new believer later to see how he is doing. Be sure the person understands the principle of Ephesians 2:8-9 that it is only through faith we are saved and not through our good works.

Not everyone you share the good news with will become a believer, but the seed you sow may be the seed used for conversion when someone else shares the Gospel. When you get the opportunity, share the good news. An eternity in heaven or hell may rest in the balance. Besides, think of the immense joy you will have when someone comes up to you in heaven someday and says, "Thanks for telling me about Jesus."

Do not underestimate the importance of building up trust with a neighbor, coworker, or friend before you witness. Find ways to talk about Jesus naturally in your conversation. Let your life and things you do, like reaching out to others in the name of Jesus, be a living testimony to your faith. When others see the joy of your salvation and your love of Jesus, they may want Jesus as their Savior too.

BELIEVERS ARE ALSO CALLED TO PRAY FOR THOSE WHO ARE SICK OR HURTING AND TO REACH OUT TO THEM.

No matter what kinds of ministry we are called to, all believers need to be ready to pray for the needs of others they know—particularly the downtrodden, the depressed, and the sick. Jesus was in the business of healing. No one was too insignificant or unimportant to be overlooked by Jesus. Jesus was concerned with each person's well-being. He wanted to bring wholeness to people's lives as well as salvation. In the last half of Matthew 25, Jesus commanded us to reach out to those who were suffering from demons, to those who were in jail, to the sick, and to those who were poor and hungry. This command includes all of us who are believers. His warning was very clear and forceful: anyone who did not reach out to the poor did not really know Him. And if they did not know Him, they were going to spend an eternity in hell.

The Bible instructs us how to pray for healing. James 5:14 is a good place to start: "If anyone among you sick? Let him call for the elders of the church, and let them pray over him, anointing him with oil in the name of the Lord." James goes on to say that the prayers offered in faith will be answered and that "the prayer of a righteous man avails much." The fact God does not always heal is God's business, not ours. Sometimes God's timing is different from ours, and we have to learn to wait on the Lord. God has His reasons for everything He does. Our business is to be obedient and ready to pray for the sick. Jesus commanded His disciples in Matthew 10:8: "Heal the sick, cleanse the lepers, raise the dead, cast out demons. Freely you have received, freely give." We should pray in faith. If we were to study all of the miracles of healing Jesus performed, most often faith was the key ingredient.

Physicians and nurses and hospitals are also gifts from God for the purpose of healing. We should honor them and always pray for them as they go about healing a loved one. Many a Christian physician has testified to the power of prayer and said that healing is a combination of prayer and good medical treatment.

Prayer for emotional wounds is not much different than prayer for physical healing. One of the first steps in praying for healing of emotional wounds is to identify the problem. Unlike physical healing, this can be much more difficult as the individual may not have a clue as to the source of the problem. Knowing what to pray for is normally the first step. Sometimes the individual has repressed memories of past painful events that caused the problem. Often, it helps to ask the Holy Spirit to bring those things causing the problem to the surface. It may be a traumatic childhood experience or some form of oppression or abandonment. Through specific prayer and working through any unforgiveness or bitterness, the Holy Spirit may do a restorative work. Again, it is very helpful to have some within the church body who are specially trained to pray for deep emotional wounds.

PRAYER ALWAYS WORKS FOR GOOD—EVEN WHEN WE DO NOT
SEE A QUICK POSITIVE RESULT.

Whether God chooses to heal someone at that time or not, prayer for healing is always a positive thing. Prayer for healing brings us closer to God. God may simply give the sick person a greater sense of peace. Sometimes God uses illness to draw a person to salvation. Few people, whether Christian or not, will turn down prayer for healing. If you ask a person if you can pray for her, usually that person will consent. If that person is not a believer, this opportunity may provide an opportunity to witness about Jesus and His saving grace. When we pray for healing, at the very least the sick person realizes someone loves and cares about him. Even if the person is not healed, often the person will improve physically and will experience less emotional stress and pain. The person who receives prayer will be blessed and so will the person who does the praying. When that sick person receives the love of Jesus through a believer, this is a powerful experience with the living God. All of us are called to a ministry of prayer.

Prayer lets us appreciate God's mercy and the blessing of good health. We should look on the opportunity to pray for another as a wonderful opportunity to spread the love of Jesus. It is a joy and a privilege. Always pray in faith. Our God is a God of love and mercy. God may not choose to heal in our timing or our way; however, God always answers our prayers because passing from this earth to eternal glory is the ultimate healing for some.

None of us can minister to all the needs of all the hurting people that we see. Nevertheless, all of us are called to do something for somebody. In Matthew 25, Jesus called all of us to love the poor and oppressed and hurting. Many people in this world go hungry every day. Even in our own cities in the United States, the richest country in the world, street people live below bridges and in cardboard boxes. Others need medical care. Many people are in prison or hospitals. Some live lonely lives at home or in an old-age home without a single person to talk to, desperately needing a visit. All of us have a most basic need, which is to be loved. Jesus calls all believers to reach out and bring the love of Jesus to those who are hurting.

ALL OF US ARE CALLED TO BE DISCIPLES AND THEN TO GO OUT AND DISCIPLE OTHERS.

Jesus, at the end of the Book of Matthew, told His disciples to go out and make disciples in all nations. Jesus tells us to do the same thing today. The word *disciple* comes from the Greek word *mathetes,* which denoted three basic things: (1) disciples learned from the one they were following, (2) disciples learned as they went about doing what they were being taught and also from practical experience, and (3) disciples imitated the life of the one they were following.

Jesus calls us to do those very things. All believers are called to learn from Jesus as they go about ministering to others, to look to Jesus as their teacher, and to imitate the life of Jesus.

Jesus is our Master and our Master-Teacher. We are continually to be discipled and to learn from Jesus all our life on earth as we go about ministering His grace to others. As we go about this lifetime task, we are also to disciple others so they too can grow in the Christian faith. We do not have to have all the answers or a seminary degree. All of us can learn and all of us can disciple others in one way or another. Even in our imperfection, we all have something from Jesus that someone else needs. And someone else always has something from Jesus that we need. Through discipleship, the church, that is Christians throughout the world, minister, teach, encourage, discipline, and assist each other in all aspects of the faith. This is called discipleship, always ongoing in order to further the kingdom of God on this earth.

Just remember, it is Jesus through the power of the Holy Spirit who will do the work. We are just to learn what we can and do what we can in accordance with the Word of God in order to make believers and disciples. God's calling on our lives and ministries is a lifetime commitment and a day-by-day journey. Jesus summarized it in a few words by saying, "Whoever desires to come after Me, let him deny himself, and take up his cross and follow Me" (Mark 8:34).

> "He [God] has sent Me [Jesus] to heal the brokenhearted,
> to preach deliverance to the captives and recovery of sight
> to the blind, to set at liberty those who are oppressed"
> (Luke 4:18).

DISCUSSION QUESTIONS

1. Why is praying for the healing of another always a positive and good thing to do?

2. How would you go about leading another to Christ? Write out what you would say, and what you would have that person pray with you to receive Christ into his or her heart?

3. How are you reaching out to the sick, those in the hospital, the poor, those in jail, or others less fortunate? Read Matthew 25 carefully, and then pray

about how Jesus is calling you to minister to the hurting. How will you become equipped? What will you do?

4. What ministry are you engaged in right now? Is that all God is calling you to do?

21

GOD'S PLAN FOR YOUR TIME AND HIS RESOURCES

"Now godliness with contentment is great gain. For we brought nothing into this world, and it is certain we can carry nothing out"
(1 Timothy 6:6-7).

IT ALL BELONGS TO GOD—EVERY HOUR WE LIVE AND EVERY PENNY WE HAVE.

Did you ever really think about time? What is time? Why is it here? We are always so busy, so how do we deal with time? Who does it belong to anyway?

Think about Jesus and time. Jesus knew all of His time belonged to the Father, and Jesus used it wisely and completely in accordance with God's will. Jesus never wasted any time, yet He was never in a hurry. He was always on time. He always had enough time. Jesus did not even own a watch. That didn't matter because Jesus did what the Father told Him to do when the Father told Him to do it. Jesus made the most of His time. In the three short years of His public ministry, Jesus changed the world. This is because Jesus had His priorities straight and was in perfect step with God. We cannot achieve that perfection, but we can put our priorities in order and use our precious time as God intends. That is out duty and that is our challenge.

First, we must put everything into perspective. We must realize that God created all the time we have and everything there is. It all belongs to Him. He gives it to us to use for His kingdom purposes, and our time is very limited on this earth. Whatever resources we have belong to Him. We must use His time and His resources wisely to carry out His purposes. This means we need to have our priorities straight. God, not us, must set our priorities.

As the saying goes, "Show me your checkbook and show me your calendar, and I will tell you what you think is important in life." This is true. We cannot just talk the talk, we must walk the walk. Jesus calls us to walk hand in hand with Him in everything we do in life. This chapter will center on setting goals for our time and money so that we are good stewards and do not squander what God has entrusted to us.

God made us and knew us before we were born. He created each one of us for a purpose. That purpose is to glorify Him and enjoy Him forever. At the same time, God has a different mission for each one of us to do in different seasons. He will call us from one thing to another on occasion. God is always full of surprises. This lets us know He is there and He cares. He uses us where we are planted. He uses us no matter what our occupation is. He expects us to do well at our regular job, and He expects to use us to share His love as we go about our normal, everyday tasks.

Time is a strange thing with God. He made all time so He stands outside of time. He is not limited by time as we are. We are confined to space and time and limited in both. Our time here on earth is short. The Bible says man's days are three score and ten. That means 70 years. Some live longer and others are taken unexpectedly at much earlier ages. Even if we live to be 100, the years will go by faster and faster with each birthday. Before we know it, we will be out of time. Our limited seasons are always drawing to a close. Each day is a precious gift so we must constantly ask ourselves what have we done of eternal significance today. Even so, we should not be frantic—just concerned and thoughtful about how God wants us to use our time. Jesus always had time for prayer. Jesus always had time to make certain His relationship with the Father was just right. Our goal should be to be more like Jesus. Then there will always be enough time to fulfill our God-given destiny.

If we are to follow God, we need to be flexible and go with God's timing. Often God will seem to start us down one path and then call us into something else—be it a new job or a new ministry or helping a new person. Sometimes God shuts a door to something we longed to do and opens another door we did not expect. Sometimes we do not understand why this is. Sometimes we do not understand why God puts us in a place that we never dreamed of being. These things happen because no one understands the mind of God. We *do* know that He cares about every hair on our heads and everything we do. We must be assured He knows what He is doing and faithfully follow.

Because our time is limited, we must use it with godly wisdom. God knows we do not need to be busy for the sake of being busy. Jesus had time to do all the things that the Father called Him to do. Jesus always had time to love others, to reach down and touch people's deepest needs and to bring those people to salvation if they were lost. A good use of time does not mean we must become workaholics or frantically see how many activities we can cram into a day. Some people work such long hours each day, trying to make money, that they have no time for God. Jesus calls us to have time for Him. How much of your leisure time, that is the time you have after working, sleeping, and caring for your family, do you spend on the things of God's kingdom, and how much on the things of this world? God should dictate that, not you.

Each day we start out with so many minutes. It is as if each day we are given 1,440 silver dollars, each one representing one minute of the day. We can spend them wisely or throw them away. Reality is that each minute not spent wisely is like tossing one of those silver dollars in the garbage because we never get them back. Time wasted is time gone forever.

One of the things most of us are called to do is to work, whether in the home or outside the home. Honest work is biblical and part of God's plan. We need to feel a peace about the kind of work we are doing. If we do not have that peace, we either need to change our attitude or ask God if we are in the right business. While we are in the workplace, we need to know that we are ambassadors for Jesus Christ wherever we go. Our lives should display Jesus just as much at work as they do at church on Sunday morning.

OUR PRIORITIES MUST BE TO GOD AND FAMILY FIRST.

The Bible teaches in a thousand different ways that our relationship with God comes before anything else. Whatever we do, we must set aside time to be with Jesus through the Word, through prayer, through praise, and through simply sitting at the Master's feet and listening to His voice. We have devoted four chapters to the Word, prayer, praise, and developing a personal relationship with Jesus. This comes first. As you plan your day and your week, put God's priorities first. God will always give us time to read His Word, to pray, to praise Him, and simply to spend time listening to His voice. Setting aside special times for these four basic things is essential. Put these on your daily schedule and in your heart.

Our next priority to God is our family. If we are married, we must be certain we are spending quality time with our spouse and nurturing that relationship. The same goes for the children. Most of us must work, and work requires a lot of time and effort. We should never get so bogged down in work that our relationships with God or our family suffer. God calls husbands and wives to be godly parents who spend time with each other and with their children. Also, we need to be good stewards of how our children spend their time. The way we spend our time either brings us closer to God or closer to this sinful world we live in. Watching junk on television, reading trashy magazines, spending countless hours at video games, or having a hobby to the point of obsession deprives us of opportunities to do God's work. This is not to mention the wounds to the soul that any ungodly activity may bring.

CHRISTIANS SHOULD MAKE GOOD USE OF THEIR SPARE TIME TOO.

At different stages of life, God places different demands on our time. A mother with little children will have time for little else except the mothering of those children. No ministry on this earth is more important than that mother's time with those children. The only equal ministry is that of a father spending quality time with his children. God set up the family as His first institution. Nothing is more important than bringing up children in the ways of the Lord. Thus, we must be sensitive to God's priorities and to the particular responsibilities we have been given at particular stages of life.

The problem with our world today is that we live in a time where there are more diversions and distractions than ever before. Modern conveniences have given us more so-called "leisure time." At the same time, the world saturates us with lustful advertisements, amusements, entertainment, and a philosophy that says the individual is No. 1. Worldly messages pollute our minds with the lie that absolutely nothing should stand in our way of pursuing the "good" life. There is only one good life, and that is living life God's way. Jesus will provide the only true joy if we follow Him.

In short, we cannot set proper priorities unless we are following God's Word and not the things of this world. The first decision we must make is to determine whom we are going to follow. Will it be the world or Jesus? Jesus tells us we cannot do both. This does not mean we cannot go to a movie, watch a decent television program, or have fun with friends. Certainly, God wants us to stay in good physical shape and take care of our health. Exercise is a good thing. Anything though, even exercise or a Christian ministry, can become an idol and the object of worship instead of God. The question is: does our activity enhance our relationship with God and achieve what He has in mind? God wants us to have an enjoyable and blessed fellowship with family and friends. Remember, God created leisure time. In fact, He orders us to rest on Sunday. When we use our spare time for rest or recreation, this time should build us up for what lies ahead. All our time should have a godly purpose.

As we live each day, we need to be good trustees of the hours and days that God has entrusted to us. After all, everything we have belongs to God. We are simply stewards while these things are in our possession. He turns over to us the years that we have on this earth as well as our jobs, our spare time, our money, and the things we possess. We must use it all for His kingdom and His glory.

PLANNING HOW TO USE OUR MONEY AND AVOIDING DEBT IS BIBLICAL.

When it comes to spending our money, we need to have a plan. Our plan needs to take into account usual expenses, our tithes, and the unexpected emergencies that come up. Like our time, we are called to use our money wisely and in a godly manner. Are you spending your money wisely? Would God be pleased? Some people spend more on entertainment than they give to the church. We have already talked about the importance of tithing and giving to God's kingdom. Make certain your budget puts God's kingdom first. God asks for the firstfruits, that is the first dollars and not the leftovers.

If you have not ever done any monetary planning, do so now. Sit down and prepare a budget. If you feel insecure about your ability to set a budget, then get some help from a Christian friend, who is wise and has financial sense. Attend a seminar or read a good Christian book on planning a budget. Mismanagement of money is much more likely to lead to bankruptcy or divorce than a lack of money. Going hopelessly in debt from buying more than one can afford is a worldwide problem that is getting worse.

Avoid going into debt. House payments can be an exception. Often, these payments are less than rent, and you end up owning your own home, which can be an important thing for the family. Borrowing to buy a home is usually a good thing if you do not spend more than you can afford, considering all of your obligations. When you borrow on a home, you also get the chance to build up equity. When you finally pay off the mortgage, then this is a good thing because you no longer have to pay house payments or rent.

It is foolish to buy what we do not need. It is even more foolish to go into debt to buy what we do not need. To borrow money to buy a fancy car when you have a good car that is paid for is an example of such foolish behavior. If you need a new car and can afford it, save the money first. Don't go into debt for a new car or some adult toy that is not necessary. There may be emergencies you cannot plan for which you have to borrow. The basic biblical principle is that we should not go through life in debt. Most people would do well to throw away their credit cards unless they pay off the entire balance each month. A credit card can be a helpful convenience or it can be a hook that leads to unnecessary spending at exorbitant interest rates. Destroy your credit cards if they are a hindrance to good spending habits. Don't be a slave to debt and take on that additional worry. Generally speaking, a Christian should be debt free. Running up debts for such things as vacations, clothes, cars, and recreation is not biblical. Do not buy now and pay later. There are enough pressures in life without having to work unreasonable hours to obtain unnecessary things you cannot afford.

Some people become enslaved to debt. Buying things that are not needed can become an addictive habit and harmful to self and to family. Many people who buy more things than they can afford are like alcoholics. People who are so addicted usually feel that owning something new will make them happy. After they buy the item, the high wears off just like alcohol. What remains is a depressing hangover of indebtedness. Have one simple rule: do not go into debt unless you have a true emergency. Even when you borrow on a home, have a short repayment plan such as ten or fifteen years. This will save you an unbelievable amount of money. Figure out the difference in the interest you will pay in a short-term and long-term loan. It is tremendous.

Saving money is a good idea. After giving your tithes and offerings and buying the necessities like food and clothing, saving money should be a high priority. We never know when the hard days will fall, and besides we need to be able to take care of our retirement expenses, education for children, and those unforeseen emergencies. You would do well to plan and set aside a certain portion of your income each month for savings. Saving is a good way to avoid going into debt.

One last thing: be aware of whom you are doing business with and where your money is going. We cannot always spend our money with those who are Christians. Maybe God has not even called us to do that. Nevertheless, we do know God does not want us spending our money on gambling, lotteries, sinful ventures, or anything that promotes immoral causes. Be careful where you spend your money. You should never purchase any pornographic, idolatrous, or other indecent thing. Is everything that you buy or possess pleasing to the Lord? That is the ultimate test.

Above all, seek God's counsel as to how to use your time and His resources. The Holy Spirit will guide you. And do not hesitate to ask for practical advice from the church.

After the Leap

"Owe no one anything except to love one another, for he who loves another has fulfilled the law" (Romans 13:8).

Discussion Questions
(Take the time to write out the following assignments.)

1. How do you spend your day? Write out how much time you spend on the following items daily, and then analyze whether you are spending your time wisely.
   - sleeping
   - going to work, working, and coming home from work
   - being with the family, excluding devotionals or prayer, but including meals
   - relaxing by watching television, working at hobbies, playing sports, reading, etc.
   - praying, reading the Bible, praising and worshiping God, family devotions, small groups, or participating in a ministry.

2. After you have filled this out (and you may want to do one for weekdays and another for weekends or nonworking days), write down two other things. First, write down those things you need to cut out or cut down on. Then, write out what those important things are that you need to spend more time doing. Now ask yourself this important question: am I spending enough time with God and with my family?

   Are you spending enough time doing God's work in whatever ministry He has called you to? Do you spend too much time watching television or engaging in other activities of less significance?

3. Now get a separate sheet of paper and prepare a budget. In that budget, be honest and list your income and all your expenses. Write down how much money goes to the Lord's work. Next, calculate how much money you are saving for your future or future family needs. Get help from someone in the church who knows about financial planning if you do not understand how to go about this budgeting process. Finally, look over your situation and ask yourself: would God be pleased with how I am spending money?

22

OVERCOMING ADVERSITY

"We also rejoice in our suffering, because we know that suffering produces perseverance; perseverance, character; and character, hope" (Romans 5:3-4, NIV).

JESUS NEVER PROMISED THE CHRISTIAN LIFE WOULD BE EASY. ADVERSITY DEVELOPS CHARACTER.

All of us will face adversity. The question is not whether or not we will face trials, but how we respond to the bad things that happen to us. That is what counts. Will the difficult and discouraging experiences of life make us bitter or better? As Romans 8:28 puts it, will our reaction to this bad experience work to the good and bring us closer to Jesus or drive us to despair and to seek an ungodly answer elsewhere? We may not be able to understand why bad things happen to us, but we can grow to understand that it is adversity and not the smooth road in life that will enable us to grow in our Christian character and our faith in God.

Many inspirational books have been written on the subject of adversity. The greatest stories appear in the Bible. In fact, the Bible is one continuous story about the different ways individuals reacted to all kinds of disaster. We need to understand fundamental concepts about how God uses adversity to develop character. And it is our character, our true character in Christ, that will determine how we will handle adversity.

First of all, we must always realize that God is in control and that He does love us. This basic fact must be foundational in our thinking. Next, we must realize that this life on earth is a training ground where God builds our character in preparation for spending an eternity in heaven. We spend a few years here while millions times millions of years in heaven will just begin our eternal stay. Hopefully, our character will continue to improve throughout eternity. We don't

After the Leap

know how that works. What we do know is that we have only a short time on this earth in which we go through testing, and God wants to use all of our experiences, good and bad, to draw us closer to Him.

God wants us to grow spiritually as a result of every experience and opportunity that life provides; therefore, we should not view life as being good or bad in accordance with the number of good or bad things that happen to us. Also, we are not to measure the goodness of life by its ease or difficulty. Read the Beatitudes to be comforted about how God blesses those who are persecuted and those who are hurting (Matthew 5:1-12). The Beatitudes demonstrate God's great love and rich blessings to those who humbly undergo hardship. To suffer for God is an honor and privilege and brings spiritual rewards that we can neither see nor measure. Certainly, we want to avoid suffering, but God will use our suffering for His glory and our benefit. We must have faith that God knows what He is doing, and that all things will work for good for those who love the Lord, as Paul said in Romans 8:28.

Our fleshly state prefers an easy life without pain or hardship, but God's ways are not our ways. One thing is for certain. We will not be able to figure out all the answers. We may not understand why we have hard times, but those times will come (2 Timothy 3:12). Just know God will use all adversity for good according to His purposes, not our purposes, if we love Him.

GOD'S WAYS ARE NOT MAN'S WAYS, AND BAD THINGS DO HAPPEN TO SO-CALLED "GOOD PEOPLE."

When we conclude that a "bad thing" has happened to a "good person," we make a judgment of who is good and who is bad. God's standards and the world's standards are different. In Jesus' day, everyone assumed that the Pharisees, who were the most religious, were good. On the other hand, the world would have said the prodigal son and Mary Magdalene were bad. Jesus showed us otherwise. Jesus' strongest and harshest words of His entire ministry were aimed at the Pharisees. Jesus loved them, but they were very bad. They only looked good. In their hearts they had no love for anyone.

If you read Jesus' sermon in Matthew 23, you will see the deadly sins of pride, arrogance, and lack of love that permeated the Pharisees' lives. Now compare Jesus' opinion of the Pharisees with Jesus' opinion of Mary Magdalene or the prodigal son, both of whom sinned greatly. Because they repented and believed, each was forgiven and stood righteous in Jesus' eyes. So when we talk about good people, we must be careful in making a judgment. Jesus said that no one was good. When Jesus said that, He was referring to us in our natural state, apart from the work of the Holy Spirit within us; therefore, since no man is good, we should avoid judging others or thinking God is being unjust to good people.

The truth is that the concept of bad people and good people doesn't exist in the way we think it does. The truth is that we are all sinners, and the Bible teaches the wages of sin is death; therefore, when something bad happens to any of us, we cannot say we do not deserve it. Whatever good health, prosperity, or any other blessings we have are not deserved, but come from the great mercy and grace of our Heavenly Father. When we take this truth deep into our hearts, we become humble. We become eternally grateful. We realize we don't deserve anything. We become overjoyed by what Jesus did for us on the cross and overwhelmed by His free gift of grace. Thus, when bad things come, we will not curse God. We will thank Him for the good things that He has given us. Even so, we do not wish for adversity. In fact, God calls on His people to pray against adversity throughout the Bible. At the same time, God wants us to put our adversity in a proper perspective and not let adversity lead us into defeat, anger, or bitterness. God will use those valleys to draw us more closely to Him.

When we look at another person, we should not see good or bad. That is for God to judge. We should know that God loves all of us even though we are all sinners. We should not condemn another person as nonredeemable nor make a judgment against any person (Matthew 7:1-2). Instead, we should praise God with a grateful heart because He has saved us when we deserved to die. When we wake up each morning and realize what God has done for us, how bad hell is, and how good heaven is, our hearts should overflow with thanksgiving.

GOD IS ALWAYS IN CONTROL EVEN THOUGH HE OFTEN TAKES US THROUGH SOME DIFFICULT DAYS.

Adversity is no fun in whatever package it arrives, but God is much more likely to use adversity to build our character if we let Him. Think about this reality. Without adversity, how would we grow and mature in our Christian character? Also, it is through our trials that we learn to appreciate life when it goes well. We would all like to live in a Garden of Eden and not have to undergo the trials of this earth. But if we lived in a perfect place, we would not appreciate the heaven that has been prepared for us—a place where there will be no more pain or suffering. It is through adversity that God brings us to our knees and makes us appreciate Him. As we go through life, we will understand how much more often than not adversity, not the easy life, brings lost souls to salvation or back to the Lord. Adversity brings people to brokenness where they cry out to God and become dependent on Him for all things instead of being filled with pride and self-sufficiency.

The opposite of adversity and failure is success. Most of us have a desire to be successful here on earth. There is nothing inherently wrong with having wealth or earthly position as long as they do not hinder our relationship with Jesus. Sometimes, however, achieving earthly goals can be detrimental. For example, many people want to be rich, and some of these people believe that riches will do away with all worldly problems and make their life easy. Some people are so ambitious and desire wealth so greatly that they spend all their energy and time to achieve that end. The only problem is that when they do achieve wealth, they experience a big letdown. Their other problems do not cease, and they discover wealth does not produce happiness. Many an ambitious person, who finally becomes rich and achieves his dream, then asks the question, "Is that all there is?" Many have become depressed and even suicidal in the discovery that wealth did not bring the intended happiness. Committed Christians have discovered that neither riches nor the easy life are the way to peace and joy. But the true gain is to live for Christ.

Wealth in and of itself is not a bad thing. In fact, wealth can be a great blessing if one puts God first and not achieving money or the things money can buy. But it will always be Jesus and not wealth that brings true peace and joy. Wealth brings a lot more responsibility and makes life more complicated. The pursuit of wealth can also become an idol and an obsession. The reality of wealth and its acquisition explains why Jesus said. "It is easier for a camel to go through the eye of a needle than for a rich man to enter the kingdom of God" (Matthew 19:24).

SUCCESS IN GOD'S EYES IS FAR DIFFERENT THAN SUCCESS IN THE WORLD'S EYES.

Our goal is not to focus on worldly success but to keep our eyes on Jesus. God's Word reminds us, "Seek first the kingdom of God and His righteousness, [then] all these things shall be added to you" (Matthew 6:33). God knows what we need, and He wants us to have what we need when we put Him first.

When we are in God's will, whatever we have, such as a simple meal or a pretty day, becomes a blessing. When we view the world from God's eyes, our values change, and we begin to see our trials as blessings because they bring us closer to Jesus. Life is not about who has the most toys or who is blessed with the best health. Life in the Spirit is all about how close a relationship we have with Jesus. Sometimes following Jesus takes us right into the face of great adversity, but Jesus will see us through it even if it is an earthly death that opens heavens' door for eternal life. If we are not following Jesus, adversity will likely make us bitter and separate us from God even further.

God has His own ways of working out His purposes. When a missionary is executed, this does not seem just or fair. The Christian faith is replete with those who were persecuted for Jesus' sake. All but one of the apostles died for following Jesus. We never know what life has in store for us, nor the day or the hour of our departure from this earth. We do know that we will share in the ultimate victory with Jesus Christ, and that heaven awaits us after our short stay here. We also know the Father loves us and will take care of us through any storm even if His solution is calling us home to heaven where there is no pain or suffering. One of the components of faith is to keep on keeping on even in the face of adversity.

We cannot lose sight of the fact that we are sinful people. Sin contributes heavily to the adversity that we face on this earth. When a child is killed in a drive-by shooting, that is a direct and terrible result of a sinful act. The young mother who is run over by a drunk driver is a prime example of how events in our lives are often beyond our control and the result of another person's sin. The only sure thing in our control is to hang on to Jesus for our salvation, knowing He will take care of us in the end. Someday God's perfect justice will prevail, but how and when is up to God. Once again, even in the face of adversity and injustice in this world, God's grace is the only thing sufficient to sustain us and see us through until we get to heaven.

The main question many of us face is: how will we react to adversity?

When adversity or tragedy strikes, we have a choice to make. That choice is: how we will react? Will the tragic event draw us closer to God? God does some of His best work in us when tragedy causes us to turn to Jesus with a greater passion. Out of such brokenness comes the crucifixion of our flesh and growth in the Spirit. Adversity will come. The mark of a Christian is how well he or she faces that adversity.

The good news is that adversity leads to brokenness, and brokenness leads to Jesus. God doesn't seem to do much to us or through us without our being broken.

After the Leap

To be broken is to lay down the flesh and pick up the cross. Paul said it best in Romans 6:6 (NIV): "For we know that our old self was crucified with him so that the body of sin might be done away with, that we should no longer be slaves to sin—because anyone who has died has been freed from sin." When we leave part of the old self on the cross, then we crucify that part of the flesh. When that part of the flesh is gone, new life takes place as the Holy Spirit takes over. Brokenness leads to true strength, the strength of Jesus in us. That is good news. Paul said, "We know that in all things God works for the good of those who love him, who have been called according to his purpose" (Romans 8:28, NIV). Paul did not say tragedy was good. Paul said God would use whatever happens to us for our own good.

THINK ABOUT THE WAYS THAT GOD BRINGS GOOD OUT OF ADVERSITY:

- Adversity causes believers to cry out to God and makes them realize their dependence on God. Through the process believers are drawn closer to God and realize that deliverance comes from God and God alone.

- Adversity gives us compassion for others who are going through pain or suffering in their lives. Also, when others know we previously suffered the same problem that they have, we gain credibility and a better opportunity to speak words of salvation, healing, and encouragement.

- Suffering reminds us that the things we take for granted are truly a blessing of God. Illness, for example, makes us appreciate and give thanks for good health. It is only through suffering that we can appreciate the absence of pain.

- When suffering and adversity are the result of sin, our eyes are opened wider to see the consequences of sin—particularly our own sin. Suffering should lead us to a greater understanding of the holiness of God.

The Bible teaches that true joy and inner peace come from being persecuted for the sake of Jesus Christ. "Blessed are those who are persecuted for righteousness' sake, for theirs is the kingdom of heaven," Jesus told us in the Beatitudes (Matthew 5:10). The apostles were beaten severely and publicly humiliated for preaching the Gospel, yet they "rejoiced that they were counted worthy to suffer shame for His [Jesus] name" (Acts 5:40-41). Suffering for Jesus, therefore, has its own rewards both on earth and in heaven.

No one wants to walk through any dark valleys during life. In the well-known and loved Psalm 23, David said, "Yea, though I walk through the valley of the shadow of death, I will fear no evil; for You are with me; Your rod and Your staff, they comfort me. . . . Surely goodness and mercy shall follow me all the days of my life; and I will dwell in the house of the Lord forever." If you have not done so, memorize Psalm 23. It is a song to the Lord that promises eternal comfort even amidst the valley of the shadow of death.

WE MUST BE READY TO UNDERGO SUFFERING AND PERSECUTION.

Jesus suffered more than any of us when He was tortured to death on the cross. His greatest suffering, which we could never fully appreciate, came from His separation from His Father. When Jesus was on the cross, He cried out, "My God, my God, why have you forsaken me?" Matthew 27:46 (NIV) We cannot imagine what it was like for Jesus, the Son of God, to be separated from the Father for even a minute. Jesus suffered beyond our capacity to comprehend when on that cross He saw all the sin of mankind and saw all the pain that resulted from that sin. Jesus grieved over the sins of the world. Jesus also knew how much His Father hated all that sin and how great the punishment would have to be in order to pay for all of that sin, sparing believers punishment. The punishment that Jesus suffered when He died in our place is so overwhelming that we cannot begin to grasp it. In going to the cross, Jesus faced the ultimate in adversity, but through His faithfulness He triumphed.

Jesus tells us: "Blessed are those who are persecuted because of righteousness, for theirs is the kingdom of heaven" (Matthew 5:10, NIV). When we follow Jesus and are persecuted and undergo hardship, we know we will be rewarded someday and that our suffering is not in vain. Only Jesus can get us through the dark times and the valleys. Our eyes must be on Him and not on ourselves. Self-pity is the weapon of the enemy. To stand in faith and rejoice in our suffering is what God tells us to do in His Word.

WE ARE CALLED TO COMFORT AND ENCOURAGE OTHERS GOING THROUGH TRIALS IN THEIR LIVES.

Be sensitive when a family member or friend is going through deep suffering. Try to see that person as Jesus would—with compassion and understand-

After the Leap

ing. If you have a friend or relative who has suffered a great loss such as the death of a loved one, be discerning and careful about what you say and what you don't say. Be cautious before you say everything is going to be all right. The loss is great, and your friend may have to go through a hard and long period of grief. Be directed by the Holy Spirit. Grief is serious and necessary to the healing process. Just be a friend and love the person who is hurting. Be a good listener. Talk about what your friend wants to talk about. Hug your friend. Pray for your friend. Let your friend cry, even if she is mad at God. That friend needs Jesus more than ever.

WORRY AND ANXIETY ABOUT THE FUTURE IS NOT A CHRISTIAN RESPONSE.

Some people worry constantly about what lies ahead. Others worry about both real and imagined oncoming adversity. Certainly, we should prepare for adversity and avoid it if we can and still be faithful to God. But worry has no place in God's kingdom. Jesus said,

> Do not worry about your life. . . . Which one of you by worrying can add one cubit to his stature? . . . Therefore, do not worry. . . . But seek first the kingdom of God and His righteousness, and all these things shall be added to you. Therefore do not worry about tomorrow, for tomorrow will worry about its own things. Sufficient for the day is its own trouble (Matthew 6:25-34). [Read the entire passage.]

In summary, we are called to live one day at a time and know that we will experience adversity. Know also God will use our suffering to develop our Christian character and bring us closer to Him. The more we can praise God for all things, the more blessed we will be. As Paul said in 2 Corinthians 12:10, "Therefore I take pleasure in infirmities, in reproaches, in needs, in persecutions, in distresses, for Christ's sake. For when I am weak, then I am strong." Always know that God is bigger than any problem you will ever have, and that God and God alone has the power to heal the deepest wound.

"God is our refuge and strength, a very present help in trouble"
(Psalm 46:1).

Discussion Questions

1. What adversity have you been through that brought you closer to Jesus? Describe the experience and how it helped develop your Christian character.

2. Why do you think it is necessary at times for God to use adversity in our lives to draw us closer to Him?

3. Why does God say that when we are weak, we are strong? Why does God say that when we are the least, we are the greatest and vice versa?

4. If a friend is facing an extremely adverse situation, what can you do? What would be your general approach to that friend?

23

JESUS WILL FREE YOU FROM YOUR PAST

"He [God] has delivered us from the power of darkness and translated us into the kingdom of the Son of His love" (Colossians 1:13).

ALL OF US HAVE THINGS IN OUR PASTS FROM WHICH JESUS WANTS TO FREE US.

By now you should have memorized Luke 4:18 in which Jesus said that His mission here on earth was to set us free from our sin, our brokenheartedness, or anything that holds us back from being the person God wants us to be. Jesus gave us the great promise of hope that He can make a difference in our lives. He can change us. He can set us free.

Jesus wants us to be free from the things of the past that hold us back. When we are born again, we begin a new life. In this new life we are to grow and become an entirely different person. We are now free from the sin that once condemned us to eternal damnation. Jesus goes much further with us, and He will set us free from any other chains that may have bound us. First, we must want to change. We must want to be free. That choice is up to us. Jesus has done the saving, and Jesus will do the freeing, but we must submit and do our part if we are to grow as new creatures in Christ.

To a large extent, we are all the products of our pasts. Our value system, our sense of right and wrong, and the way we look at the world are influenced mostly by our childhood and our adult experiences. God has set His standards that we are to live by, but this world, our flesh, and our mortal enemy will do all they can to hinder our growth. Too often we live according to the lies of this world, and these lies as well as old habits hold back our Christian growth from its full potential.

All of us are unique. No two people have the same characteristics. What makes us what we are? God, of course, created us and made each one of us different. We are also what we are because of who our parents are, how they raised us, and how they modeled life for us. We are what we are in part because of what we learned in our homes, in school, on the streets, in the church, and on the athletic field. Our friends and their opinions about life help form the way we view the world. So do the things we see, read, and hear on television and movies, and in books and music. We also are influenced by those good and bad experiences in life that help mold our character and our belief system. Many things help form our view of the world and God. These personal viewpoints cause us to make life choices based on lies instead of the truth of God. The enemy, who is the father of lies, contributes greatly to the lies of this world. And we know he is full of hate, cruelty, and injustice. In short, we become bombarded by things that are not true. Thus, instead of being molded by God, we are molded by our past and pick up a lot of worthless baggage we do not need.

Our parental heritage plays a big part in who we are. Because so much of our view of the world comes from our parents, children have a strong tendency to develop the same traits their parents had. For example, the person in prison is much more likely to have other relatives in prison than someone in the free world. The alcoholic is much more likely to have a father or mother who suffered from the same problem. The sins of the parents can easily be passed down to the third and fourth generation as the Bible warns—unless Jesus intervenes.

Whatever our problem and whatever our background, Jesus wants to free us from our past. Jesus is the way and the truth and the life. Jesus came to show us the truth. When we are adopted into God's family and begin to listen to our Heavenly Father, then we will begin to change. Jesus came to change us. Jesus wants us to get rid of any idea or lifestyle from our past that is sinful. He wants to cleanse us of all of our bad habits. Jesus does not want us to conform to the things of this world.

Many of us are like robots. We want to copy those people who we admire and who appear to have it all together. Most teenagers are prime examples of the strong influence of the world as they work hard trying to dress, talk, and act in accordance with whatever is "in" at the time. God doesn't want us parroting the behavior of others. God wants us to walk in truth and be the man or woman He has called us to be. We must not live by the lies of this world, but by the truth of God. Fundamental changes in our thinking must take place. This requires a commitment to change and the power of the Holy Spirit to overcome.

Most all of us want to be somebody. Most of us want to fulfill a destiny that we believe is ours. Most of us, who are born-again Christians, want to follow Jesus and change into the person He desires us to be. The problem we face is that without the work of the Holy Spirit, true change of the heart does not come. Often, we try to break an old habit or a thought pattern. We manage well for a few days or weeks, and then we fall back into sin. We become discouraged. The enemy tells us we are no good and will never change so we might as well indulge ourselves in sin. We get stuck in a rut. We feel helpless. We lose faith. Then we become sitting ducks for the enemy to take a further toll on our lives.

One basic problem is often our lack of faith that Jesus can change us. We believe Jesus can save us, but we do not accept the fact we can become new creatures in Christ. Thus, many people will stay captives to certain sins all of their lives—even after they have accepted Jesus as their Savior. Make no mistake about it. Jesus came to set the prisoners free (Luke 4:18). Jesus is not talking about those in jail. He is talking about those enslaved to the sins of the past.

FIRST OF ALL, WE NEED TO LOOK HONESTLY AT OURSELVES AND DISCOVER WHAT OUR PROBLEMS ARE.

Some people know exactly what their problem is. Others do not have a clue. Our first step must be to take an honest assessment of ourselves. We must be open and honest with ourselves. Even though God knows everything about us and sees our every flaw, we also need to know what needs to be fixed so we can seek and pray for the right kind of help. Also, we need to confess our sins fully and bring each one of them to God for His forgiveness. We need to know our weaknesses so with God's help we can know what needs fixing.

If we were to make a list of all of the things that hold people back from coming to the Lord or serving Him, the list would be long indeed. Such a list would certainly include the following:

- Addictions such as drugs, alcohol, tobacco, sex, gambling, compulsive spending, overeating, and many more.

- Overwhelming feelings of anger, anxiety attacks, paranoia and persecution, feelings of insignificance, guilt shame, fear, hopelessness, and lack of reason for living.

- Ego problems such as pride, thinking that one is better than others, unbridled ambition, and desire for power.

• Apathy, shutdown emotions, inability to express feelings, depression, iner-
tia, fear of being vulnerable, or entering into relationships with others.

Chances are that most human beings face one or more of the problems listed above. All of these problems are stumbling blocks to a productive life of joy
and peace. Sometimes the discovery process about our past is not easy. Some
Christians would be well-advised to seek Christian counseling so that things can
be recalled, brought up, and discussed. Then solutions can be forthcoming.
Sometimes deliverance from demonic influences is in order. Always prayer is in
order. God's response is sometimes immediate and sometimes slow, but prayer
will work if we are open and teachable and committed to change.

This chapter cannot go into any detailed solutions for particular types of
problems. Problems are many, and personalities vary widely, but there are many
good Christian books, seminars, and counseling available to enlist God's help for
healing. Have faith that God has a solution for you if you are open to change and
willing to take your problem to the church or trusted Christian adviser. One of
the reasons the church exists is to call on the healing power of God to intervene
in the lives of one another. God uses all sorts of ways to heal us. These include
individual prayer, elders laying on hands and praying, a prayer partner, small
groups, the pastor, professional Christian counseling, principles learned from the
Bible, and that old basic remedy of repentance and confession.

FIND OUT THE WAY THE LORD HAS IN MIND TO DEAL WITH
YOUR PAST SO YOU CAN BE FREE.

God uses many different ways and means to work healing. The Bible illustrates different patterns and models for us. Jesus healed in different ways. One
thing Jesus always did was to listen to the Father as to exactly what to do. We
need to do likewise. Always take the problem to the Lord in prayer and ask that
He reveal to you the nature of the problem so you will know how to pray.
Consult your pastor or leader in your church to receive both their prayers and
advice as to what to do. Talking to a mature Christian friend whom you trust and
who has sound Christian discernment is a good idea. What you do not want to
do is get someone's advice simply because that person is a close friend. You need
to be assured that the advice you are receiving is biblical. You need someone who
is mature in the faith, has sound judgment, and believes Jesus does have the power
to heal you from your past. Reading the right Christian book can be very helpful, but do not go to the bookstore and buy a book. Seek advice from your pas-

After the Leap

tor or a mature Christian friend, who has knowledge and experience with the problem that you face. Bad advice can be worse than no advice at all.

God must have your full cooperation and honesty in the process. He wants you to bring the problem to Him. He will lead you to a solution. How He does it is up to Him, but usually He will not force healing on you. You must want to change and cooperate fully. Being open to radical change is a giant first step in the healing process; therefore, go to Jesus constantly in prayer and ask Him to change you. Ask Him to draw you closer to Him. Ask Jesus to transform you more and more to His likeness. As Jesus said, "Ask, and it will be given to you; seek, and you will find; knock, and it will be opened to you" (Matthew 7:7).

You must stay focused on Jesus and have faith that you are a new creation in Christ.

Some individuals have grown so used to their addictions or bad habits that they simply do not want to give them up. They cannot imagine life without whatever it is that they crave to do. When this is the case, the individual must ask for God's help and make a strong resolve to break from the habits of the past. At first, this is usually very hard and painful. But day by day with God's help, the chains will be broken and freedom will emerge. When we are content with the worldly ways of our past, we will not change. The Bible refers to the unwilling- ness to change as hardness of heart. Hardness of heart will prohibit our growth in the Lord the same as it did with the Pharisees. Unless we are willing to make radical changes in our lives, little is likely to happen.

The world is full of people who have chosen to stay enslaved to the past and refuse to let Jesus change them. Let me illustrate a few common examples and patterns. John had a father who was an alcoholic. John's father lived to drink whiskey. This father told John that drinking whiskey would make him a man. John's dad started giving John whiskey when John was young, and the father often drank with John like a buddy during those teenage years. John is now an alcoholic. John likes to drink and believes that is the way real men act. Now John is not only addicted to alcohol, but he believes he will always be a drunk like his father. With that thought pattern, John will pass on the same lie and flawed thinking that "real men always drink" to his son.

George lives to please his mother. George's dad died at an early age. George's mother was a perfectionist. George's mother taught George that his value and worth as a person was based on how well he performed in school and sports. George did well at both. He lived for his mother's praise. Even though George graduated years ago and now has a wife and children, he still lives for his mother's praise. His sense of worth as a person depends on his mother's reactions. George has never grown up. George will never believe he is significant because he will never live up to his mother's expectations. George needs to be free of that lie on which his life is based.

Mary was a victim of child abuse from her father. She felt unloved, dropped out of school, and pursued one boyfriend after another in her search for love. Mary is now a Christian, but she cannot seem to break free of her desire to seek sexual relationships. This leads her into depression, as she feels unclean and unworthy. She is immobilized by the resulting guilt and shame from seeking the wrong kind of love in the wrong kind of places,

In the above cases, the people are living lives based on lies about who they are in Christ. You could no doubt think of many other examples from among those you know. In each example the individual has based his or her life on a false assumption. Lives based on such deceptions are empty and fruitless. The reason is that if we like money, we will never have enough money. The same is true for sex, pleasure, alcohol, power, or anything else of the world. To be free in Christ, we must accept the truth about ourselves and be willing to conform to God's solution with the faith that Jesus can and will do a good work in us.

Whatever false premise you have previously based your life on must be set straight by Jesus. It is never too late to change and become a productive citizen in God's kingdom. The Bible says, "By His stripes we are healed" (Isaiah 53:5). That statement refers to Jesus' completed work on the cross and the unlimited power of His grace.

GOD HAS GIVEN US A VERY SPECIAL RELATIONSHIP WITHIN THE FAMILY OF GOD. WE SHOULD ACT LIKE IT.

You must understand that when we take Jesus into our hearts, we receive many rich blessings, including a new identity, a new family, a new position in Christ, a new heart, a new spirit, and a host of other miraculous life-changing things. Although we previously looked at some of the things we are in Christ, please take a few moments to ponder and consider this awesome list of things describing how close we are in Christ.

- **You are now a child of God** (1 John 3:1), **and an heir of God** (Galatians 4:7).
- **You are a new creation** (2 Corinthians 5:17), **having been chosen by Jesus**

before the beginning of the world (Ephesians 1:4).
- You have been given the mind of Christ (1 Corinthians 2:16).
- You have been firmly rooted in Christ and are now being built up in Him (Colossians 2:7).
- You have been made complete in Christ (Colossians 2:10).
- You have died with Christ and died to the power of sin over your life (Romans 6:1-6).
- You now have direct access to God (Ephesians 2:18).
- You may approach God in faith, boldness, and confidence (Ephesians 3:12).
- You have been given a spirit of love and self-discipline (2 Timothy 1:7).
- You can come with confidence before God to receive His mercy and grace (Hebrews 4:16).
- You are a citizen of heaven (Philippians 3:20) and are chosen and dearly loved by God (1 Thessalonians 1:4).
- You are Jesus' friend (John 15:15).
- You are a member of the body of Christ (1 Corinthians 12:27).
- You are now a stranger to this world (1 Peter 2:11) and an enemy of the devil (1 Peter 5:8).
- You are now reconciled to God and a minister of reconciliation (2 Corinthians 5:18-19).
- Finally, you are God's workmanship, created in Christ for good works, which God prepared beforehand that you should walk in them (Ephesians 2:10).

What a list! Take all of these things from the Word of God and take them fully into the depths of your heart and soul. Just knowing who we are in Christ should be an inspiration. How He loves you! It is beyond comprehension, but it is true. You may want to copy this list to put on the refrigerator door or carry in your Bible or wallet. If you ever have doubts about who you are in Christ, get out this list and absorb it once again. We know the enemy will come in and try to steal the joy and confidence we should have from our relationship to Jesus; therefore, we need to always remind ourselves of our standing in Christ. No one can separate us from His love. Now we need to live like it. What a mighty God we serve.

"I have been crucified with Christ; it is no longer I who live, but Christ lives in me" (Galatians 2:20).

DISCUSSION QUESTIONS

1. Is there anything from your past that is holding you back in any way? If so, what is it? Make a list.

2. Now write out what you plan to do about this so Jesus might free you.

3. Do you need prayer or good Christian counseling to be healed of anything from your past? For what do you need prayer the most?

24
DEVELOPING CHRISTIAN CHARACTER

"But the fruit of the Spirit is love, joy, peace, longsuffering, kindness, goodness, faithfulness, gentleness, self-control. Against such there is no law" (Galatians 5:22-23).

THE CHRISTIAN LIFE IS A PROCESS OF THE DEVELOPMENT OF OUR CHRISTIAN CHARACTER, WHICH COMES BY WAY OF THE HOLY SPIRIT.

God is concerned with our hearts first and foremost. When the Bible refers to our hearts, it is speaking of who we really are deep down inside. Thus, when we talk about our heart and our character, we are talking about the same thing.

Our Christian character is who we are in Christ right now—how close our hearts are to Jesus. Jesus is in the business of transforming our hearts, and He is never through with us during our lifetimes. It is a constant process. Before we knew Jesus, our characters were molded by our flesh. Now Jesus has us. He is our Lord and King, and He wants to change us. The question is: are we being changed or are we content with being the same? As Jesus works to clean up our past, we need to have a keen awareness of our Christian character.

We all need to take a good close look at our true selves and then ask what it will take to produce change. To put this another way, will we allow our flesh or Jesus to determine our character? We have a choice. Development of strong Christian character is the work of the Holy Spirit, but to grow in character, that is to grow in Christ, will require a strong commitment on our part.

Our true character comes from down deep in our being. Our character is who we are when no one is watching. The dictionary defines character as "those peculiar and personal qualities, which are impressed by nature or habit upon a person and which distinguish him from all others." Character is not how we seem to look to others on the outside, but character is who we are on the inside. Our character includes such things as our integrity, our love for others, our patience. Do we tell the truth or lie? Do we love or hate? Do we persevere or give up easily? If we find a bunch of money and no one sees us find it, will we keep the money or seek to find the owner? These things are reflections of our character.

Jesus is the best character builder. In fact, He is the only true and good character builder. The truth is that our character will always have its roots in one of two places. It will come from our own weak and sinful flesh or from the Spirit of God. All goodness, righteousness, and truth come to us through God's Holy Spirit (Ephesians 5:9). We cannot have life without the Spirit. The Spirit gives life, as John tells us (John 6:63). "The mind of sinful man is death, but the mind controlled by the Spirit is life and peace" (Romans 8:6, NIV). Jesus came not just to save and heal us, but also to develop our Christian character so that He can draw us close to Himself and use us in His work. Jesus comes to live in us through the Holy Spirit so that the Holy Spirit will change our hearts. To change the heart is to change the character.

Although God made each one of us different and unique, we all have the capacity to develop a Christlike character. Our only alternative is to walk in our old ways and be brought down by our old selfish habits. Different people struggle with different sins. Some sinful habits, which are character flaws, are so debilitating and destructive that they keep people from functioning in a normal way. Such sin gives the enemy a wide entryway to come in and do great damage. The combination of a weak flesh and evil spiritual forces can keep people enslaved unless Jesus sets the prisoner free. All of us have character flaws that need healing by the power of Jesus through the Holy Spirit. All Christians need to constantly work on their character by becoming more Christlike. All of us need a closer relationship with Jesus. The closer we are to Jesus, the more our character will grow and produce the good fruit of the Spirit.

Anyone who suffers from longstanding character defects such as dishonesty, any addiction, or serious character flaw needs special help from the church. This is one of the reasons why the church, the body of Christ, exists. This chapter will not explain in detail how a Christian should deal with problems such as bitterness, addictions, lust, anger, or whatever. All I can stress here is that you must have faith that Jesus can deal with any problem. You must seek the right kind of help. You can start by talking to your pastor or very mature Christian friends in order to know how to proceed. Jesus can and will bring all of us from weakness to strength if we let Him. The purpose of this chapter is to explain which character traits come from the Holy Spirit and which come from our flesh. Do not

After the Leap

be discouraged. Jesus is not finished with you yet.

THE FOLLOWING CHARACTER TRAITS ARE NOT DESIRABLE. DO YOU IDENTIFY WITH ANY OF THESE?

Galatians 5 gives us an excellent summary of character traits that are sinful as well as traits that reflect the life and love of Jesus. Turn to Galatians 5 and read the chapter carefully. According to Galatians 5:19-21, the bad character traits that come from the flesh and on which Satan preys are as follows:

- **Adultery, fornication, uncleanness, licentiousness.** Anyone who has a sexual relationship outside marriage has a problem. This includes any lustful habits such as pornography. Jesus wants us to have pure hearts and minds.

- **Idolatry and sorcery** represent any worship of other gods or dabbling in the occult or the supernatural.

- **Hatred, contentions, jealousies, outbursts of wrath, dissensions, heresies, murders.** These traits are the opposite of the love Jesus demonstrated and calls us to. God does not want us to have any malicious thoughts about someone else.

- **Selfish ambition and envy** should not be a part of our character. These grow out of coveting, which we discussed before in the Ten Commandments.

- **Drunkenness, revelries, and the like.** Wild living has no part in the Christian life. Getting drunk and going to wild parties will be an open door to the enemy and other sins.

How are you doing with every issue raised on the list above? If we look at this list of character weaknesses set forth by Paul in Galatians 5:22-25, we see the same sins as when we studied the Ten Commandments. Jesus said, "He who has My commandments and keeps them, it is he who loves Me. And he who loves Me will be loved by My Father, and I will love him and manifest Myself to him" (John 14:21).

Your character traits largely depend on what your most basic desires are. A good test is to ask yourself: what is my heart focused on? What do you desire most in life? What does your mind dwell on? Jesus said, "For out of the heart proceed evil thoughts, murders, adulteries, fornications, thefts, false witness, and blasphemies" (Matthew 15:19). As you can see in this verse, Jesus has focused on most of the Ten Commandments and reminded us that our character flaws and our character strengths come from the heart. The heart that seeks after the flesh, that is to please our natural desires, will produce sin and weakness of character. The heart that seeks after Jesus will produce godly character and the good fruit mentioned next by Paul in Galatians 5.

THE FOLLOWING CHARACTER TRAITS, FROM THE HOLY SPIRIT, ARE WHAT WE SHOULD LONG FOR.

Paul tells us of another list of character traits that come from Jesus through the Holy Spirit. These are the fruit of the Spirit that make up a strong Christian character and stand in direct contrast to the last list. Galatians 5 tells us this fruit of the Holy Spirit includes, love, joy, peace, long-suffering or patience, kindness, goodness, faithfulness, gentleness, and self-control. Let's examine the fruit of the Spirit.

- **Love** comes first, of course, and love in its fullest sense includes everything else. Remember, God is love. Jesus is love. Love is the unselfish giving of ourselves to others as Jesus did for us. If we are full of love, the other traits should follow.

- **Joy** is the mark of a Christian. Jesus does not want us to lead dull or unhappy lives. Jesus does not want us to look as if we just got run over by a freight train. Jesus brings us joy. We should be joyful. The Psalms tell us time and time again to be joyful in our praise of our Lord and joyful with one another. "The joy of the Lord is your strength" (Nehemiah 8:10). There is no strength in bitterness or discontent.

- **Peace** comes from God and God alone. Jesus said, "Come to Me, all you who labor and are heavy laden, and I will give you rest. Take My yoke upon you and learn from Me, for I am gentle and lowly in heart, and you will find rest for your souls" (Matthew 11:28-29). God is our refuge and our strength. He is our peace, which is a gift of the Spirit of God.

- **Patience,** or long-suffering, as some translations of the Bible say, is a godly characteristic. We are called to hang in there and know that God will come to our rescue. We are called to be patient, which, in other words, means to wait on the Lord and have faith. Remember that suffering produces perseverance. Perseverance produces character and character produces hope. Patience is the ability to persevere without anxiety.

- **Goodness** comes from the Holy Spirit also. As a believer, we should have goodness. We should be people of God and follow His commandments. When we do this, our lives demonstrate goodness. True goodness comes only from God, as Jesus said. It comes out of our heart when Jesus is living in us.

- **Kindness** is a form of love. When we are kind, we are thoughtful and considerate. When we are kind, we express the love of Jesus to others through the little things we do for them. When we are kind, we are not selfish or harsh or judgmental. Kindness includes being courteous to others in the little things of life. To be kind is not to be mean, rude, overbearing, or controlling.

- **Faithfulness** means we will keep on following God and His ways even when we cannot see the end of the road. We act in faith from the knowledge that God is there and that He will take care of us and provide for us. Being faithful means we believe in the promises of God and stand on them even though we cannot see how everything is going to work out.

- **Gentleness** is a form of meekness and humility. Gentleness is when we are very sensitive to another person's feelings. Gentleness is to be very tender in our relationships with others. We will not do things or say things that will be hurtful to the other person when we act out of gentleness. Gentleness is to be thoughtful and soft-spoken as opposed to harsh, loud, rough, or meanspirited.

- **Self-control** is the last fruit of the Spirit in this list and is so necessary for the Christian life. People who lose their temper frequently are usually out of control. To be addicted to anything is to be out of control because that individual cannot say no. We are not called as Christians to give in to our raw emotions and say or do hurtful things, no matter how strong the urge. If we are walking closely with Jesus, a lack of self-control will not be a problem.

HUMILITY IS ONE OF THE MOST IMPORTANT CHARACTER TRAITS WE CAN HAVE. HUMILITY IS THE OPPOSITE OF PRIDE AND ARROGANCE.

As we mentioned earlier in the book, pride is the worst of sins. The proud person believes that the important thing in life is to seek glory for oneself. The proud person puts self first and God second or not at all. The proud person does not know God, does not fear God, and gives God no credit. Yet, God is due all the credit and all the glory. The proud person is full of his own self-importance. In a sense, the proud person is his own god. Pride was behind the first sin and the fall of Adam and Eve in the Garden of Eden when they ate of the forbidden fruit. The basic problem was pride because Adam and Eve wanted to be independent of God and do their own thing.

The opposite character trait of pride is humility. God wants us to be humble, and God will bless the humble person. God makes that promise time and time again in the Bible. Humility is defined as being submissive, not proud or arrogant. It also means to be respectful and meek and to have a modest opinion of oneself. Paul said that we are to show true humility to all men (Titus 3:2). God wants us to seek humility and righteousness (Zephaniah 2:3). We are instructed: "Do nothing out of or selfish ambition or vain conceit, but in humility consider others better than yourself" (Philippians 2:3, NIV). To be humble is to recognize the truth about our own inadequacies and shortcomings and the truth about our perfect and all-wise God.

God has strong warnings for the proud and great comfort for the humble. God said, "I will halt the arrogance of the proud, and will lay low the haughtiness of the terrible" (Isaiah 13:11). To be prideful is to be wicked. God said He would look at every proud man and bring him low (Job 40:12). Yet, the humble receive the blessing of God. God said, "This is the one I esteem: he who is humble and contrite in spirit and trembles at my Word" (Isaiah 66:2, NIV).

The ultimate example of humility was Jesus. Jesus did the most humble act of all time when He suffered the humiliation of the cross. Jesus' entire life was one of humility as He took the form of a servant. Jesus said: "Take my yoke upon you and learn from me, for I am gentle and humble in heart" (Matthew 11:29, NIV). Ephesians 4:2 (NIV) tells us to follow Jesus' example and "be completely humble and gentle."

God's blessing upon the humble is great. Luke 1:52 (NIV) says, "He [God] has brought down rulers from their thrones, but has lifted up the humble." First Peter 5:6 (NIV) says, "Humble yourselves, therefore, under God's mighty hand,

After the Leap

that He may lift you up." Proverbs 11:2 says that with humility we obtain wisdom. Proverbs 22:4 says, "Humility and the fear of the Lord bring wealth and honor and life."

JESUS GAVE US THE BEATITUDES, WHICH ARE ABOUT HUMILITY AND LOVE.

In the most important sermon of all time, the Sermon on the Mount, Jesus spoke of attitudes and character traits that Jesus says we are to have. These traits are called "Beatitudes." They flow from the work of the Holy Spirit in us as we become more like Jesus. These traits have the common characteristic of love, humility, and servanthood, where the lowly in mind and spirit are blessed beyond measure (Matthew 5:3-12). Turn to this passage and read it now. The word *blessed* or *happy* (as some translations render the word) refers to a deep inner peace that comes as a result of such an attitude. Basically, the Beatitudes teach us that when we are broken of our own fleshly desires, we can take on the things of the Spirit. To be broken means to crucify our own flesh, pushing ourselves out of the way so the Holy Spirit can transform us.

Every Christian should do an in-depth study of each Beatitude. The first one, **"Blessed are the poor in spirit, for theirs is the kingdom of heaven"** teaches us that when we realize we have no good spiritual state without God and that Jesus provides it all, then we will be blessed. That, of course, is what salvation is about and that is why the reward for those who are poor in spirit is to "inherit the kingdom of heaven."

"Blessed are those who mourn, for they shall be comforted." Jesus wept over Jerusalem because He saw so much sin and so many who were lost among God's chosen people. To mourn is to suffer because of the sin in this world and its dire consequences. Those who mourn with the compassion of Jesus will be comforted.

"Blessed are the meek, for they shall inherit the earth." To be meek is to be submissive to Jesus and His ways and to put our own ways and our own pride aside.

"Blessed are those who hunger and thirst for righteousness, for they shall be filled" means we should hunger and thirst for Jesus and His righteousness. God's law and His Word are so important to our lives that we should desire them from the depths of our souls.

"Blessed are the merciful, for they shall obtain mercy" means we should have great love and compassion for those who are hurting, and we should do something about it. To be merciful is to extend the love of Christ in a tangible way to those less fortunate.

"Blessed are the pure in heart, for they shall see God" refers to that purity we receive from God in the form of total forgiveness because of Jesus' death on the cross. This is the only way we can be cleansed, and this leads us to a greater understanding of God and His amazing grace.

"Blessed are the peacemakers, for they shall be called sons of God" refers to those who work to bring salvation, that is reconciliation and peace between God and man. Also, as we go about ministering to others, we bring God's peace to men and between men as well.

"Blessed are those who are persecuted for righteousness' sake, for theirs is the kingdom of heaven." In this last beatitude, Jesus makes it clear that it is an honor to be persecuted for His sake as we go about His business. He reminds us that our reward will be great. These Beatitudes challenge us and make us examine our hearts and our minds from deep inside. Christians should always ask themselves: how am I doing in my "beatitudes?"

THE HOLY SPIRIT DOES THE WORK, BUT JESUS CALLS US TO COMMITMENT AND OBEDIENCE.

Without the work of the Holy Spirit, we will not be able to grow in our Christian character. It is from the Spirit that the good fruit comes. In order for this fruit to come, we must humbly submit to the will of God and look forward to the change He will make in us. And we must do this with the love of Christ, who embodies fully all perfect attributes of character. So, put on the character traits of Jesus.

Colossians 3:12–17 sums up the character that we are to take on as a new person in Christ. We are to:

> put on tender mercies, kindness, humbleness of mind, meekness, longsuffering; bearing with one another and forgiving one another . . . even as Christ forgave you, so you also must do. But above all these things put on love, which is the bond of perfection. And let the peace of God rule in your hearts. . . . Let the word of Christ dwell in you richly in all wisdom, teaching and admonishing one another in psalms and hymns and spiritual songs, singing with grace in your heart to the Lord. And whatever you do in word or deed, do all in the name of the Lord Jesus, giving thanks to God the Father through Him.

The ultimate question is this: will you take such full responsibility for your life that you will do what God wants instead of what you want? Will you love Jesus so much and obey Him so much that He will be able to do a good work in you? Yes, it is true that only the Spirit of God can change your heart, but this is only possible if you let Him. This is only possible if you obey and turn control of your life over to Him. Who is in control of your life? Ask yourself that eternal question. Is it your flesh or is it Jesus? Which one are you sold out to? You cannot have it both ways.

"Do not be conformed to this world, but be transformed by the renewing of your mind, that you may prove what is that good and acceptable and perfect will of God" (Romans 12:2).

DISCUSSION QUESTIONS

1. Make a list of the good traits just discussed from Galatians 5. Then on a separate sheet of paper make a list of the bad traits mentioned in Galatians 5. Now write out how you are doing in each of the good character traits (the fruit of the Spirit). Then do the same for each bad character.

2. Which of the bad traits do you need to work on? What is your plan to change these traits in your character?

3. Which of the character traits from the good list do you need to improve on? How do you plan to go about this? Write it out. Keep your plan in your prayer journal and check on yourself every month to see how you are doing.

4. How would you evaluate your openness and willingness to make major changes in your life?

25
WALKING IN THE SPIRIT OR THE VICTORIOUS LIFE

"Our old man was crucified with Him, that the body of sin might be done away with, that we should no longer be slaves of sin"
(Romans 6:6).

JESUS WANTS US TO WALK IN THE SPIRIT, NOT THE FLESH.

The first 24 chapters of this book covered many basic biblical principles. In one way or another all of these principles teach us how to walk in the Spirit. Walking in the Spirit begins with the moment of salvation when we humbly admit we must put our faith in Jesus for our salvation. Then, as we give up our own flesh and turn our lives over to Jesus more each day, we are on the road to walking in the Spirit. Walking in the Spirit begins with repentance and salvation and grows to the extent we come to love and obey Jesus.

Walking in the Spirit is a matter of control. We cannot walk in the Spirit of God if our flesh is in control. As that praise song says, "I surrender all." We must surrender our flesh and take up our cross and follow Jesus. We will either follow the desires of our flesh and let the enemy gain a stronghold, or we will follow Jesus. Which will it be? Who is in control? If Jesus is in control, then we will walk in the Spirit indeed.

Jesus has called us not to a spirit of fear but to a spirit of boldness. He wants us to courageously take up our cross and follow Him (Matthew 16:24). He calls us to do this on a daily basis. Jesus will give us the victorious life because He defeated Satan once and for all with His death on the cross, giving us our salvation from sin; therefore, we are not to be discouraged but to be joyful as we realize we serve the King and are on the winning side.

After the Leap

As we journey through life and grow spiritually, we will come to know the great truth that "It is the Spirit who gives life; the flesh profits nothing" (John 6:63). That is why our life on this earth is a constant process of relinquishing control from our old self to God, in order to make room for the Spirit. When we have emptied ourselves of ourselves, then the Spirit of God will come in, will change us, and will empower us to be disciples of Christ.

Of course, we will never finish our battle against our own flesh while we are here on this earth. Paul walked in the Spirit, yet he realized the battle against the flesh was a daily battle and none of us are without sin. Paul said, "For the good that I will to do, I do not do; but the evil I will to not do, that I practice" (Romans 7:19). Paul realized he would fight his own flesh until the day he went to heaven; nevertheless, Paul also realized that he no longer was a slave to sin but had been set free from the power of sin by Jesus. In Paul's early life, he was a prisoner to sin as he relentlessly pursued his fleshly pride and ruthless ambition. The reign of sin in Paul's life was so great that he persecuted hundreds of innocent Christians and ordered many to be stoned to death. Then Paul met Jesus and was saved. Paul began a life of obedience to Jesus. He gave his all to Jesus. He obeyed Jesus everywhere, including dark damp dungeons, shipwrecks, beatings, and in the worst of places. As Paul obeyed and surrendered his life to Christ, the Spirit of God took control of Paul's life.

Paul kept his eyes on Jesus. Paul focused his mind on God's will and not his own. Paul tells us to set our minds on Jesus: "For those who live according to the flesh set their minds on the things of the flesh, but those who live according to the Spirit, the things of the Spirit" (Romans 8:5). Even though we, like Paul, will never finish battling our own flesh, we can have the Spirit reign in our lives. And when the Spirit is in control, we will not only have joy and peace, but we will also be empowered by the Spirit to fulfill God's purpose for our lives. We still must do our part.

To walk in the Spirit is to be reliant on God for everything. This includes our purpose and vision for life. It is Jesus through the Holy Spirit who will give us a vision for life. The Bible says that "without a vision the people perish." The Spirit gives us our purpose since in Him we have our very being. Jesus wants us to have that vision and fulfill the purpose that God had in mind for us long before we were born. God has now sent His Spirit to breathe new life and real life into the earthly, sinful vessels we call bodies. By the power of the Holy Spirit, we can have life and have it abundantly for the first time as we grow in Christ.

Mother Teresa said, "The worst condition in life is to be nobody to nobody." With a strong faith in God, a close intimate walk with Jesus, and the Holy Spirit living in power within us, we know we are somebody. We can overcome the old ways. We can climb those mountains we dared not climb in those fleshly bodies of the old self. Life becomes exciting as we see God do a work in us in areas we never dreamed could be changed.

WALKING IN THE SPIRIT REQUIRES A STRONG COMMITMENT OF OBEDIENCE FROM US.

As we begin this walk, we must commit ourselves to obedience in Christ that starts with a personal relationship with Him. Through prayer and praise and staying in the Word, we are called to love others as we unselfishly reach out to those who are hurting in the name of Jesus. As we obey and keep our eyes on Jesus and not the things of this world, something miraculous begins to happen. Jesus starts to transform us into His image. As Romans 12:2 tells us, "Do not be conformed to this world, but be transformed by the renewing of your mind." This transformation has taken place in millions of Christians. It is a miracle of God and only possible by the power of the Holy Spirit. That power is now available to all of us who believe.

As we grow in Christ as citizens of His kingdom and soldiers in His army, we align ourselves, especially our hearts, with the living God. We begin to realize that truly "He who is in us is greater that he (the enemy) who is in the world." We begin to realize that as we throw ourselves into this thing called the Christian faith that the things of this world do become strangely dim and insignificant. And we begin to see light at the end of the tunnel that truly we can "be conquerors in Christ."

God has an unlimited storehouse of blessings for us. God's Spirit is unlimited in power as to what He might do for us. But first of all, we need to want it. To receive God's Holy Spirit more abundantly, we must desire it deeply from our hearts. Developing a loving and intimate personal relationship with Jesus is the key. This relationship grows out of our love and obedience to Jesus as we focus on what He wants us to do. That is why the basics of the faith are so important. There are just certain things we must do to grow in Christ. Are you praying constantly? Are you reading the Bible daily? Are you loving your time of praise and worship? Are you reaching out to others? Are you part of a church body that stands together and ministers together? Do you repent and confess when you do wrong? Do you love Jesus more than anything else?

Is there any habitual or constant sin that is a roadblock to walking in the Spirit? Are you obeying God's commandments? Walking in the Spirit is hard work and a matter of submitting to God rather than our own fleshly desires. It

After the Leap

also involves a totally different way of thinking. God will increase His Holy Spirit in direct proportion to our love and obedience. As the Spirit lives more and more in us, the flesh will become less and less.

One good test of how well we are walking in the Spirit is our reaction to our own personal sin. How do you see your sin? Do you see sin in a totally different light than you once did? Does your sin and its consequences break your heart? Do you weep over it as Jesus did? Are you seeing sin through the eyes of Jesus who wept over the sin of Jerusalem? To walk in the Spirit is to mourn over sin. The person who mourns over the consequences of sin will be blessed by God, as Jesus tells us in the Beatitudes (Matthew 5). Do you mourn over your own sin and the sins of others and the consequences of sin that you see about you in the world? The person who walks in the Spirit takes sin very, very seriously; and that person cannot wait to confess and get right with God when sin invades his or her life. What is your reaction to sin and particularly to your own sin?

When we are walking in the Spirit, we will see God's greatness and the power of His love, grace, and mercy. Our eyes will be opened to understand better about "Amazing Grace," that grace that includes salvation when we did not deserve it. As that favorite old hymn goes, "[I once] was blind, but now I see." The Spirit removes the blindness and draws our hearts toward the living Jesus. To walk in the Spirit is not just to *understand* more about His grace but also to be ready to *receive it* in much greater abundance.

Colossians 2:6-7 spells it out clearly: "As you therefore received Christ Jesus the Lord, so walk in Him, rooted and built up in Him and established in the faith, as you have been taught, abounding in it with thanksgiving." Paul goes on to say not to walk in deceit or the empty traditions of men or according to the world because "you are complete in Him," Christ Jesus (Colossians 2:8-10).

WHEN WE WALK IN THE SPIRIT, WE ARE NOT ALONE. WE ARE PART OF GOD'S ARMY.

We live in a time when Jesus wants all of His people mobilized for battle. The harvest is plentiful, but the workers are few, as Jesus told His disciples (Matthew 9:37). Today both the harvest and the workers are growing. But more harvesters are needed. The truth is we live in an exciting time. We may live in the most sinful time in history when we consider the millions murdered by abortion and the civilized countries abandoning God's laws for lawlessness. At the same time God is moving in history as never before. Record numbers are coming to Christ daily. Nearly all the people groups of the world are being reached for

Christ. Today, there is a great manifestation of the work of the Holy Spirit as all kinds if miracles are taking place throughout the world. There is a growing spirit of unity within the church as more churches are joining together to do God's work. We live in a time of a great worldwide prayer movement. It is prayer that breaks down the strongholds of the enemy. God is doing wonderful things through His people, and the opportunity to serve the kingdom has never been greater. Those who are walking in the Spirit are doing those things that Jesus said His believers would do.

We are being called to join Jesus in His marvelous work throughout the world. Of course, we can do nothing for God's kingdom on our own power. Only when we are empowered by the Holy Spirit can we do great things in the name of Jesus. What a mighty God we serve. Our God desires to bring all people to Himself. The Bible tells us so. God enjoys reaching down to a sinful soul and bringing forth a new birth in Christ. God wants to nurture that infant believer so He can develop a heart for Christ that can be used in God's army. When we grow in Christ and are used by Him, we are on the way to living the victorious life. We are called to step out in faith. Although we receive our salvation through faith and not our good works, remember that faith without works is dead (James 2:17). What James is saying is that faith without any works is not faith at all. It is just talk. We demonstrate our faith by our actions and how we live.

God fulfills His promises and lives up to everything that His Word declares. Every gift that God provided those early Christians in the Book of Acts is also available to us today. Jesus said He was leaving so that the Holy Spirit would come for all His disciples (John 15:26). Jesus also said that we would do greater things than He did (John 14:12). Of course, we are imperfect humans and will never approach the perfection of Jesus. Jesus meant that when He left this earth all believers would have access to the miraculous work of the Holy Spirit. Jesus meant that God would move miraculously through believers around the world for generations to come, and that the mighty Holy Spirit would produce miracles in even greater abundance, all for God's glory. By the power of the Holy Spirit, God can do for us and through us whatever He desires. As Paul said, "Through Christ, all things are possible."

GOD WANTS US TO BE EQUIPPED AND READY, WILLING, AND ABLE TO JOIN IN THE WORK HE HAS PLANNED FOR EACH ONE OF US.

At this time in history, God is calling His church, that is all of His followers to serve Him. The question for each of us is: are we ready? The time may be short. The church is called from being lukewarm to become the radiant and perfect bride of Christ (Revelation 3:14-22). Instead of locking our church doors so the unwanted cannot come in, we must open the doors and welcome the lost with open arms. Thus, we must take to the streets, the prisons, and the neighborhoods where Jesus ministered, to be used by God to reclaim what the enemy has taken. The Spirit of God makes the impossible possible.

The old walls of religion must come down while new walls must be built on the solid rock of Jesus. The dead church serves no purpose of God and has no place in the kingdom. Jesus said He would spit the lukewarm church out of His mouth (Revelation 3:14-16). Jesus wants His church to be on fire with the fire of the Holy Spirit. Jesus is raising up a new church, His holy bride, who will be triumphant at the end of the age (Revelation 21:9; 22:5).

None of us has long to live on earth whether the Second Coming occurs tomorrow or whether we die a few months or decades from now. Each day is important to God. Each day is a blessing, a day God has made, so rejoice and be glad in it and serve the Mighty King.

The Prophet Isaiah proclaimed that Jesus was coming to set the prisoners free (Isaiah 61:1). Jesus fulfilled that promise by His own admission: "The Spirit of the Lord is upon Me, because He has anointed Me to preach the gospel to the poor. He has sent me to heal the brokenhearted, to preach deliverance to the captives" (Luke 4:18-19, 21). This is a powerful message that will radically change the lives of all who take Jesus into their hearts. Jesus will save. He will deliver. He will heal. He will set the prisoners free. As believers, we have been crucified with Christ that we should no longer be slaves to sin (Romans 6:6). Jesus who is in you is greater than he (the devil) who is in the world (1 John 4:4). As Jesus makes us into new people, He is also calling us into His service.

JESUS HAS OVERCOME THE ENEMY. JESUS HAS WON. SO GET ON THE WINNING TEAM AND RUN THE RACE BY THE POWER OF THE HOLY SPIRIT.

What we all must realize is that Jesus has overcome the enemy. John tells us: "Whatever is born of God overcomes the world. And this is the victory that has overcome the world—our faith. Who is he who overcomes the world, but he who believes that Jesus is the Son of God?" (1 John 5:4-5) Remember "the sufferings of this present time are not worthy to be compared with the glory which shall be revealed in us" (Romans 8:18).

The Spirit-filled life is one of praise and joy and thanksgiving. First

Thessalonians 5:16-18 tells us to: "Rejoice always, pray without ceasing, in everything give thanks; for this is the will of God in Christ Jesus for you." Is your life so full of praise and prayer and thanksgiving that you continually invite the Holy Spirit to come in and strengthen you for the living of your days?

The words of Paul ring out again in Romans 8:37 (NIV), "In all these things we are more than conquerors through him who loved us." Just think, all who believe in Christ are conquerors of this world through Christ. "To live is Christ, and to die is gain" (Philippians 1:21). Jesus said, "And he who does not take his cross and follow after Me is not worthy of Me. He who finds his life will lose it, and he who loses his life for My sake will find it" (Matthew 10:38-39).

We have a choice. We can play the "poor me" game and keep our heads in the sand, or we can step out in faith and begin to soar like an eagle on God's power and under His wing. What will it be? Step out in faith. Try it God's way. We do not have to run the race on our own because we have Jesus at our side. All we have to do is enter the race and start running and never give up. We will win the race, not by our own power or might, but by the power of Jesus living in us. What we are called to do is to take the first step, then the next, and the next with the faith God will empower us to finish the race. We are to "run with endurance the race that is set before us" (Hebrews 12:1). When we finish we will be victorious. This is because if God is for us, who can be against us? (Romans 8:31)

Remember, the important thing is not how your life starts but how it ends. How will you be remembered? Will it be as one who followed Jesus and reflected His love? This is the mark of a good disciple. And finally, when the race is over, will we hear those cherished words of the Master at the gate of heaven, "Well done, good and faithful servant" (Matthew 25:21). So finish the race and fulfill the purpose Jesus has called you (Acts 20:24). Grow in Christ.

What a glorious thing awaits us as at the end of this life on earth when our souls enter heaven to be with Jesus forever. Revelation 21:4, 7 says, "God will wipe away every tear from their eyes; there shall be no more death, nor sorrow, nor crying; and there shall be no more pain, for the former things have passed away. He who overcomes shall inherit all things, and I will be his God and he shall be My son." And Revelation 21:9-27 describes the glory of the New Jerusalem that awaits those whose names are written in the Lamb's Book of Life, thanks to Christ Jesus, our Lord and Savior.

"I have fought the good fight, I have finished the race, I have kept the faith" (2 Timothy 4:7).

After the Leap

Discussion Questions

1. Write out the vision that God has given you for your future. Spend some time thinking and praying about this first.

2. How can you receive more of the Holy Spirit? What can you start doing to insure a greater increase?

3. How does reaching out in faith and ministering to others relate to walking in the Spirit?

26

EXAMINE YOURSELF

"Examine yourselves as to whether you are in the faith. Prove your-selves. Do you not know yourselves, that Jesus Christ is in you?—unless indeed you are disqualified (2 Corinthians 13:5).

The last command Jesus gave us in the Book of Matthew was, "Go and make disciples of all the nations." Jesus came to save us, and now He calls us to a greater purpose, that is to be His disciples. We are to be trained and equipped and then sent forth to train and equip others, all for the purpose of glorifying God and bringing others into the kingdom.

Our entire purpose in living is to love Jesus so much that our love for Him overflows into the lives of everyone we meet. We were born to serve our Savior. In fact, the Bible says that we were created for good works. Right after Paul tells us in Ephesians 2:8 that we are saved only through faith and not by our good works, Paul tells us in verse 10, "For we are His workmanship, created in Christ Jesus for good works, which God prepared beforehand, that we should walk in them." The Bible says also that once we get to heaven, we will be rewarded in accordance with our good works. Therefore, doing good works by the power of Christ and for Christ goes to the heart of why we exist in the first place.

Are you doing good works and growing as a disciple? Are you just sitting back and missing out on all of the joy from doing those good works God has planned for you? The way to know is to examine yourself honestly and objec-tively. Did you know the Bible says that every time you take communion that you are to examine yourself? (2 Corinthians 13:5) Only by taking a personal invento-ry of your spiritual life can you have any idea about your walk with Christ. Only then can you know whether or not your personal relationship with Jesus is grow-ing. Are you becoming equipped to do God's work? Are you working within the

After the Leap

church to advance His kingdom? Are you reaching out in love to those who are sick, hungry, or in prison? Are you sharing your faith and discipling others how to walk with Christ?

Where do you stand at this moment in this eternal race of life? Are you standing still, coasting, walking, or running the race? What did you do this day or this week that had eternal significance? What would Jesus say about you if you were being judged this very day? Someday, and it will be soon, you will stand before the King of Kings and Lord of Lords, and Jesus will ask you, "What did you do to further My kingdom?" As He looks into your eyes, you will know He knows the answer and that He knows your every act of love in His name. Are you getting ready for that day?

Every Christian is accountable to God. We all must be accountable to other people in our lives as well. We must be accountable to our church, to our family, to those we work for, and to ourselves. All of us need some special person or a small intimate group of people to hold us accountable in our Christian walk. The ultimate object of this is to insure our accountability to God. Taking responsibility for our lives is a must for the Christian.

Our spiritual life is of eternal significance. We must grow in Christ and our walk in the Spirit. This will not happen by accident. This chapter focuses on the inventory each of us should take in order to determine where we are in our spiritual walk with Christ. The Bible says we will be known by our fruit. How much fruit are you producing? How much is God using you to share His love in a lost and hurting world? Remember, we are the branches and He, Jesus, is the vine. How attached to the vine are you on a daily basis? This inventory will help you measure that. Are you living for Christ or for yourself? Are you a citizen of heaven and part of God's kingdom, or are you still too much in this world? You can only have one citizenship.

Remember, you were put here for a purpose, that is God's purpose, and you are called to run the race and fight the good fight—not on your own power but with His power. Are you doing that? Read these following words from Philippians 3:8-14 slowly and carefully and ask yourself if they describe your attitude, your vision for life, and your heart.

> But indeed I also count all things loss for the excellence of the knowledge of Christ Jesus my Lord, for whom I have suffered the loss of all things, and count them as rubbish, that I may gain Christ and be found in Him, not having my own righteousness, which is from the law, but that which is through

faith in Christ, the righteousness which is from God by faith; that I may know Him and the power of His resurrection, and the fellowship of His sufferings, being conformed to His death, if, by any means, I may obtain to the resurrection of the dead.

Not that I have already attained, or am already perfected; but I press on, that I may lay hold of that for which Christ Jesus has also laid hold of me. Brethren, I do not count myself to have apprehended; but one thing I do, forgetting those things which are behind and reaching forward to those things which are ahead, I press toward the goal for the prize of the upward call of God in Christ Jesus (Philippians 3:8-14).

At this time, go off in a quiet place and take the time you need to answers the questions in this personal inventory. Make an honest appraisal of where you are in your Christian life. Your answers will tell you how you are doing and will suggest to you how to grow in Christ.

As you consider the following areas of your life, please read the passages from the Bible to remind you where God stands on these subjects.

Prayer life—Matthew 6:9-13; Matthew 14:23; Mark 11:24; Romans 12:12; Philippians 4:6; Colossians 4:2; 1 Thessalonians 5:17.
• Do you pray daily and for how long?
• Do you keep a prayer list?
• Do you keep a prayer journal and write down each prayer that is answered?

The Bible—Psalm 12:6; Psalm 119; John 1:1; John 1:14; Romans 15:4; 2 Timothy 3:15-17; James 1:22-23.
• How often do you read the Bible?
• What is your personal plan for Bible study?
• What is your plan to memorize verses?

Praise and worship—Psalms 145—150.
• How often do you just praise and worship the Lord?
• How much do you enjoy worshiping the Lord?
• How do you praise and worship the Lord when you are alone?

Intimate Christian friends—John 15:12; John 15:17; Romans 1:11-12; Romans 15:5-7; 1 Peter 3:8; 1 Peter 4:8-10.

After the Leap

- Are you in a small group?
- Do group members hold each other accountable?
- Do those in your small group feel free to talk about their personal lives?

What old sins in your life do you need to deal with?
- What are the specific sins you need to deal with?
- Have you taken these to the church or others in the faith for prayer and counsel?
- What are you doing in your life to get rid of bad habits and sins?

What are you doing to further the kingdom of God right now?
- Write down any ministry in which you are currently serving Jesus.
- What is your spiritual obligation to your own family? Write down what you are doing and also what you should be doing. Pray about it.
- What particular things do you feel that God is calling you to do for His kingdom right now? Write them down and write down how you plan to respond.
- What further equipping or assistance do you need to be more effective? How do you plan to go about becoming equipped for God's work?

How are you spending your time and money?

Go back and review your answers in chapter 21. Are you are satisfied that you are where God wants you to be? What adjustments do you need to make in your budget, your giving to the work of God's kingdom, and the use of your time?

Where are you in your walk with Jesus? Forget about the sins and failures of the past. Forget about the years you feel you have wasted. God wants you right now. Start afresh to step out in faith to serve Jesus. You are part of God's army in a mighty battle that has eternal significance. There are people out there waiting to be saved, and others waiting to be discipled. You are being called right now to join in this great kingdom battle—to be part of the body of Christ to save the lost, disciple believers, and to reach out to the poor and hurting in the name of Jesus. Go take the love of Jesus to a lost and dying world and receive the joy and peace that He has for you as you obey. This is what the victorious Christian life is all about.

"What then shall we say to these things? If God is for us, who can be against us?" (Romans 8:31)

APPENDIX A: AN OUTLINE FOR TEACHING THE COURSE

You do not have to be a gifted teacher to disciple others. You do not have to be a gifted teacher to teach from this book. If you have a heart for Jesus, you can teach others the basics of the Christian faith. All of us are called to be disciples and to disciple others. This is the way God's kingdom works.

God, through the power of the Holy Spirit, will do the teaching. The Spirit imparts the truth. The teacher's job is to speak it. The teacher's role is to present the biblical truths clearly.

When you teach, pray before each class that the Holy Spirit will guide you in your presentation. Pray that each student will have an open heart and mind to receive God's Word. Keep in mind that the purpose of discipling is to bring the disciple to a closer relationship with Jesus.

Do not be bound to the content of this book. As God leads you, share your own testimony or experiences that glorify God. Be flexible. If God leads you to omit a chapter or discuss something not covered in these pages, do it.

Spend time in the Word yourself and have your own prayer life in order. Be sure you understand the Bible verses for each chapter. Have faith that God will give you more ideas about how to share these biblical truths than what is suggested here. Students need to be challenged to know the basics of the faith and at the same time begin to practice the Christian life.

Have students memorize the Bible verses. These verses appear in the bold print at the beginning and the end of each chapter. Memorizing verses will allow those truths to become a part of the student's heart. You may want to have the students say the verses together out loud either as you begin or end the class.

If you have time, involve the students in discussion so they can witness to each other. Use the discussion questions to elicit honest answers. If you have the time to get the students into a discussion, this will be a rich learning experience. Be certain each student has a notebook and takes notes and writes down the answer to each and every discussion question. Students who examine their own walk in Christ will get a lot more out of this course. Some questions are very personal so do not force students to recite their answers unless they want to. Students should keep their written answers so they can look back in a year or so and measure their growth in Christ.

You can teach these chapters in several ways. If you only have a few days to teach the entire course, you will be limited to one hour or less per chapter. If you have weekly sessions, you can teach the course in 26 weeks or less. You can cover a chapter a week and assign homework. The homework is to read the chapter in advance, memorize the verses, and write out the answers to that week's discussion questions. Be sure each student brings a Bible to class and becomes familiar with the books of the Bible and how to look up verses.

It is best if each student has a copy of this book. If everyone does not have a book, you can still teach if the students have a Bible, a notebook to take notes, a pencil or pen, and are given the discussion questions each week for their homework. The teacher should make up his or her own plan for presenting each lesson. The teacher must decide in advance how much time to give to a particular chapter, which Bible verses to use, which discussion questions, if any, to use for discussion during classroom time. The teacher must decide how much time to allot to the lecture and to discussion. The teacher needs to be flexible

This is an easy book from which to teach. Keep your presentation simple and do not think you have to cover every point. Decide in advance which points you will emphasize. Finally, have faith that the Lord wants to do a good work in every student's life, and pray the Holy Spirit will lead you every step of the way.

A SUMMARY OF HOW TO TEACH FROM THE BOOK ONE CHAPTER AT A TIME

1. Have students bring a Bible, a notebook, and something to write with. Encourage students to take notes during the lecture and to write out their answers to all of the discussion questions at the end of each chapter.

2. Prepare the lecture or presentation and know how long you will talk. Try to get the class involved by asking a fairly simple question here and there during the lecture. Before you start, be familiar with the Bible verses and the text. Know what you will say and be sure to cover the main points of the chapter.

3. Before your weekly presentation of a particular chapter, have students do some preparation. (If they do not have a book, you will have to hand out the Bible verses and discussion questions or say them so the student can write them down in advance.)
   • Students should look up all the Bible verses mentioned in the chapter.
   • Students should memorize the verses at the beginning and end of the chapter.

• Students should read the chapter either in advance or after the lecture.
• During or after class, have students answer the discussion questions. If they cannot do it then, ask them to write out the answers later. This will challenge students in their faith.

4. If you have time, break the class in small groups after your presentation so that students can talk about the discussion questions. If you only have a small group of students, or you are teaching the course to only one person, then you will probably want to discuss those questions after your presentation.

A SUMMARY FOR TEACHING ALL OF THE CHAPTERS IN A SINGLE WEEK

If you are teaching this course in a week or over several days, you obviously will have to cut out some things. If your time is limited, you may want to try the following suggestions:

1. Have students get a copy of the book and read it prior to the seminar.

2. During the seminar, omit the memory work and the discussion questions. Suggest students do this later by self-study. (See self-study tips that follow.)

3. Make your presentation of each chapter shorter and save time to answer questions from the students if you can.

4. Be sure that each student has a notebook to take notes during the lecture.

5. If these students may be teaching from this book later on, consider spending some time in discipling the students about how they could teach the course to others.

SUMMARY ON HOW TO DO A SELF-STUDY

Any student can take this book and do a self-study discipling course. Here are four simple steps to accomplish such a study.

1. Have a plan in mind, such as covering one chapter a week. Get into a routine and set aside a particular time during the week to do the course.

2. Each week (or time period that you have chosen) read one chapter and look up the Bible verses cited in that chapter.

3. Memorize the two Bible verses at the beginning and end of your study chapter.

4. Write down the answers to the discussion questions at the end of the chapter.

Appendix B: A Summary of Topics

Salvation
Chapter 1: The Big Picture and Salvation
Chapter 2: Repentance and Forgiveness

Understanding the Trinity
Chapter 3: God
Chapter 4: Jesus
Chapter 5: Holy Spirit

How to Grow in Christ
Chapter 6: Bible
Chapter 7: Prayer
Chapter 8: Praise

Spiritual Warfare
Chapter 9: The Two Kingdoms and Our Enemy
Chapter 10: Overcoming the World and the Flesh

Obeying God (The 10 Commandments) and Having the Right Heart
Chapter 11: The Great Commandment
Chapter 12: God (Commandments 1–4)
Chapter 13: Family—Parents and Children (5th Commandment)
Chapter 14: Family—Marriage
Chapter 15: Murder (6th Commandment)
Chapter 16: Adultery—Your Body (7th Commandment)

Chapter 17: Integrity (Commandments 8–9)
Chapter 18: Coveting versus Grace (10th Commandment)

God's Plan for You
Chapter 19: In the Church
Chapter 20: In Your Ministry
Chapter 21: In Your Life

Developing Christian Character
Chapter 22: Overcoming Adversity
Chapter 23: Freedom from the Past
Chapter 24: Developing Christian Character
Chapter 25: Walking in the Spirit
Chapter 26: Examine Yourself

After the Leap

About the Author

The author, Carol Vance, has combined an interesting background in the law and criminal justice, with Christian discipleship and evangelism.

Carol served as District Attorney of Harris County (Houston), Texas for 14 years and was President of the National District Attorney's Association. Carol is an outstanding trial lawyer and a member of the American College of Trial Lawyers. Since 1979, he has been a senior partner in the law firm of Bracewell & Patterson, L.L.P.

Carol also served as Chairman of the Texas Board of Criminal Justice, which governed one of the two largest prison systems in the United States. Since 1992, he has been active in encouraging many ministries and new programs within the Texas Department of Criminal Justice. In 1997, Carol was helpful in inviting Prison Fellowship to start the first prison in the United States with all Christian programming just outside of Houston.

Carol has been an active follower of Jesus in numerous ways. He has traveled overseas to present the Gospel in Malawi, Africa, and recently returned from Kenya where he taught this book to new church leaders. He has preached often in jails and prisons and is currently active in the ministry at the Jester III prison unit outside of Houston, one of the many places where this book has been used for discipling. The book is also being used extensively in the Texas prisons.

In 1996, Carol helped form an inner-city church that reaches out to those in need. Carol has been an elder in the Presbyterian Church for nearly 30 years and is a frequent speaker before professional, business, and Christian groups. Carol and his wife Carolyn have 5 children and 12 grandchildren.

Carol understands Jesus' command to be a disciple and that believers are called to disciple others. Using the Bible as the only source, Carol put together basic biblical truths covering 26 basic topics that every Christian should know.